Apple Pro Training Series

Getting Started with Motion

Mary Plummer

Apple
Certified

Apple Training Series: Getting Started with Motion
Mary Plummer
Copyright © 2005 by Mary Plummer

Published by Peachpit Press. For information on Peachpit Press books, contact:

Peachpit Press
1249 Eighth Street
Berkeley, CA 94710
(510) 524-2178
Fax: (510) 524-2221
http://www.peachpit.com
To report errors, please send a note to errata@peachpit.com.
Peachpit Press is a division of Pearson Education.

Editor: Judy Ziajka
Apple Alliance Manager: Serena Herr
Series Managing Editor: Kristin Kalning
Technical Editor: Tim Snell
Technical Reviewer: Jeff Guenette
Copy Editor: Hon Walker
Production Coordinator: Pat Christenson
Compositors: David Van Ness and Tina O'Shea
DVD Production: Eric Geoffroy
Indexer: Karen Arrigoni
Interior Design: Frances Baca
Cover Illustration: Alicia Buelow
Cover Production: George Mattingly

ISBN 0-321-30533-7
9 8 7 6 5 4 3 2 1
Printed and bound in the United States of America

Acknowledgments

My deepest thanks to my husband and partner in business and life, Klark Perez, for your inexhaustible patience and support in carrying the weight for both us and our company, InVision Digital and Media Arts, while I was writing.

Thanks to Patty Montesion for your support, unwavering enthusiasm, this extraordinary opportunity, and my career as an Apple Certified Trainer. Thanks also to Kirk Paulsen for the invitation to write this book.

Huge thanks to Damian Allen for your exceptional Motion training; Dion Scoppettuolo for your guidance in planning this book; and Guido Hucking, Greg Niles, and the entire Motion team for creating this revolutionary motion graphics application.

Thanks to Serena Herr and the amazing Peachpit Press team for making this book a reality in record time: Kristin Mellone Kalning, Pat Christenson, David Van Ness, Tina O'Shea, Karen Arrigoni, Eric Geoffroy, Frances Baca, Alicia Buelow, and George Mattingly. Special thanks to Judy Ziajka for your leadership and keen eye for details and for making this writing marathon such an enjoyable experience; and to Hon Walker for your invaluable editorial touch. Thanks also to Tim Snell and Jeff Guenette for your notes and motion graphics expertise.

Thanks to Pamela Tuscany-Warren, Senior Director Marketing and Business Development, Universal Studios Florida Production Group/22A, and to everyone at Universal Studios Florida for the opportunity to have a production company and Apple Authorized Training Center on the lot. Thanks also to my talented friends Jeffrey A. Graves, Mark Magin, and Annie M. Zadie for providing such beautiful media, and to J. Issac Royffe for your help.

Extra special thanks to my family for their unconditional love throughout my freelance career. Thanks "Meem," Lee, Dad, Ginny, Chris, Sessely, Jorin, Landon, Kim, Guy, Emily, Chris, Jackson, Peg, Jim, Bill, Paula, Warren, Loretta, Chase, Sergio, Virginia, Kent, Klark, and my dog, Niki.

animation

action

creation

Contents at a Glance

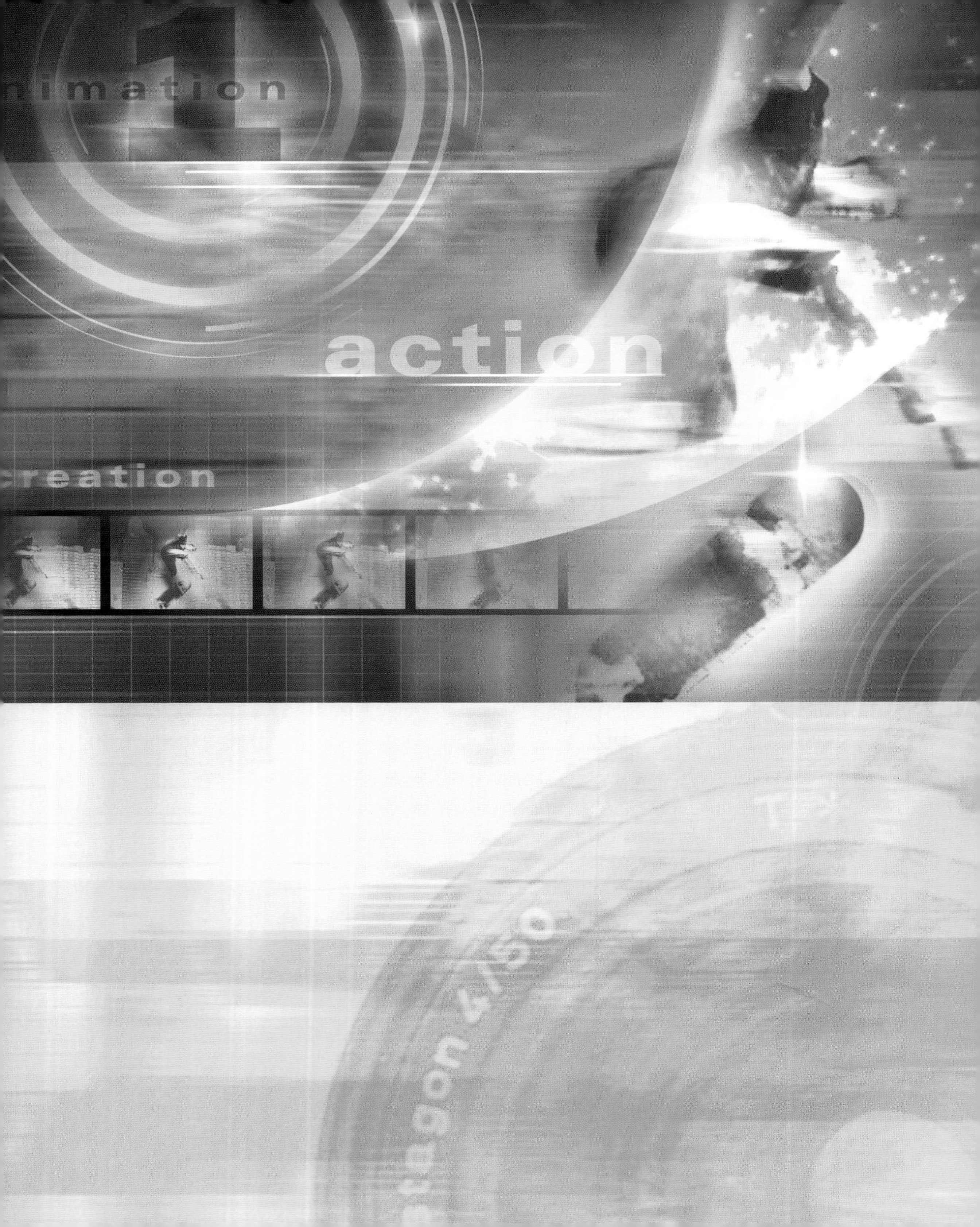
nimation
action
reation

Table of Contents

Lesson 8

Working in the Timeline 395

Lesson 9

Working with Audio and Keyframe Basics 445

animation

action

creation

Introduction

Getting Started

Welcome to the official introductory training course for Motion, Apple's dynamic and powerful motion graphics compositing software. This book is a detailed guide to creating motion graphics projects using Motion and the library of more than 4 GB of royalty-free content that is included with the software. It is based on the premise that a training book should go beyond a basic tour of the application, providing you with practical, professional techniques that you will use on a daily basis to add professional-quality motion graphics to your projects.

Whether you are a seasoned graphic designer or have never tried compositing images before, you will learn how to use Motion for a variety of real-world scenarios, creating multi-layered composites from scratch, animating objects and text with behaviors for a point-of-purchase advertisement, enhancing a dramatic news bumper with filters and generators, creating particle systems and visual effects, and more.

The Methodology

This book emphasizes hands-on training. Each exercise is designed to help you learn the application inside and out, starting with the basic interface and moving on to more advanced Motion features and design techniques. The book assumes a basic level of familiarity with the Apple OS X operating system. If you're new to Motion, you'll want to start at the beginning and progress through each lesson in order, since each lesson builds on information learned in previous ones. If you're already familiar with Motion, you can start with any section and focus on that topic.

Course Structure

This book is designed to be an introduction to Motion and is not meant for those who have a lot of experience using this program. Video editors, digital photographers, Web designers, and graphic artists interested in expanding to motion graphics will have the most to gain by reading this book. But this doesn't mean that the book's lessons are basic in nature. Motion is sophisticated software, and along with the application, the lessons cover all aspects of motion graphics. A lot goes into building exciting, professional-quality motion graphics, so to help you thoroughly understand the processes involved, this book is divided into four sections:

Lessons 1–3   Using the Motion interface and building motion graphics

Lessons 4–7   Working with behaviors, filters, particles, and text

Lesson 8–9   Editing in the Timeline, mixing audio, and keyframing

Lessons 10–11   Managing media, setting preferences, and exporting

In addition, a glossary of motion graphics terms appears on the DVD that accompanies this book.

Using the Motion Interface and Building Motion Graphics

Lessons 1 through 3 lay the groundwork for your work in Motion by introducing you to the Motion interface, windows, and transport controls as you explore the basic elements of graphic design. You'll start with still images, basic shapes, and text and then bring your project to life with moving pictures, behaviors, and particles. Then you'll build a complex layered composite from the background up while learning to import objects and organize layers.

Working with Behaviors, Filters, Particles, and Text

Lessons 4 through 7 focus on Motion's specialized design features—in particular, behaviors, filters, particles, and text. You'll work on more than a dozen projects in these action-packed lessons as you learn each feature, from the basic to the advanced. Along the way, you'll pick up some motion graphics tips and techniques that you can apply to your own projects.

Editing in the Timeline, Mixing Audio, and Keyframing

Once you've mastered the interface, layers, and primary Motion features, you're ready to move on to some advanced motion graphics techniques, such as Timeline editing, audio mixing, and precision animation with keyframes. Lessons 8 and 9 take your projects to the next level as you explore the Timing pane, Timeline, Audio Editor, Keyframe Editor, and Record button for recording keyframes.

Managing Media, Setting Preferences, and Exporting

Lessons 10 and 11 cover the essentials for successfully managing and sharing your finished projects. These lessons are at the end of the book, so that if you are following the lessons sequentially, you learn in the last lesson how to export your finished projects. However, these lessons are also self-contained, so that if you run into trouble with missing media files or want information on exporting a project, you can do the exercises in these lessons at any time, as needed. Lessons 10 and 11 also include bonus sections, which are in PDF format on the DVD in the MOTION_INTRO Book Files folder. The bonus section for Lesson 10 (Bonus 10) covers Motion preferences that allow you to tailor the interface for different types of projects and customize your workspace. The bonus section for Lesson 11 (Bonus 11) covers additional importing and exporting options, including options to import and export image sequences, work with layered Photoshop files, save a project as a template, and export with Compressor.

System Requirements

Before beginning to use this book, you should have a working knowledge of your computer and its operating system. Make sure that you know how to use the mouse and standard menus and commands and also how to open, save, and close files. If you need to review these techniques, see the printed or online documentation included with your system. Motion also supports the Wacom Intuos tablet family for gestures.

Motion takes advantage of the Power Mac G5 to deliver highly interactive, real-time performance. Some systems provide greater interactivity than others, and it is important to choose the right system for your needs. Performance depends on the processor speed, the amount of RAM, and the graphics subsystem.

Minimum System Requirements

▶ Macintosh computer with 867 MHz or faster PowerPC G4 or G5 processor

▶ 512 MB of RAM (2 GB or more recommended)

▶ Mac OS X 10.3.3 or later

▶ QuickTime 6.5 or later

▶ Display with 1024 × 768 resolution or higher (1280 × 1024 recommended)

▶ One of the following graphics cards: NVIDIA GeForce 6800 Ultra, NVIDIA GeForce 6800 GT, NVIDIA GeForce FX 5200 Ultra, NVIDIA GeForce FX Go5200, ATI Mobility Radeon 9600, ATI Radeon 9600 Pro, ATI Radeon 9700 Pro, ATI Mobility Radeon 9700, ATI Radeon 9800 Pro, or ATI Radeon 9800 XT

▶ 10 GB of disk space for application, templates, and tutorial

▶ DVD drive for installation

Recommended System

▶ Dual 2 GHz Power Mac G5

▶ 2 GB of RAM or more

▶ Mac OS X 10.3.3 or later

▶ ATI Radeon 9800 Pro graphics card or better

Using the Motion Trial Software

Many of the exercises in this book use content that is included with the full Motion installation. If you are using the Motion trial version for the exercises in this book, you will not have all of the Motion content that ships with the full version of the application. You should find the content that you need for the exercises in the Additional Motion Content folder, located in the MOTION_INTRO_Book_Files folder. If you do not find the content that you need in the Contents folder of the Library, simply use the File Browser to navigate to the Additional Motion Content folder and choose the appropriate media file from the folder. If you open a project that requires media that is missing, search for the missing file in the Additional Motion Content folder. Also, the save features are disabled in the trial version. You can still build projects; you just won't be able to save them. For installation instructions, see the Motion Install ReadMe file in the Motion Trial Software folder on the DVD.

Copying the Lesson Files

This book includes an *APTS_MOTION_INTRO* DVD of all the files you will need to complete the lessons. The MOTION_INTRO Book files folder contains the numbered Lesson folders, which contain the applicable projects and media files. While installing these files on your computer, it's important to keep all of the numbered Lesson folders together in the main MOTION_INTRO Book Files folder on your hard drive. If you copy the Lesson folders directly from the DVD to your hard drive, you should not have to reconnect your project files to the media.

Installing the Lesson Files

1   Put the *APTS_MOTION_INTRO* DVD into your computer's DVD drive.

2   Drag the MOTION_INTRO Book Files folder from the DVD to the Desktop of your computer.

3   To begin each lesson, launch Motion; then follow the instructions at the beginning of the lesson to open the project files for that lesson.

Reconnecting Broken Media Links

In the process of copying the media from this book's DVD, you may break a link between the project file and the media file. If this happens, the next time you open a project file, a window will appear saying that Motion can't find a file and asking you to reconnect the project files. Reconnecting the project files is a simple process. Just follow these steps:

1   When the Missing Media window appears, click the Search button.

2   Navigate to where the MOTION_INTRO Book Files folder resides on your hard drive; then go to the specific Lesson subfolder for the current lesson.

3   In the Lesson folder, select the name of the missing media file. Then click the Open button to reconnect that media file.

4   Repeat steps 2 and 3 as necessary, until all the project files have been reconnected.

About the Apple Pro Training Series

Apple Pro Training Series: Getting Started with Motion is part of the official training series for Apple Pro applications, developed by experts in the field and certified by Apple Computer. The series offers complete training in all Apple Pro products. The lessons are designed to let you learn at your own pace. Although each lesson provides step-by-step instructions for creating specific projects, there's room for exploration and experimentation. You can progress through the book from beginning to end or dive right into the lessons that interest you most. Each lesson concludes with a review section summarizing what you've covered.

Apple Pro Certification Program

The Apple Pro Training and Certification Program is designed to keep you at the forefront of Apple's digital media technology while giving you a competitive edge in today's ever-changing job market. Whether you're an editor, graphic designer, sound designer, special effects artist, or teacher, these training tools are meant to help you expand your skills.

If you are interested in Motion end-user certification, please see www.apple.com/software/pro/training for more information. Certification is offered in Motion, Final Cut Pro, DVD Studio Pro, Shake, and Logic. Successful certification as an Apple Pro provides official recognition of your knowledge of Apple's professional applications and allows you to market yourself to employers and clients as a skilled, pro-level user of Apple products.

To find an Authorized Training Center near you, go to www.apple.com/software/pro/training.

For those who prefer to learn in an instructor-led setting, Apple also offers training courses at Apple Authorized Training Centers worldwide. These courses, which use the Apple Pro Training Series books as their curriculum, are taught by Apple Certified Trainers and balance concepts and lectures with hands-on labs and exercises. Apple Authorized Training Centers have been carefully selected and meet Apple's highest standards in all areas, including facilities, instructors, course delivery, and infrastructure. The goal of the program is to offer Apple customers, from beginners to the most seasoned professionals, the highest-quality training experience.

Resources

Apple Pro Training Series: Getting Started with Motion is not intended to be a comprehensive reference manual, nor does it replace the documentation that comes with the application. For comprehensive information about program features, refer to these resources:

- ▶ The Reference Guide. Accessed through the Motion Help menu, the Reference Guide contains a complete description of all Motion features.

- ▶ Apple's Web site: www.apple.com.

1

Lesson Files

Time

This lesson takes approximately 1 hour to complete.

Goals

Launch the Motion program

Explore the Motion interface

Explore the Utility window

Work with the Dynamic Guides

Modify an object in the Canvas

Create an object using the Create tools in the toolbar

Work with the Dashboard window

Add a drop shadow to an object in the Canvas

Create text in the Canvas

Change text color in the Dashboard

Save a Motion project

Lesson 1
Working with the Basic Interface

Welcome to the world of motion graphics.

By definition, graphics are representations of something in the form of images. Graphics include pictures, text, shapes, and objects, all of which can be grouped together to create an overall image called a *composite*. These composite images can be used for anything from a business card to a billboard.

Motion graphics, on the other hand, are exactly what their name implies: graphics in motion. Motion graphics are more than just graphics that move, however; they can grow, spin, fly, glow, wiggle, explode, and just about anything else you can imagine.

Over the years, I've worked with many frustrated editors and graphic designers who struggled to create dynamic motion graphics without spending days calculating and plotting, and who often settled for less than what they desired.

That was before Motion. This software is different. You don't have to be a computer engineer or graphic designer to create motion graphics. You don't even have to be an artist. If you can click a mouse, you can turn your Mac into a motion graphics studio—it's really that simple.

It's a good idea to learn to walk before you run, so prepare yourself for a brisk walk through the basic Motion interface as you build a graphic composite. Along the way, you'll learn some useful keyboard shortcuts as you get to know the program.

Getting Started

Before you start, you need to load the Motion program and content onto your hard drive. You also need to copy the lesson files from the DVD in the back of the book to your computer.

The instructions for loading the software and files are in the introduction to this book.

Once you have the Motion program and lesson files loaded onto your hard drive, you're ready to begin this lesson.

Launching Motion

There are three ways to launch Motion:

▶   Double-click the Motion application icon in your hard drive.

▶   Click once on the Motion icon in the Dock.

▶   Double-click any Motion project file.

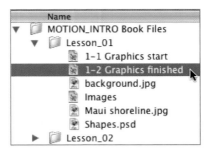

For this exercise, you'll launch Motion by opening a project file.

1   Locate the MOTION_INTRO Book Files folder on your computer.

> **NOTE ▸** If you haven't copied the Lessons folder for this book to your hard drive, do so at this time.

2   Select the Lesson_01 folder; then double-click the **1-2 Graphics finished** project file to open the project and launch the program.

When Motion opens, you will see two windows displaying the project **1-2 Graphics finished.**

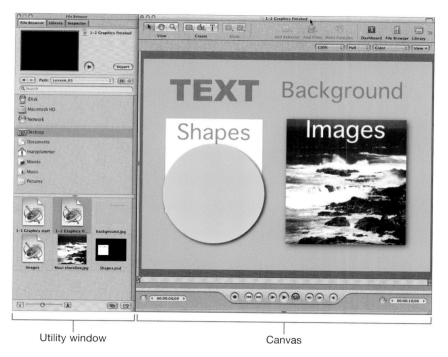

Utility window   Canvas

The long window at the left is the Utility window. The Utility window helps you organize and modify your project's elements. The larger window at the right is the Canvas, which is where you create and preview your project.

The current project in the Canvas window is a literal example of a graphic composite using elements common in graphic design, including text, shapes, images, and a background.

In the next series of exercises, you will build this project from scratch to better understand the basic elements of graphic design.

Closing and Opening a Project

Now that you've seen the finished composite and know what you're aiming for, let's close the project so we can rebuild it.

There are three ways to do almost everything in Motion, including close a project. You can use a menu, a button, or a keyboard shortcut. In this exercise, we'll use the menu method.

Like most software applications, Motion offers a series of menus across the top of the screen that you can access at any time by clicking the menu name.

1 Locate the File menu toward the upper left of your screen.

2 Click once on the File menu to open it.

3 Select Close from the File menu to close the current project.

> **NOTE** ► The shorthand for steps that involve menus will be written as Choose File > Close. In other words, File is the title of the menu, and Close is the selection within that menu.

The Canvas window containing the current project closes.

NOTE ▸ If you made any changes to the project file that was open, you will see a dialog box asking you if you want to save changes. For now, click the Don't Save button to close the dialog box.

Now let's practice the menu method again to open the project **1-1 Graphics start**.

1   Choose File > Open to open a project on your computer.

An Open window appears.

2   Inside your MOTION_INTRO Book Files folder, navigate to the Lesson_01 folder and select **1-1 Graphics start**.

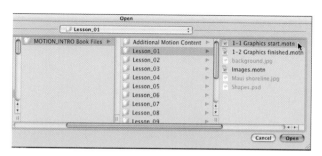

The entire path to your project file is APTS_MOTION_INTRO > MOTION_INTRO Book Files > Lesson_01 > 1-1 Graphics start.

3   Click the Open button at the lower right of the Open window to open the selected project.

1-1 Graphics start opens in the Canvas window.

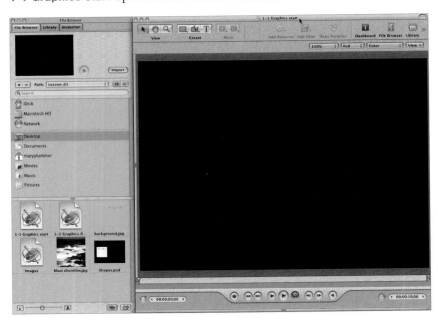

Exploring the Utility Window

One of the many advantages of Motion is the simplicity of the interface. As with other Apple Pro applications, Motion provides two main windows—the Canvas and the Utility window—as your base of operations. Let's start with the Utility window, since that is where you find and modify the content and media that you use to build your projects.

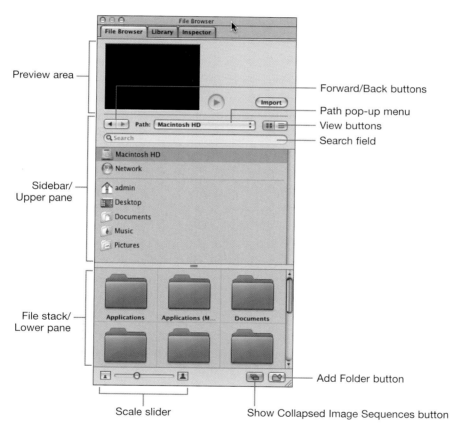

The Utility window has three primary functions: You use it to browse for files, organize elements, and modify elements.

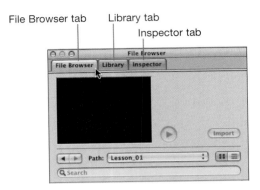

The Utility window separates its primary functions onto three tabs:

▶ File Browser — Browse, select, and import media files, including single images, image sequences, QuickTime movies, and audio files.

▶ Library — Access Motion content such as gradients and preset particles, plus browse, select, and apply effects and filters to objects in your project.

▶ Inspector — Adjust the parameters for all objects and effects in your project.

We'll use the File Browser tab to locate the elements we need to create our project.

NOTE ▶ You'll work with the Library and Inspector tabs in the next lesson.

Working in the File Browser

One of the first things you'll need to do with any Motion project is locate, preview, and bring in media files from your computer. You can accomplish all of these goals using the File Browser.

The upper pane of the File Browser contains icons for locations on your computer, including your hard drives, servers, and home folder. The lower pane displays the folders and contents for whatever location you have selected in the upper pane.

Let's explore the File Browser and see how it works.

1　At the upper left of the Utility window, click the File Browser tab if it is not already selected.

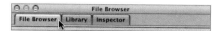

　　Notice that the name at the top of the Utility window is File Browser, to indicate that the File Browser tab is active.

2　In the upper pane of the File Browser window, click the Desktop icon to open your Desktop in the lower pane.

3　In the lower pane, double-click the MOTION_INTRO Book Files folder to open it. Then double-click the Lesson_01 folder to open it in the lower pane of the File Browser.

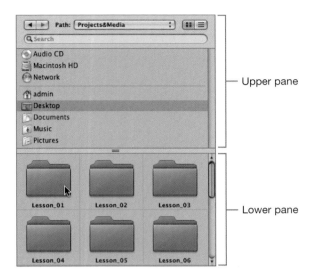

The Lesson_01 folder contains all of the projects and media needed for this lesson.

Changing the File View

Now that you have opened the Lesson_01 folder in the lower pane of the File Browser, let's take a look at the different ways that you can view your files.

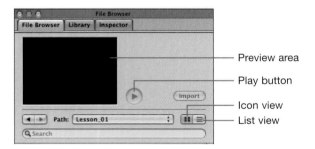

The Motion File Browser allows you to view your files in either List or Icon view. To change the way you view your files, you simply click the appropriate view button. Once you've changed to either List or Icon view, the Motion Browser will remain that way until you change it again. The Utility window, including the File Browser and view selection, is part of Motion, not specific to a particular project. Therefore, whichever view is selected when you quit Motion will be the default when you relaunch the program.

Let's modify the file view in the File Browser. The previous task showed the files displayed in the Icon view, so let's switch to the List view.

1	At the middle right of the File Browser, click the List view button.

It's a small button with three horizontal lines on it, representing a list.

The files in the lower pane of the File Browser now appear in the List view. List view is very useful if you are working with a lot of files and want to sort them alphabetically.

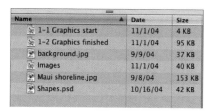

2	Click the Icon view button, located to the left of the List view button, to change back to the Icon view.

The Icon view button has four squares on it.

The Icon view is very useful if you want to see a visual representation of your files.

You can resize the icons using the Scale slider located at the bottom left of the File Browser.

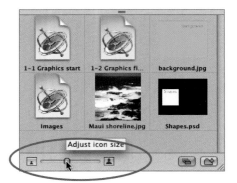

3   Click and then drag the Scale slider to the left to make the icons smaller; drag right to make them larger.

4   Resize the icons until you can easily see all files included in this lesson.

Previewing Files in the File Browser

With your files displayed in the bottom pane, you can easily preview any of them in the Preview area at the top of the File Browser.

To preview a file in Motion, you simply click the file icon to select it. You can preview a file in either the List view or the Icon view.

1   Locate the file called **background.jpg** and click to select it.

The file opens in the Preview area of the File Browser.

The Preview area includes a viewer, a Play/Pause button for video and audio files, and information about the file.

2   Select the file **Maui shoreline** to preview it.

The still photo titled Maui shoreline opens in the preview area.

3   Select the remaining two files, Images and Shapes, to preview them in the File Browser.

These are the files you'll use to build your first composite project.

NOTE ▶ You cannot view the Motion Project files **1-1 Graphics start** or **1-2 Graphics finished** in the Preview area.

Now that you're familiar with the Utility window, let's move on to the Canvas window.

Exploring the Canvas Window

The Canvas window is the interactive, hands-on creative environment where you'll be dragging, dropping, resizing, modifying, moving, tweaking, previewing, and adding effects and filters to the various objects in your project.

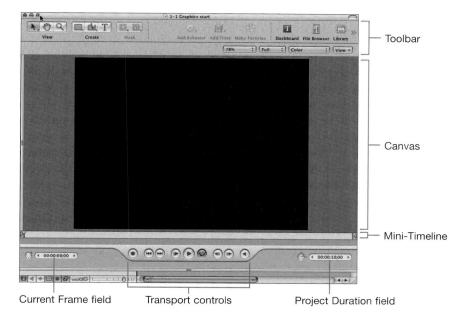

Let's take a quick tour of the Canvas window.

▶   Toolbar — Use the buttons to show and hide the interface components, transform objects, add effects, and change the view of your composite.

▶   Canvas — Add files, view and modify the objects in your composite, and use the transport controls to easily navigate and preview your project.

▶   Current Frame and Project Duration fields — Display the current location of the playhead and the project duration in either frame or timecode increments.

▶   Transport controls — Use to play or scrub through your project and enable keyframing and audio playback. You'll learn more about these in Lesson 2.

▶   Mini-Timeline — Use to add, move, and trim objects within your project without having to open the Timing pane, which contains the full Timeline.

Adjusting the Window

Since the Canvas window is essentially your creative workstation, you should be sure that you understand how to adjust it before you dive into the creative process.

Motion was designed for Macintosh OS X, and the Canvas window works the same as other OS X windows do. If you're new to the Mac or to OS X, follow these steps to get some practice zooming, moving, and minimizing the Canvas window.

If you're already a master at Mac OS X window features, feel free to skip this exercise.

There are three buttons in the upper-left corner of the Canvas window: Close (X), Minimize (–), and Zoom (+).

1   Click the Zoom button (+) to zoom the Canvas window so it fills your
computer screen.

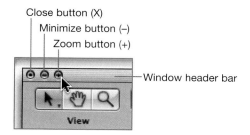

The Canvas window will resize to fill your screen.

NOTE ▶ Make sure your screen resolution is set to 1024 × 768 or higher
in the display preferences for your computer. You can find more information on changing your screen resolution in the Mac OS X documentation
that came with your computer.

You can also adjust the window by dragging the size control in the lower-
right corner of the window.

2   In the lower-right corner of the window, click the size control (the diagonal
lines) and drag upward to make the window smaller.

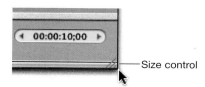

Notice that the viewable area of the Canvas becomes smaller as you
change the size of the window. You can also see the Utility window behind
the Canvas window on the Desktop.

To move the Canvas window, you drag the gray header bar at the top of
the window.

3   Click the top of the window near the name of the project. Don't release your mouse.

4   Drag the window to the lower-right corner of your screen. Release the mouse.

5   Click the Zoom button (+) again to zoom the window back to full-screen size.

If your window is already full screen, clicking the Zoom button will make your window revert to its previous size and position.

TIP ▶ If you're using a laptop or a large studio display, the Zoom button is a very useful tool for maximizing the size of your workspace. Also, any time you can't see the entire window because part of it is offscreen, you can click the Zoom button to bring the entire window into view.

You can also minimize or hide the Canvas window without quitting the program. When you minimize the window, it moves to the Dock near the Trash. To reopen the window, simply click the window's icon in your Dock.

6   Click the Minimize button (−) to hide your Canvas window in the Dock.

7   Locate the Canvas window icon in your Dock and click it to unhide the window.

NOTE ▶ You can also double-click the header at the top of the Canvas window to minimize and hide the window. If you click the Close button (X), you will close the actual project and will need to open it again from the File menu.

Changing the Window Layouts

Now let's go back to the standard window layout. One way to change the layout is with the Window menu.

1   Choose Window > Layouts > Standard to reset the windows to the standard layout.

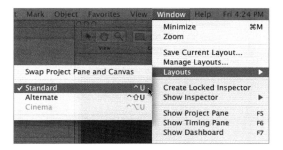

The windows return to the standard layout, with the Utility window on the left and the Canvas on the right.

Another way to control the windows and reset them to the standard layout is with a keyboard shortcut.

2   Click the Zoom button on the Canvas window so that the window fills the screen.

3   On your computer keyboard, press Ctrl-U (the Control key plus the U key).

The windows return to the standard layout.

TIP ▶ To remember the keyboard shortcut for the standard window layout, just think about controlling the windows. If you were to talk to the windows, you might say, "I want to control you"—or Ctrl-U. This shortcut also works in Final Cut Pro and Final Cut Express.

Now let's put the Canvas to use and begin building a project.

Zooming In and Out of the Canvas

As you work in the Canvas, you'll often want to zoom in and zoom out for a better view of your work. There are three ways to zoom in on and out of the Canvas:

▶ Use the Zoom tool in the toolbar.

▶ Choose View > Zoom In or Zoom Out.

▶ Press Cmd-= (equals sign) or Cmd-– (hyphen).

If you want to make your project fit in the Canvas window, you can simply use the shortcut Shift-Z.

Zooming is something you will want to master quickly, so let's go right to the keyboard shortcut for this exercise.

1 Press Cmd-= several times to zoom in on the Canvas.

By default, you zoom in on the center of the Canvas.

2 Press Cmd-– to zoom out of the Canvas.

3 Press Shift-Z to fit the project to the Canvas window.

NOTE ▶ On the Apple keyboard, the Command key is next to the space-bar and has an Apple icon on it.

Adding Files to the Canvas

You create composites by placing objects on top of each other. A good place to start is the background. There are two easy ways to add the background file from the File Browser to the Canvas window:

▶ Select the file and click the Import button.

▶ Drag the file from the File Browser to the Canvas window.

We'll use the drag-and-drop method to import the Background file. Then we'll use the Import button to add the Shapes file. We'll also use Motion's guides to align the Background object.

1   In the File Browser, select the `background.jpg` file. Do not release the mouse.

2   Drag the file to the center of the Canvas window.

A small green circle with a plus sign (+) appears to show you are adding a file to the Canvas.

NOTE ▶ A yellow crosshairs appears in the Canvas when the object is centered.

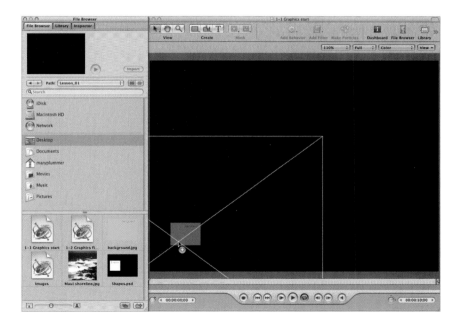

3   Release the mouse to add the Background file.

The Background file appears in the Canvas as a light blue rectangle the same size as the Canvas.

Working with Dynamic Guides

Did you notice the yellow lines that appeared as you dragged the Background file over the Canvas? Those lines are called Dynamic Guides, and you can use them to help align your objects in the Canvas.

To see the guides again, click the Background object in the Canvas and drag it up, down, right, or left. The yellow guides appear, showing you whether your object is aligned in the center of the frame or to another object.

1   In the Canvas, drag the Background object (the light blue rectangle) and move it around the center of the frame until you see a both the horizontal and vertical yellow guides in the center.

When the yellow lines appear as a cross in the center of your object, it is aligned in the center of the frame.

Now let's add the Shapes object to the project using the Import button method.

2   In the File Browser, select the Shapes object to load it into the Preview area.

Notice that it looks like a white square on a black background. The black around the white square is an alpha channel (an area that appears invisible); you will not actually see the black portion of the Shapes file when you add it to the project.

MORE INFO ▶ You will learn more about alpha channels in Lesson 5.

3   At the lower right of the Preview area, click the Import button to import the file into the project.

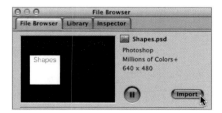

The Shapes file is added to your project above the Background layer and is centered in the Canvas window automatically.

When you import a file using the Import button, the entire file is centered in the Canvas, so anything within that file will keep its original place. The Shapes file used in this exercise was designed in Photoshop with the white square placed exactly where it should be for the final Motion composite.

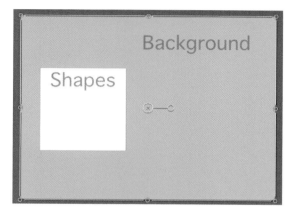

Excellent work. However, the layer is called Shapes, and there is only one shape. Either we should change the title or add a shape. We'll add a shape that we create ourselves. First, let's save our work. If you are using the trial version of the software, you won't be able to save your work because the save features are disabled.

Saving a Motion Project

Now that you've added several objects to your Motion project, it's a good idea to save it. Saving in Motion works just as in any other Apple application. First you decide where you want to save your finished project; then you actually save it in that location.

You should create a new folder on your Desktop for your exercises while you're working with this book. That way, you won't accidentally overwrite the original files in your Lessons folder, and if you want, you'll be able to go back and work on a project again.

To keep things simple, you should use the same folder for storing all of the projects you create as you work through this book.

To save a file to a new location, you use the Save As command.

1   Choose File > Save As.

The Save As window opens.

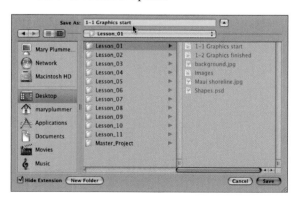

Full Save window

The Save As window shows the current filename and includes the Mac OS X Finder to navigate to a different location on the computer.

If you see a condensed Save As window, click the downward-pointing triangle to the right of the Save As field to expand the window.

Condensed Save window

2   At the left of the Save As window, click the Desktop icon.

3   At the lower left of the Save As window, click the New Folder button to create a folder for your saved projects.

A New Folder window opens.

4   In the Name field, type *My Motion Projects*.

5   At the lower right of the New Folder window, click the Create button to create the new folder.

Your folder is created. Now let's change the project name.

6   In the Save As field, type *Graphics*.

7 At the lower right of the Save As window, click the Save button to save your project.

Your Graphics project is now located in the My Motion Projects folder on your Desktop. As you continue to work on the project in this lesson, you can save your progress by pressing Cmd-S.

Creating a Shape from the Toolbar

This lesson is all about getting to know the interface, and now is as good a time as any to learn how to create your own shapes. For this exercise, you'll use the Circle tool in the toolbar to create a circle.

The toolbar is located along the top of the Canvas window. Throughout this book, you'll be using tools from the toolbar. The tools are grouped into categories, including the View set, the Create set, and the Mask set.

Tools in the View set are used to change the view and manipulation method in the Canvas. The Create set contains tools that add new content, such as shapes and text, to the project. The Mask set contains tools to add a mask to an existing layer or object.

Motion has three types of Create tools:

▶ Shapes — Create squares, rectangles, ovals, and circles.

▶ Bézier — Create unusual or complex shapes.

▶ Text — Create text.

In this exercise, you'll use the Circle tool to create a circle.

To create a circle, you select the Circle tool; then drag in the Canvas to create the shape. Let's try it. The Circle tool is located on the pop-up menu with the Rectangle tool.

1   In the toolbar, click and hold the Rectangle tool to open the pop-up menu.

2   From the menu, select the Circle tool.

The Circle tool becomes visible in the Create tool set, and your cursor changes to crosshairs.

3   Move the crosshairs cursor to the center of the Canvas, below the letter *B* in the word *Background*.

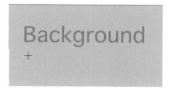

4   Drag down and to the right. Release the mouse.

Congratulations. You've created a shape, and if you're lucky, it's a circle. If, instead, you created an oval, you can easily try again. This time, to make sure you get a circle, you will constrain the proportions. Try this next task even if you created a circle on the first try—you'll find your next circle much easier to create.

First, you'll undo your work.

Using Undo and Redo

Creating graphics is like creating music: Sometimes you have to hear it—or see it—to know whether you like it. And often, what seemed like a good idea doesn't work so well once you add it to your project. There's also the possibility of human error, like drawing an oval instead of a circle.

Like most programs, Motion has Undo and Redo features. You can undo any step in Motion, even after you've saved your project, as long as the program remains open.

To undo, you simply select Undo from the Edit menu. To make undoing your work really easy, Undo is always at the top of the menu. Let's try it.

1   Choose Edit > Undo Add Circle.

Notice that the Undo option in the menu tells you what you will be undoing—in this case, the option reads Undo Add Circle.

Now bring back your oval—redoing a change is just as easy as undoing it.

2   Choose Edit > Redo Add Circle.

You'll likely be using Undo a lot as you work through the exercises in this book, so the keyboard shortcut for this task is a good one to learn.

3   Press Cmd-Z to undo the oval again.

NOTE ▶ Cmd-Z also works as the Undo shortcut in other Apple applications.

Constraining Proportions

When you draw a circle, it is important that the height and width stay in proportion. To do that, you simply hold down the Shift key while you draw your circle.

1   On the toolbar, click the Create Circle tool.

Notice that the Circle tool still shows in the Create tool set, because it was the last tool used.

2   On the Canvas, hold down the Shift key and drag the crosshairs down and to the right. Release the mouse.

Now you should have a perfect circle.

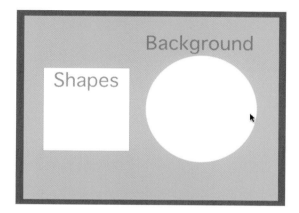

The circle isn't quite the size we want here. In the next task, we'll resize it.

Transforming Objects

You can resize or transform objects on the Canvas using the Select/Transform tool. It's the tool at the left that looks like an arrow.

1   On the toolbar, click the Select/Transform tool to select it, or press Shift-S.

The circle you created is now inside a bounding box with handles (dots) on the corners and edges. These handles are the points where you can transform the object.

NOTE ► If you don't see the Select/Transform tool on the left, you may have opened a different tool accidentally. Click the tool button to open the pop-up menu and choose the Select/Transform tool, or press Shift-S.

2   Drag any of the handles (dots) around the circle to change the size or proportions of the circle.

Chances are, you just turned your perfect circle into an oval again. That's okay; you can always undo your work.

3   Press Cmd-Z to undo your last move if you transformed your circle.

If you transformed more than one part of the circle, undo as many times as necessary to get back to your original circle.

You can also use the Shift key to constrain proportions as you transform or resize an object, the same way you used it to constrain proportions when you created the object.

4   Hold down Shift and click the handle at the upper right of the circle; drag to the left or right until the circle is approximately the same size as the white square in the Shapes object.

As you transform the size of an object, a box appears indicating the amount of change in the shape's size.

Using the Dashboard

You can also change the color of your circle. The task is simple, thanks to the Dashboard. In your car, a dashboard is the easy-to-read instrument panel that is always in front of you so you can see it at a glance while continuing to drive. In Motion, the Dashboard is a small, interactive floating window that allows you to modify your objects while you continue to create your composite.

The Dashboard controls include check boxes, color wells, sliders, and knobs, depending on the parameter you want to modify.

There are three simple ways to activate the Dashboard window:

- ▶ Choose Window > Show Dashboard.
- ▶ Press F7.
- ▶ Press D (for Dashboard).

Let's use the Dashboard to add color to our circle.

1 Press D to open the Dashboard window.

A small floating window opens.

The Dashboard window shows controls for whatever you currently have selected—in this case, the circle.

You can move the Dashboard window by dragging its header bar.

2 Click the Dashboard header bar and drag the window to move it to the left of your circle object.

Now we'll use the Dashboard to change the circle's fill color. To change the fill color, you click the fill color well and select the color you want from the color wheel. By default, whenever you create a shape in Motion, the Fill box is checked and the fill color is white.

3 On the Dashboard, click the Fill color well.

A Colors window with a color wheel appears.

NOTE ▶ If your Colors window does not show the color wheel, select the wheel at the top left of the Colors window. If you do not see a wheel, click the button at the upper right of the Colors window to expand the window and reveal the color selection choices.

4 Drag the dot in the center of the color wheel to the upper right to turn your circle yellow.

Notice that the Fill color well in the Dashboard changes along with the color of your circle on the Canvas.

5   Click the Close button (X) at the upper left of the Colors window to close the window.

Adding a Drop Shadow from the Dashboard

Graphics, whether they are static or in motion, can be greatly enhanced by the addition of a simple drop shadow. If you look at your yellow circle on the light blue background, you'll notice that the image appears "flat"—it looks like a light blue background with a yellow circle painted on it. The circle could be part of the background pattern, because there is nothing separating the two elements.

In the real world, if an object is in front of a flat wall, the object usually casts a shadow on the wall. The same principle works in graphics. If the yellow circle casts a shadow on the background, it gives the illusion of being in front of— and not part of—the background.

If you add a drop shadow to an object, the shadow will appear on any object directly below it in the composite image.

Let's try it.

1   Press D to open the Dashboard, if it is not already open.

2   Near the middle of the Dashboard, select the Drop Shadow check box.

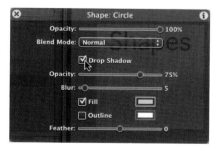

A check appears in the check box, and a drop shadow appears below the yellow circle.

Circle without a drop shadow

Circle with a drop shadow

You're now done with the Dashboard.

3   Click the Close button (X) at the upper left of the Dashboard window, or press F7, to close the Dashboard.

> **NOTE** ▶ If you are using a laptop, you will need to hold down the Function (Fn) key located at the lower left of the keyboard when you press the F7 key.

Selecting and Deselecting Objects

As you work with the Motion interface, it's important to know what you have selected at all times. Many of the Motion features change depending on what is selected. To select an object, you simply click it with the Select/Transform tool. To deselect that object, you click the empty space outside of the frame. Let's try deactivating the circle.

1   Click the circle to select it.

2   Press Cmd-− (hyphen) to zoom out one level.

3   Click the empty space outside of your light blue Background object in the Canvas to deselect the circle.

To select the Shapes object without selecting the Circle object, you need to click an area of the Shapes object that doesn't include the circle.

4   Click the the white square on the Shapes object to select Shapes object.

A bounding box appears around the entire Shapes object.

5   Click the empty space outside the background to deselect the Shapes object.

6   Press Shift-Z to again fit the project to the Canvas window.

> **NOTE ▶** If you accidentally press the Z key by itself, you'll activate the Zoom tool. To get back to the Select/Transform tool, simply press Shift-S.

Project Tasks

Now it's your turn to apply what you've learned so far to your composite. First you'll move the circle so it overlaps the lower half of the white square. Then you'll add and resize the Images object on the Canvas. Finally, you'll add a drop shadow to the Images object on the Canvas. Use the illustration at the end of the steps as a visual guide.

1   On the Canvas, click the yellow circle to select it.

2   Drag the circle to the left until it overlaps the lower half of the white square.

3   Click the empty space outside the background to deselect the circle.

4   In the File Browser, select the Images file and drag it to the center of the Canvas. Use the Dynamic Guides to place it in the center of the frame.

5   Press Cmd-– (hyphen) to zoom out one level so you can clearly see the bounding box around the Images file.

6   Press and hold Shift; then click and drag the handle at the upper right of the Images object to resize the object until it is about the same size as the combined square and circle.

7   Drag the Images object toward the right of the frame so the top is even with the top of the white square. Leave an equal amount of background visible between the right and left sides of the Images object.

8   Press D to open the Dashboard for the Images object.

9   Add a drop shadow to the Images object; then close the Dashboard.

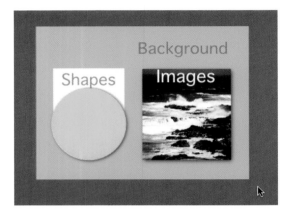

Creating Text in the Canvas

Creating text in Motion is as easy as creating a circle or a square. To create text, you first need to select the Text tool. There are two easy ways to select the Text tool:

▶   Click the Text tool in the toolbar.

▶   Press T.

Since you already know how to click to select a tool in the toolbar, let's use the keyboard shortcut.

1 Press T to select the Text tool.

The selection arrow changes to the text cursor.

2 Move the text cursor to the upper left of the frame and click once.

A flashing-line cursor appears where you clicked the Canvas. This is where you will type your text.

3 Type *TEXT*.

The word *TEXT* appears on the Canvas.

4 Press Esc to change from the Text tool to the Select/Transform tool.

You will now change the text size, color, and style in the Dashboard.

5 Press D to open the Dashboard.

Move the Dashboard so you can see the text as you change it.

6 In the Dashboard, click the Font pop-up menu to open it. Select Arial Black as the font.

You can scroll through the fonts and see a live update of the different fonts on your selected text object.

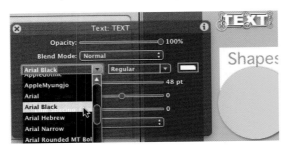

7   Drag the Size slider to change the font size to 68 points.

The width of the text should be about the same as that of the white square below.

8   On the Canvas, drag the text object to align its center with the center of the yellow circle and white square. Use the Dynamic Guide to center the text object on the shapes. A vertical Dynamic Guide will show you when the text and shapes are aligned properly. Keep the text object above the white square.

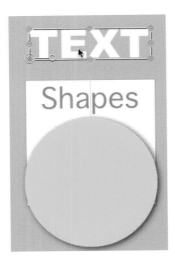

Your text is in position. Now change the color.

9   Click the color well on the right side of the Dashboard to open the Colors window.

Choose a bright red from the color wheel.

10   Close the Colors window and the Dashboard.

11   Press Shift-Z to make your project fit the Canvas window.

12   Press Cmd-S to save your finished project.

Congratulations! You just completed your first composite graphic in Motion. This is also the last static composite you'll ever create in this book. From now on, your projects will include motion graphics.

What You've Learned

▶   You can launch Motion in three ways: Double-click the Motion icon in the Applications window, click the Motion icon in the Dock, or double-click a Motion project file.

▶   The Motion interface has two primary windows: the Utility window and the Canvas window.

▶   The Utility window has three tabs—File Browser, Library, and Inspector— that are used, respectively, to browse, organize, and modify project elements.

▶   The File Browser is divided into three sections: the Preview area plus an upper pane and a lower pane.

▶ You can view files in the lower pane of the File Browser in either List view or Icon view.

▶ The Scale slider at the bottom of the File Browser allows you to adjust the size of the icons in the lower pane of the File Browser.

▶ To reset the Motion windows to their standard layout, choose Window > Layouts > Standard or use the keyboard shortcut Ctrl-U.

▶ The Canvas window is a hands-on, interactive environment for adding, viewing, and modifying objects in your project.

▶ You can add files to the Canvas by selecting a file and clicking the Import button in the File Browser or by dragging the file from the File Browser to the Canvas.

▶ Adding a file to the Canvas by using the Import button in the File Browser automatically places the file in the center of the frame in the Canvas window.

▶ Dynamic Guides are yellow lines that appear as you move objects to help you align objects to the center of the frame or to other objects.

▶ The Create tools in the toolbar can be used to create shapes or text.

▶ Hold down the Shift key while creating or transforming an object to constrain the proportions of the object and create a perfect circle, for example.

▶ The Dashboard is a floating window that allows you to see and modify your objects in the Canvas.

▶ There are three ways to display the Dashboard window: Choose Window > Show Dashboard, press F7, or press the D key.

▶ Pressing Cmd-S saves the project, and pressing Shift-Cmd-S opens the Save As window so that you can change the name or location of a project as it is saved.

2

Lesson Files

Time

This lesson takes approximately 1 hour to complete.

Goals

Use the transport controls

Work with the mini-Timeline

Change the play range In and Out points

Add a motion background from the Library

Add a particle emitter from the Library

Explore the Current Frame and Project Duration fields

Change a region's timing in the mini-Timeline

Add an audio file to the project

Add a text behavior

Add a basic behavior to a layer

View the Project and Timing panes

Lesson 2
Creating Motion Graphics

If a still picture is worth a thousand words, then what is a moving picture worth? If it's an exciting and dynamic motion graphic used for a company logo, a commercial, a movie's opening title sequence, or a promo, it can be worth millions.

In this lesson, you'll bring a composite to life with motion graphics as you use the transport controls and tour the Project and Timing panes. You'll also get an introduction to behaviors and particles, which are some of Motion's most powerful design tools.

Opening a Project from the File Browser

In Lesson 1, you learned how to open a Motion project using the File menu. Now let's look at another way to open a project, from the File Browser. Our goal in this exercise is to navigate to the Lesson_02 folder, locate the project **2-1 Motion Graphics start**, and open it without leaving the File Browser.

1   Launch Motion, if it is not already open.

2   Choose File > Close to close the current project, if you have a project open.

3   In the File Browser, near the top, click the Path pop-up menu to open it.

The Path pop-up menu shows recent paths you have searched in the File Browser.

4   In the Path pop-up menu, choose MOTION_INTRO Book Files.

The MOTION_INTRO Book Files folder opens in the lower pane of the File Browser, revealing all your lesson folders.

NOTE ► If you do not see MOTION_INTRO Book Files in the Path pop-up menu, click the Desktop icon in the upper pane, and then navigate to APTS_MOTION_INTRO > MOTION_INTRO Book Files.

5 In the lower pane of the File Browser, double-click the Lesson_02 folder to open it.

> **NOTE** ▶ You may want to adjust the icon size using the Scale slider to make the icons in the Lesson_02 folder easy to see.

You've opened the folder; now you need to open the actual lesson file. You'll use a contextual menu.

Working with Contextual Menus

What's a contextual menu? Good question. Contextual menus are convenient hidden menus that change depending on the context of where you are and what you may want to do. There are two ways to open a contextual menu:

▶ Ctrl-click.

▶ Click the right mouse button (requires a two-button mouse).

> **NOTE** ▶ If you have a three-button mouse, feel free to right-click anytime; however, for the written exercises, I'll refer to the Ctrl-click method.

1 In the lower pane of the File Browser, locate the **2-1 Motion Graphics start** project.

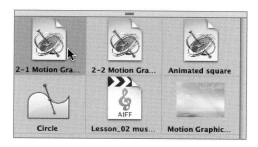

2 Ctrl-click the **2-1 Motion Graphics start** project to open the contextual menu.

A small contextual menu appears with three options: Reveal in Finder, Rename, and Move to Trash. You don't want to rename the file or move it to the Trash, so that leaves only the first option: Reveal in Finder.

3   In the contextual menu, choose Reveal in Finder.

A Finder window opens, revealing the actual lesson files located on the hard drive.

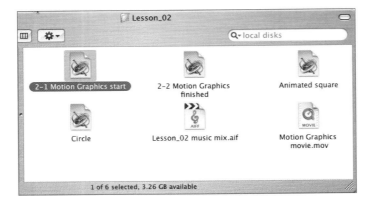

4   In the Finder window, double-click the **2-1 Motion Graphics start** file to open the project.

The project opens in the Canvas window.

There you have it—an easy way to open project files from within the File Browser using a contextual menu.

Previewing a File in the Viewer

There are two ways to view media files in Motion: You can view a small version of a file in the Preview area of the File Browser, or you can play the file in the

Viewer. Let's take a look at a QuickTime movie of our finished project using both viewing methods.

1   In the lower pane of the File Browser, click the **Motion Graphics movie.mov** file to play it in the Preview area.

The file will automatically play in a loop, which is great for quick previews but can also be annoying after a while.

2   Click the Play/Pause button in the Preview area to stop previewing.

The Preview area is useful for a quick view to see what your file looks like. However, it shows you only a very small version of your media, which may not let you see enough detail.

For a full-scale preview of your media files, you can open the file in the Viewer. To open your media file in the Viewer, you simply select Open in Viewer from the contextual menu.

3   In the File Browser, Ctrl-click the **Motion Graphics movie.mov** file.

Because this is a media file and not a project file, the contextual menu presents different choices.

4   In the contextual menu, choose Open in Viewer.

A Viewer window opens containing a full-scale version of your media file.

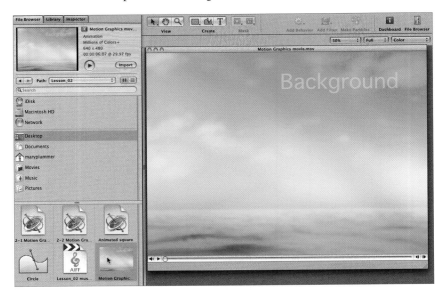

5   Click the Play button at the lower left of the Viewer to play the movie.

As you can see, the full-scale version of the finished movie gives you full-resolution details of the project you are about to complete.

6   Play the video one more time in the Viewer to see what you're going to be building in this lesson.

7   Click the Close button (X) in the upper-left corner of the Viewer window to close it.

Now that you've opened the project and previewed the final movie, let's get started.

Adding a Motion Background from the Library

There's a big difference between the project you built in Lesson 1, which was a still composite, and the one you're about to create here. However, the finished motion graphics project uses many of the same graphics building blocks that you used in the previous lesson, including a background, shapes, images, and text. They're just a lot more active.

Let's start with a background movie. Motion comes with more than 4 GB of content, including some great-looking backgrounds that you can use for your projects.

What makes a great-looking background? Good question. Of course, anything you do in the creative world of graphic design is subjective. However, for me, a great-looking background helps set the tone of a piece. It can enhance the mood and bring a project to life without distracting you from the main subject. Think of a background movie as moving wallpaper for your project. You'll notice if it isn't there or if it's really loud and tacky, but if it fits the project, it can add class and production value to the overall composite.

Graphic design is all about catching someone's attention, getting their eyes to focus on the right elements, and hoping they'll remember the important parts long after the experience.

Imagine walking into an empty room with blank walls and nothing but an Exit sign—you're likely to feel the stark barrenness of the room and want to head for that exit. On the other hand, a tastefully decorated room with an Exit sign will likely feel more inviting, and you may choose to stay awhile before exiting. Either way, you'll feel differently about the experiences, and chances are good that the second one will be more memorable.

Now that you understand the importance of a great background, let's go get one. Fortunately, all of the Motion content is conveniently organized in the Library. To view the Library content, you simply click the Library tab in the File Browser.

Then you click the Content folder to view the Motion content. The column on the right shows all of the categories of content available. If you're using the trial version, use the File Browser to find the files for this exercise in the Additional Motion Content folder in the Motion Book Files folder.

Let's narrow the content to the Seasons category.

1   In the Utility window, click the Library tab to open the Library pane.

2   Click the Content folder to see the Motion Content files.

3   Click the Seasons category to narrow the content to only the files that pertain to seasons.

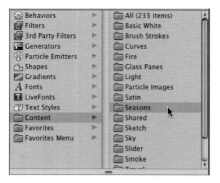

Icons for the Seasons content appear in the lower pane of the Library.

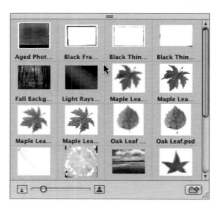

Narrowing the Content Search

To narrow the search for a specific filename or subject, you can use the refine search field located below the Preview area in the Library.

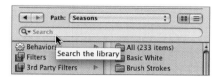

For this project, you are going to use a summer background, so let's narrow the search to backgrounds that use the word *summer*.

1   In the refine search field, type *summer* and press Return.

One file, called **Summer Background.mov**, remains in the lower pane.

2   Click the **Summer Background.mov** file icon to see the file in the Preview area.

Now that you've located the background file for the project, you can add it to the project.

3   Drag the **Summer Background.mov** icon from the Library to the center of the Canvas and release the mouse. Use the Dynamic Guides to center the background file in the Canvas.

4   Delete the word *summer* from the refine search field.

TIP It's a good idea to clear the refine search field whenever you are finished using it. That way, the next time you go to find something in the Library, you won't be confused or limited by the narrowed selections from a previous search.

Saving Your Project

Now that you've added the first object to your project, it's a good time to start saving your project in the My Motion Projects folder on your Desktop.

1 Choose File > Save As to open the Save As window.

2 Select the My Motion Projects folder on the Desktop.

3 Click the Save button or press Return to save your project.

Viewing a File in the Mini-Timeline

Two things just happened when you added the background movie to your project. First, the Summer Background movie appeared in the Canvas. Second, a Summer Background region appeared in the mini-Timeline.

What's the mini-Timeline? It's a condensed (miniature) Timeline that shows selected elements from your project. Your project elements appear in the mini-Timeline as long, barlike regions.

The mini-Timeline is located at the bottom of the Canvas window.

In this case, since the background file is selected in the Canvas, the Summer Background region appears as a blue bar in the mini-Timeline. Objects and media files appear as blue regions in the mini-Timeline.

1 Locate the mini-Timeline at the bottom of the Canvas window.

2 Choose Edit > Deselect All to deselect the Summer Background file in the Canvas.

NOTE ▶ The shortcut for Deselect All is Shift-Cmd-A.

Notice that the Summer Background region disappears from the mini-Timeline. Remember that the mini-Timeline shows only what is selected in the Canvas. If nothing is selected, the mini-Timeline is empty.

You'll work more with the mini-Timeline later in this lesson.

Playing a Project in the Canvas

Before you start playing your project, it's a good idea to know how to set your project duration and move the playhead. By default, the project duration in Motion is 10 seconds. You can change the duration in the Preferences window or in the Project Duration field.

The Project Duration field is located at the lower right of the Canvas window.

Viewing Project Timecode and Frames

You can view the project duration in timecode or frames depending on your workflow. If you work with video, you're probably more familiar with timecode. If your background is graphic design and you are more accustomed to working with frames, you may prefer to view the duration in frames. If you're not familiar with either measurement, you will be by the end of this book.

Let's start with timecode. The timecode you'll be using is the North American broadcast standard rate of 29.97 frames per second and is written from left to right as hours, minutes, seconds, and frames.

To change from timecode to frames, you can use the Stopwatch button to the left of the Project Duration field.

1   Locate the Project Duration field at the lower left of the Canvas window.

2   Click the Stopwatch button to the left of the Project Duration field to change from timecode to frames.

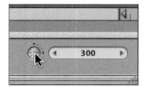

The timecode rate for the project is 29.97 frames per second, which translates to 30 frames per second when you work in frames mode. Since the project is 10 seconds long and the frame rate is 30 frames per second, the project is 300 frames total.

3   Click the Stopwatch again to change the field back to timecode.

MORE INFO ▸ You can find more detailed information about timecode in the Motion documentation that came with the application.

Changing a Project's Duration

You can change the project duration by double-clicking the Project Duration field and typing a new duration, clicking the incremental arrows, or dragging in the field.

Let's try all three methods to change the project duration. Setting timecode with the incremental arrows is like setting your digital alarm clock. You can change the timecode one frame at a time by clicking, or you can click and hold the incremental arrow until you reach the timecode you want. And the control is a little easier to set than an alarm clock, because if you overshoot your mark, you can click the opposite arrow to go the other direction, one frame at a time.

1   Click once on the small incremental arrow to the right of the Project Duration field to increase the duration by one frame.

2   Click and hold down the incremental arrow to the right of the Duration field to increase the duration to 00:00:11;00.

3   Click and hold down the mouse over the Project Duration field.

4   Move the mouse to the right or left to change the duration in the direction you are moving.

5   Click and drag the mouse again to change the timecode to 00:00:05;00.

Now let's try the last method, and actually type the duration. The good news is that timecode works from right to left, so you don't have to type the entire thing, just the part you need. For this exercise, you need to change the timecode to 6 seconds (00:00:06;00). Since the hours and minutes are zeros, you can skip those and just type *6.00*.

6   Click the timecode in the Project Duration field.

The field darkens to show it is selected.

7   Type *6.00* and press Return to set the timecode duration for the project.

The project duration is now set to 6 seconds.

NOTE ▶ Make sure that you type the period between 6 (seconds) and 00 (frames) and then press Return. If you don't type the period, you will be entering 600 frames–which changes the duration to 20 seconds. If you changed the duration to 20 seconds, simply type *6.00* and press Return to change the duration to 6 seconds.

Scrubbing the Playhead

One of the key features that allows us to see our project is the playhead. The playhead is the thin vertical bar with the yellow arrow on top, located in the scrubber area directly above the mini-Timeline. The playhead moves along your project as it plays and allows you to view one frame at a time in the Canvas. If the playhead is paused, as it is in your project, you will see only the current frame. If the playhead is moving, you will see each frame sequentially, which allows you to see movement over time.

There are many different ways to move the playhead to view your project. One method is to drag the playhead in the scrubber area—this method is called *scrubbing*. The playhead turns green when you drag it, to show that it has been selected. You can also move the playhead one frame at a time forward or backward using the left and right arrow keys. Let's try both methods to move the playhead.

1   Locate the playhead at the bottom of the Canvas window.

2   Click and drag the playhead to the right and then to the left to view different frames in the Timeline.

3   Tap the right arrow key several times to move the playhead one frame at a time to the right.

   When the playhead moves to the right, you are moving forward in time through your project.

4   Tap the left arrow key several times to move the playhead one frame at a time to the left.

   When the playhead moves to the left, you are moving backward in time (reverse) through your project.

Changing the Current Playhead Position

You have set the duration of your project and learned how to scrub the play-head; now let's look at the Current Frame field, which indicates the current playhead position.

The Current Frame field is located at the lower left of the Canvas window and works the same way the Project Duration field does.

Let's change the current frame.

1   Click the Current Frame field and type *5.00* and then press Return.

    The playhead moves forward in time to 5 seconds in the project (5;00). The image in the Canvas changes to show the project 5 seconds from the beginning.

2   Click and drag the cursor over the Current Frame field to the left to move the playhead in reverse and change the current frame to 1;11.

Now that you know how to move the playhead and change the current frame, let's set the play range for the project.

Setting a Project Play Range

A project's duration determines how long a project can be from start to finish. I stress that the duration is how long it *can* be, because you may also set a play range for your project that is shorter than the actual duration.

However long you make your project, you may want to view only a portion of the project at a given time. For instance, if your project's duration is 10 seconds and you need to work on only the first 2 seconds, then you may want to play only the first 2 seconds of the project while you work. The portion that you want to view is called the play range and is indicated by In and Out points.

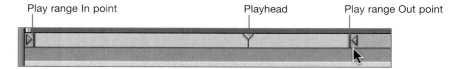

There are two easy ways to set play range In and Out points:

▶ Choose Mark > Mark Play Range In or Mark Play Range Out.

▶ Use keyboard shortcuts: Option-Cmd-I for In and Option-Cmd-O for Out.

By default, the play range In point is the beginning of the project.

Let's set the play range Out point at 3 seconds so you will play back only half of the 6-second project.

1 Drag the playhead to the right until the Current Frame field reads 3;00.

You can also type *3.00* in the Current Frame field and press Return.

2 Press Option-Cmd-O (that's the letter O, for Out point).

The play range Out point appears at the playhead position (3;00).

Now that you've set the play range, let's play the project with the transport controls.

Working with the Transport Controls

One of the first things you'll need to know as you start adding motion to your graphics is how to play your project to see how it looks.

Fortunately, there is a handy set of buttons called the transport controls that will help you play and navigate through your project.

The transport controls are located at the bottom of the Canvas window.

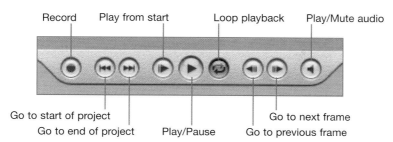

The transport controls consist of the following buttons:

▶ Record — Enables automatic keyframing, which creates and records keyframes for all parameter changes made in the Canvas, Dashboard, or Inspector.

▶ Go to start of project — Moves the playhead to the start (first frame) of the project.

▶ Go to end of project — Moves the playhead to the end of the project. The end of the project is determined in the Project Duration field.

▶ Play from start — Plays the project from the play range In point.

▶ Play/Pause — Starts or pauses playback in the Canvas.

▶ Loop playback — Loops playback within the project play range.

▶ Go to previous frame — Allows you to move the playhead toward the beginning of the project one frame at a time.

▶ Go to next frame — Allows you to move the playhead forward one frame at a time.

▶ Play/Mute audio — Toggles the project audio on or off during playback in the Canvas.

The Record button is a more advanced feature, so we'll save it for Lesson 9.

The rest of the transport controls are pretty self-explanatory; however, the best way to learn is by doing, so let's take the transport controls for a test-drive.

1   Click the "Go to start of project" button, which looks like a line with two arrows pointing left.

The playhead moves to the beginning of the project.

Notice that the current frame is 00:00:00;00, which indicates the very beginning of the Timeline.

2   Click the Loop playback button to turn loop playback off.

By default, loop playback is turned on.

3   Click the Play button, which is the largest button in the center of the transport controls, to play the project once.

Notice that the playhead stops at the play range Out point, instead of the end of the project. That's because the play range Out point determines what part of the project you will see during playback.

4   Click the Loop playback button again to turn looping back on.

When loop playback is on, the entire play range will repeat (loop) over and over until you stop playback.

5   Click the "Play from start" button, which is located just to the left of the Play button.

The project will begin playing from the beginning. The Play button becomes a Pause button while the project is playing.

6   Click the Pause button to pause playback.

Using Keyboard Shortcuts for Transport Control

Like most professional applications, Motion is full of easy-to-learn keyboard shortcuts for quick navigation through your project. Here are a few shortcuts for starters.

1   Press the spacebar to play your project.

2   Press the spacebar again to pause.

3 Press the Home key to move the playhead to the beginning of the project.

4 Press the End key to move the playhead to the end of the project.

> **NOTE ▶** If you are working on a laptop computer, you will need to hold down the Function (Fn) key before you press the Home (left arrow) or End (right arrow) key.

5 Press Shift-Cmd-A to deselect any objects selected in the project.

6 Press Shift-I to move the playhead to the play range In point.

7 Press Shift-O to move the playhead to the play range Out point.

   Shift-I and Shift-O move the playhead to the play range In or Out point, unless you have an object selected in the project. If an object is selected, Shift-I and Shift-O move the playhead to the first or last frame of the selected object.

8 Hold down the Shift key and tap the right arrow key to move 10 frames to the right.

9 Hold down the Shift key and tap the left arrow key to move 10 frames to the left.

Project Task

Let's apply your new skills to the project. Here is your goal: Change the play range Out point to the end of the project (5;29). Why 5;29 if the project is 6 seconds long? Because the first frame of the project timecode is 00:00:00;00. You can change the first frame from 00;00 to 00;01 in the Preferences window. If the first frame is 00;01, then the last frame will be 06;00. Both timecode scenarios are exactly 6 seconds long.

If you'd like a little guidance through this task, follow these steps:

1 Press the End key to move the playhead to the end of the project, or click the "Go to end of project" button in the transport controls.

2   Press Option-Cmd-O to set the play range Out point to the playhead position.

Notice that the Current Frame field shows that the playhead is at 5;29, while the Duration field shows that the duration is 6;00.

Adding and Modifying Objects During Playback

One of the great features of Motion is that it was designed to be used while a project is playing. That means that you can add files and even adjust them while the playhead is moving—in real time! Anyone who's worked with motion graphics over the past decade will appreciate the magnitude of this feature.

Real time means that you can see live updates to your project as you make changes. You don't need to stop, render, take a nap, and come back in a few hours to see the changes. It all happens before your eyes in the Canvas.

So let's add a prebuilt yellow circle to your project while the playhead is moving.

> **NOTE ▶** One point to remember is that an object will always start at the beginning of the project if you add it while the playhead is moving. You can also change the Motion preferences to add all new objects at the playhead position. The default setting is for objects to start at the beginning of the project.

Then you'll add a drop shadow and move the circle into position to add some animation.

The circle is part of the content in the Lesson_02 folder.

1   Press the spacebar or click the Play button in the transport controls to begin playback.

2   Click the File Browser tab to change from the Library to the File Browser pane.

3   Locate the Circle icon in the lower pane of the File Browser.

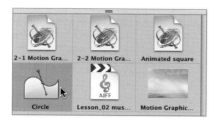

NOTE ▶ If the lower pane of the File Browser does not show the contents of your Lesson_02 folder, navigate to the Lesson_02 folder in the File Browser and double-click the Lesson_02 folder to reveal the contents.

4   Drag the Circle icon from the File Browser to the center of the Canvas and release the mouse.

Two things happen when you release the mouse: A yellow circle appears in the middle of the Canvas in front of the Summer Background movie, and a blue region called Circle copy appears in the mini-Timeline.

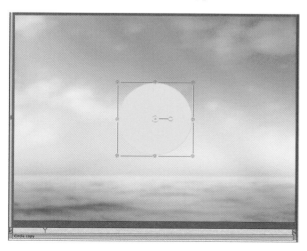

Let's separate that circle from the background by adding a drop shadow.

5 Press D to open the Dashboard.

6 Click the Drop Shadow box in the Dashboard to add a drop shadow to the circle.

Now let's reposition the circle so it will enter the frame from the right as it moves instead of appearing in the middle.

7 Press Cmd-– (hyphen) to zoom out in the Canvas by one level.

8 Drag the circle and place it just outside the frame in the upper right of the Canvas window.

Why place the circle outside the frame instead of inside the frame? Good question. For the circle to enter the frame, it must originally be placed outside the frame, just as when you want to show someone entering a room, the person must start the scene outside the room.

Circle object outside the upper-right corner of the frame

NOTE ▶ Whenever you move an object outside the viewable frame area, you will not be able to see the object, only the bounding box around the object.

9 Close the Dashboard window.

10 Press Cmd-S to save your progress.

Great! You have successfully imported a shape over a background, added a drop shadow, and moved the object out of the frame. Now all you need to do is make the shape move.

Animating an Object with Behaviors

Another really exciting feature of Motion is the ability to add behaviors to your project elements. Behaviors allow you to animate objects using simple, graphical controls. You'll be working with many different behaviors throughout the course of this book. For this exercise, you'll apply two different behaviors from the Library.

Before you add a behavior to an object, it's a really good idea to have a goal. If you know what you want to accomplish, it's much easier to choose the right behaviors for the job. Your goal in this exercise is to have the yellow circle enter the frame on the right, move across the screen toward the left, bounce off the left edge of the frame, and exit the screen frame right.

It's also a good idea to apply behaviors while the playhead is moving, so let's change the play range for the entire duration of the yellow circle's onscreen debut.

For this project, the yellow circle should be visible on the screen for the first 4 seconds. That means you should change the play range for the yellow circle's performance so that it ends at 4 seconds.

Dragging the Play Range Points

Let's move the play range Out point to 4;00. To do this, as you learned earlier in this lesson, you can move the playhead to 4 seconds and then press Option-Cmd-O. You can also drag the play range Out point to move it.

When you drag the play range In or Out point, you will see a small yellow display that shows you the new current frame for the In or Out point.

Since you haven't tried that method yet, this is a good time to test it out.

1   Click the play range Out point and drag toward the right.

A yellow dialog window appears to show the changing timecode of the play range Out point.

2   Drag the play range Out point until the window shows that the timecode is 4;00.

3   Press Shift-Cmd-A to deselect all of the objects in the project.

The mini-Timeline shows only the play range points.

4   Press the spacebar to play the project.

Now you're ready to animate the yellow circle.

Previewing a Behavior in the Library

The icon for behaviors in Motion is a gear, because behaviors represent a mechanical part, or movement. The Basic Motion behaviors are located in the Library; these are basic behaviors that are commonly used in motion graphics. Let's go to the Library and find the Basic Motion behaviors.

1   Click the Library tab, or press Cmd-2, to open the Library pane.

2 Click the Behaviors icon at the top of the upper pane of the Library.

Motion comes with more than 180 premade behaviors that are organized into categories.

3 Click the Basic Motion behaviors folder in the right column of the upper pane.

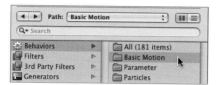

Remember your goal: to make the yellow circle move across the screen. Behaviors have simple names to make it easy to understand what they do. To move an object, all you need to do is *throw* it.

4 Click the Throw behavior to view it in the preview area at the top of the Library window.

Throw behavior selected in File Browser Throw behavior in Preview area

Applying a Basic Motion Behavior

Now that you've previewed the Throw behavior in the Library, it's time to apply it to the yellow circle.

To add a behavior to an object, you simply drag and drop the behavior on the object, or select the behavior and click the Apply button. Let's try the first method and throw the behavior (pun intended) onto the circle.

1   Press the spacebar to start playback if you stopped it in the last exercise.

2   Click the Circle object to see the bounding box, if it's not already visible.

3   Drag the Throw behavior icon from the Library to the circle in the Canvas; release the mouse.

   A purple region named Throw appears in the mini-Timeline. Behaviors and filters are always represented by purple regions in the mini-Timeline.

Now that you've added the behavior, you need to show it what to do.

Modifying Behaviors in the Dashboard

In the old days of motion graphics, we had to plot graphs, calculate motion vectors, and apply more math than creativity to make a simple object move across the screen. Fortunately, those days are over. What once took hours or days to accomplish can now be done in seconds. Not only that, but Motion also does all of the calculating for you. All you need to do is use the graphical interface in the Dashboard to adjust the behaviors.

1   Press the spacebar to begin playback if your project is not already moving.

2   Press D to open the Dashboard if it is not already open.

   The Throw behavior is represented by a circle in the Dashboard.

The crosshairs in the center of the circle represent your object. To make the object move, simply click and drag your pointer in the direction you want the object to go. An arrow appears in the direction that you drag the mouse. The longer the arrow, the farther and faster the object will be thrown.

3   Drag toward the lower left of the Throw display in the Dashboard to throw the circle.

Your circle moves toward the lower left of the screen.

NOTE ▶ If you wish to extend the arrow longer than the graphical interface allows in the Dashboard, you can adjust the Zoom slider on the right side of the Dashboard. The Zoom slider allows you to zoom into or out of the graphical interface. Dragging the Zoom slider upward zooms out of the interface so that you can extend the arrow the farthest distance.

4   Drag the Throw display again to adjust the angle so the circle exits about one-third from the bottom on the left side of the frame.

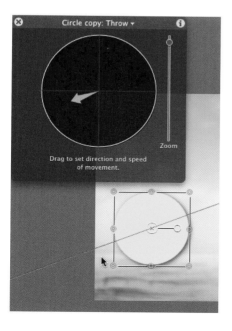

Your circle follows a red line that indicates the motion path that you just added with the Throw behavior.

Keep your playback moving for the next exercise.

Working with a Simulation Behavior

As you can see, basic behaviors are very easy to apply and adjust. There are also Simulation behaviors that use complex mathematical physics and geometry to simulate acts of nature such as gravity, wind, and orbit. Once again, Motion takes care of the calculations; all you need to do is apply the behavior and adjust it in the Dashboard.

To make an object bounce off the edges of the screen, you use a Simulation behavior called Edge Collision. When the yellow circle collides with an edge of the frame, it will bounce off in a different direction. How far it bounces is based on how hard (fast) you throw the object against the edge of the frame.

Let's add an Edge Collision behavior so the yellow circle bounces off the left and bottom edges of the screen, sending it back out the way it came in, from frame right.

1   Click the Simulations folder in the right column of the upper pane in the Library.

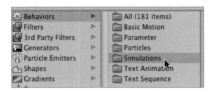

2   Locate the Edge Collision behavior in the lower pane of the Library.

3   Drag the Edge Collision icon from the Library to the moving circle; release the mouse.

Notice the Edge Collision interface in the Dashboard. Also notice how the motion path bends as the circle bounces off the different edges of the frame.

NOTE ▶ Make sure you release the behavior on the yellow circle. If you accidentally drop it on the background, press Cmd-Z to undo and try again.

You want the circle to collide off only the left and bottom edges of the frame, so your next step is to set this in the Dashboard.

4 Uncheck the boxes in the Dashboard for the top and right edges to change the motion path created by the Edge Collision behavior.

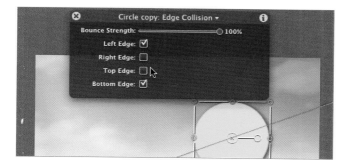

If your circle is not exiting on the right side of the frame, you may need to adjust the angle and speed of your Throw behavior. You'll do that in the next exercise.

Adjusting Behavior Timing in the Dashboard

Remember the original goal for these behaviors. You've accomplished part of the mission by throwing the circle against the left edge of the frame and having it bounce off in the other direction. The other part of the goal is to have the circle exit frame right at 4 seconds.

Take a moment to watch your project play back and see if the circle is completely out of frame by the time the playhead reaches the end of the play range. If it isn't, you can easily change that by adjusting the throw controls in the Dashboard.

1   Press the D key to cycle from the Edge Collision behavior to the Throw behavior in the Dashboard.

2   Drag the arrow in the Dashboard toward the edge of the circle display to throw the circle faster.

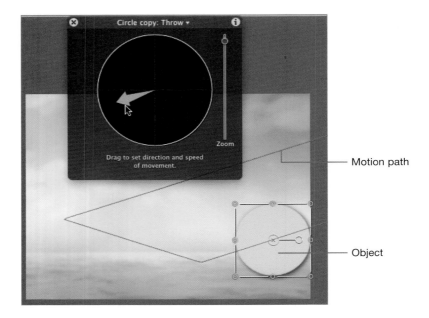

Remember: The longer the arrow, the faster and harder you are throwing the object.

You can use the red motion path as a guide to see where the circle enters and exits the frame.

3   Adjust the speed of the throw (length of the arrow) until the circle exits completely at the end of the play range.

4   Adjust the angle of the throw to make sure the circle exits on the right side of the frame.

Mission accomplished! You're ready to move on with the rest of the project. First, though, let's hide the motion path.

Hiding the Motion Path

The red motion path is a visual guide that lets you see the direction and movement of an object. However, it can also be distracting as you try to build your project. To hide the motion path, simply deselect the object that is moving.

1   Click the empty (gray) space outside the frame to deselect everything in the Canvas.

The circle continues moving, but the motion path and Dashboard disappear.

If you want to see the motion path again, simply click the moving object to select it.

2   Click the yellow circle while it's moving to select it again.

The red motion path appears along with the bounding box around the circle, to show that the circle is selected. A blue region called Circle copy appears in the mini-Timeline.

3   Press Shift-Cmd-A to deselect everything again.

Now that you're armed with a basic knowledge of behaviors, let's move on to particles.

Working with Particles

The next exciting feature in our Tour de Motion is the wonderful world of particles. If you thought adding a behavior was fun, wait until you see the particles in action.

Particles are used in motion graphics to create smoke, fire, snow, falling leaves, and other special effects that require many objects created from one primary object (cell). The particle cell is multiplied through a particle emitter. For example, with a particle emitter you can turn a single raindrop (cell) into many particles to create a torrential rainstorm.

The icon for a particle emitter in Motion looks like a cone erupting with sparkles. The cone represents the emitter, and the sparkles represent the particles.

Remember: This chapter is just an introduction to many of the Motion features. You'll get a chance to work more with particles in Lesson 6.

Let's take a look at some of the particle emitters that come with Motion. Because the particle emitters are part of the Motion content, you'll find them in the Library.

1 Click the Library tab or press Cmd-2 to open the Library, if it's not already open.

If the Utility window closed, press Cmd-2 again to reopen the Library in the Utility window.

2 Locate the Particle Emitters icon in the upper pane of the Library.

3 Click the Nature folder to narrow the selections to the Nature category.

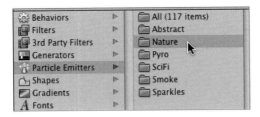

4 Click the icon for the Big Rain particle emitter in the lower pane to preview the emitter at the top of window.

The Big Rain particle emitter creates a continuous stream of rain in the lower half of the preview area.

Using the Particle Emitter Preview

Okay—so you can preview the Big Rain particle emitter in the lower half of the preview window. Wouldn't it be nice if you could see the rain as it covers the entire window? Well, you can.

Not only can you preview a particle emitter, but you can also change its position while it is previewing.

To change the position in the preview window, simply click and drag your pointer over the preview window. Wherever the pointer goes, the particle emitter follows. Let's try it.

1   Click the Big Rain particle emitter to begin playback in the preview window if the emitter isn't already playing.

2   Click and drag your pointer toward the lower portion of the preview window.

    The rain follows the pointer and begins at the bottom of the window.

3   Drag your pointer toward the top of the preview window.

    The rain follows, now covering the entire preview window.

    Now let's try another particle emitter.

4   Click the Bubble Machine particle emitter located just to the right of the Big Rain particle emitter in the lower pane of the Library.

5   Click and drag your pointer to different corners of the preview window to move the stream of bubbles.

Let's apply some bubbles to our project.

Adding Particles to the Canvas

Now that you've had a chance to view a few different particle emitters, you're ready to add one to the project. You can add a particle emitter to your project in either of two simple ways:

▶   Select an emitter in the Library and click the Apply button.

▶   Drag and drop an emitter from the Library to the Canvas.

For this exercise, you'll use the second method.

1   Press the spacebar to begin playback in the Canvas, if the project is not already playing.

2   In the Library, select the Bubbles Rising particle emitter; it is located next to the Bubble Machine particle emitter.

3   Drag the icon for the Bubbles Rising particle emitter from the lower pane of the Library to the center of the Canvas; release the mouse.

The Bubbles Rising particle emitter adds a flurry of bouncing bubbles to the center of your project.

That was easy. You've successfully added particles to your motion graphics project. So what do you think of your project now?

Focusing the Audience's Attention

I like the bubbles floating about the screen. The only problem is that they compete with our flying yellow circle. This may not be a real-world project, but we should still apply real-world aesthetics and professional design techniques.

Throughout this book, I'll throw in some basic motion graphics design rules I've come up with over the years. Keep in mind that rules are meant to be broken and that motion graphics design is very subjective, so there are no absolutes. These "rules" are more like guidelines to help you make your Motion projects visually effective.

Rule #1: Decide where you want the audience to focus its attention, and direct your motion graphics scene accordingly.

This may seem like an obvious concept, but it's often overlooked, especially by those who are new to motion graphics. The various elements of your project are like characters in a scene. There are main characters—for instance, the product in a television ad—and supporting characters—like bubbles—that enhance the mood or action in a scene without stealing all the attention. If this were an ad for bubbles, you'd be on the right track, but it's not.

In the project we've been creating, the moving yellow circle is a main character. When you play the project, your eyes are immediately drawn to the circle as it enters the frame. Unfortunately, the bubbles arrive too early and attract your attention and keep it. If this were an ad for the yellow circle, you would have just lost your audience, and your client.

Watch the project again to see how your eyes become distracted from the circle.

So how do you keep the bubbles and your job? Simple. Start the bubbles later, when the circle is on its way off the screen. That way, the circle gets its solo debut, and the bubbles become a pleasant addition to the cast rather than stealing the show.

Trimming in the Mini-Timeline

Motion offers two simple ways to trim a region in the mini-Timeline:

▶ Drag the edge of the region to extend or shorten it.

▶ Move the playhead to the place you want to trim, and press I to edit the beginning (In point) or O to edit the ending (Out point).

Let's use the second method, using the playhead and the keyboard shortcut.

1 Click the bubbles in the Canvas to select the Bubbles Rising layer in your project.

The blue region called Bubbles Rising should appear in the mini-Timeline.

NOTE ▶ If your mini-Timeline has anything in it other than Bubbles Rising, deselect everything and try again.

2 Press the spacebar to pause playback.

This method of trimming a region requires that you stop playback.

3 Select the Current Frame field and type *2.15* and then press Return.

The playhead moves to 2;15 in the mini-Timeline. Notice that the yellow circle is on its way out of the frame.

4 Press the I key to trim the Bubbles Rising region so that it starts at 2;15.

The blue Bubbles Rising region changes in the mini-Timeline so that it starts at the playhead position.

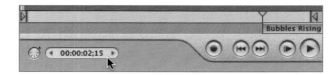

5 Press the spacebar again to resume playback.

6 Press Cmd-S to save your progress.

Importing Motion Projects into the Canvas

Not only can you import media files and particles into a project, but you can also import a Motion project file. When you import a Motion file into your project, all the elements in the project remain intact and can be adjusted in the new project.

To import a Motion project, you can either drag it to the Canvas or select it and click the Import button. If you drag it, you can place the file contents anywhere on the screen. If you click the Import button, the file contents will maintain the same positions as in the original project.

In this exercise, you'll import a Motion project into the current project. The Motion project you'll be adding includes a moving white square that turns into a moving image of clouds wrapped in a delicate black frame—compliments of the Motion content in the Library.

1 Click the File Browser tab or press Cmd-1 to view the File Browser.

2 Locate the Animated square Motion project icon.

3 Click the Animated square project icon to select it.

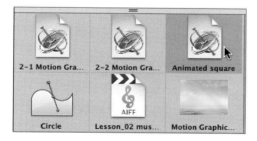

4 Press the spacebar to begin playback in the Canvas, if the project isn't already playing.

5 At the top of the File Browser window, click the Import button to import the file to the project.

A white square slowly moves onscreen and continues toward the center. Notice that the white square doesn't really compete for our attention until the image inside changes to clouds. This also coincides with the yellow circle's exit at frame right.

Notice that because the bubbles are behind the square image, they act more as accents than distractions. That's because the Animated square object was added *after* the bubbles, so it is above the previous objects, including the background, yellow circle, and bubbles.

You'll work more with object order and layers in the next lesson.

Animating Text in the Canvas

In the preceding lesson, you learned how to create a text object and color it. In this exercise, you'll create text, adjust the timing, and animate the text with text behaviors.

We'll start by creating the text. Remember to keep your playback going the entire time.

1 Press T to select the Text tool.

2 Click the text cursor below the Images (square) object in the center of the Canvas.

NOTE ▶ Don't worry if your cursor isn't exactly where you want it; you can always move the text object after you create it.

3 Type *TEXT* and then press the Esc key to return to the Select/Transform tool.

NOTE ▶ The Select/Transform tool is the default tool that you use when working with Motion.

TEXT appears in the Canvas inside a bounding box.

4 Press D to open the Dashboard.

5 Open the Font pop-up menu in the Dashboard and change the font to Arial Black.

6 Drag the Size slider to change the font size to 68 points.

7 Click the color well (the white rectangle) to open the Colors window; choose red from the color wheel, and then close the Colors window.

8 Drag the TEXT object to reposition it below the Images object.

You've created the text. Now you will animate it.

Adding Text Behaviors

Adding behaviors to text is as easy as adding behaviors to any other object in your project. You simply select the behavior and then drag it to the text object or click the Apply button. The text behaviors are located in the Library along with the other Motion behaviors.

Text behaviors do one of three things:

▶ Make text appear in the project.

▶ Make text disappear from the project.

▶ Make text flash, glow, bounce, wiggle, or act in some similar way.

In this exercise, we'll make text appear in the project by applying a text behavior to our TEXT object.

1 Click the Library tab, or press Cmd-2, to switch to the Library tab.

2 Click the Behaviors icon to select it in the Library.

The Behaviors icon looks like a gear and is located at the top of the upper pane in the Library.

3 Click the Text Sequence category of behaviors to view the text behavior categories.

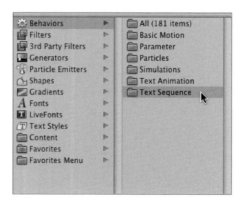

4   Locate the Text-Move folder in the lower pane of the Library.

5   Double-click the Text-Move folder to open it.

There are quite a few Text-Move behaviors to choose from. Let's change to List view to make them easier to see.

6   Click the List view button located at the top of the Library window.

7   Click the accordion icon in the lower pane of the Library to see the behavior in the preview area at the top of the window.

The words *Text Behavior* unfold like an accordion, mimicking the behavior of text appearing in the project.

You can scroll through the various behaviors in the list by using the up and down arrow keys on your keyboard.

8   Click the down arrow to move down the list until you reach the Drop In Random behavior. Then, watch the selected Drop In Random behavior in the preview area.

Now you can apply the behavior to the TEXT object. To add the behavior, make sure your object is selected in the Canvas.

9   Drag the Drop In Random icon from the Library to the TEXT object in the Canvas; release the mouse.

The text is now animated, and a purple region appears in the mini-Timeline. Remember: Objects appear as blue regions in the mini-Timeline, and Behaviors appear as purple regions.

Changing Animated Text Timing

Earlier in this lesson, you adjusted the timing of the Bubbles Rising particle emitter so that it began exactly at the 2;15 position in the mini-Timeline. Our goal with the text is to make it look like it is dropping out of the Images square. To do that, the Images square needs to be in its final position *before* the text appears.

Let's apply what you've learned so far to adjust the timing of the text.

1   Press the spacebar to stop playback.

2   Press Shift-Cmd-A to deselect everything in the Canvas.

3   Drag the playhead to scrub forward in the project until the Images square stops in its final position (3;00).

4   Click the TEXT object in the Canvas to select it.

A bounding box appears around the word *TEXT*, and a blue text region appears in the mini-Timeline.

5   Drag the blue text region in the mini-Timeline until it begins at the playhead position (3;00).

Why drag the region instead of pressing I to trim it? Because if you drag the region for an object, you move not only the object but also all its behaviors. If you trim an object that has behaviors attached, you may also trim the behaviors, which will change the timing of the behavior.

6   Press Shift-Cmd-A to deselect all elements in the project.

Resetting the Play Range

Your project is almost complete. Let's take a look at the entire project. To do that, you need to reset the play range. When you reset the play range, the play range In point moves to the first frame of the project, and the play range Out point moves to the last frame of the project. There are two methods for resetting the play range:

▶   Choose Mark > Reset Play Range.

▶   Press Option-X.

Since you haven't used a menu in a while, let's use the menu method to reset the play range.

1   Choose Mark > Reset Play Range.

The play range Out point moves to the end of the project (6;00).

2   Press the spacebar to play the entire project.

Looks pretty good for a motion graphics interface demo! It could use a little music, though.

Adding Audio to a Project

MORE INFO ▶ The last step in your demo project is adding music. The project has an overall happy, bubbly, techno feel—to fit the mood, I created a simple tune in the Apple Pro application Soundtrack.

Adding audio is as easy as adding any other file to a project. You simply select the file in the File Browser and then drag or click the Import button.

1   Press Cmd-1 to open the File Browser, or click the File Browser tab.

2   Locate the **Lesson_02 music mix** file in the lower pane of the File Browser.

3   Click the Lesson_02 music mix icon to preview (listen to) the file.

4   Drag the Lesson_02 music mix icon to the Canvas to import it into the project.

A green region representing the audio file appears in the mini-Timeline. All audio files appear as green regions in the Motion Timeline.

Congratulations! You've just completed a motion graphics project with Motion's user-friendly interface.

MORE INFO ▶ You can find more information about Soundtrack on the Apple Web site and in *Soundtrack*, another Apple Pro Training Series book by Mary Plummer, from Peachpit Press.

Viewing the Project and Timing Panes

Before you move on to the next lesson, I'd like you to take a quick look at the Timing pane. Up to this point, you have built two complete projects using only the Canvas window. There are two additional ways that you can view and interact with your project.

The *Project pane* shows all the different layers and media in the project. If you are accustomed to working with layer-based design software such as Adobe Photoshop, then the Project pane will look very familiar.

The *Timing pane* shows a timeline view of your project with different tracks for each layer, behavior, and effect. If you are accustomed to working with timeline-based software such as Final Cut Pro, then you will find this pane familiar.

You'll get to work with each of these panes in later lessons. For now, let's just take a look to see where they are and how to show and hide them.

Motion offers three easy ways to open the Project and Timing panes:

▶ Choose Window > Show Project Pane or Window > Show Timing Pane.

▶ Drag the left edge of the Canvas window to open the Project pane or the bottom edge of the Canvas window to open the Timing pane.

▶ Press F5 to open the Project pane or F6 to open the Timing pane.

NOTE ▶ If you are using a laptop computer, you'll need to hold down the Function (Fn) key before you press a numbered function key.

The keystroke shortcuts are easy to use. Let's try them here.

1 Press F5 to open the Project pane.

The Project pane opens on the left side of the Canvas window. This pane contains all the objects used in the project.

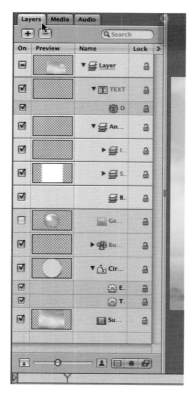

If your Project pane looks different from the one in the illustration, don't worry—you'll learn how to organize the objects and layers in the next lesson.

2 Press F5 again to close the Project pane.

3 Press F6 to open the Timing pane.

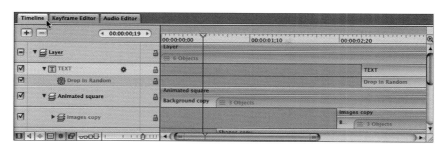

As you can see, all the different objects and their regions are visible on the Timeline tab of the Timing pane. You'll work more with the Timing pane throughout the book, especially in Lesson 8.

4 Press F6 again to close the Timing pane.

Saving and Closing Your Project

Now that you've finished your tour of the Motion user interface, it's time to save and close your project.

1 Press Cmd-S to save the project.

2 Choose File > Close to close your project.

The Canvas window closes, and you're ready for the next lesson.

What You've Learned

▶ You can use contextual menus in the File Browser to open files in the Viewer or reveal projects in the Finder to open them.

▶ Motion comes with more than 4 GB of content, including background movies.

▶ The Motion content is located in the Library pane in the File Browser window.

▶ You can narrow the search for content in the Library by typing the file-name in the refine search field.

▶ The mini-Timeline displays a colored region for the selected element in the Canvas. The different region colors represent different types of elements: blue for media files, purple for behaviors or filters, and green for audio files.

▶ You can view or change the project duration as frames or timecode in the Project Duration field.

▶ There are many different ways to move the playhead, including dragging the mouse, using keyboard shortcuts, changing the Current Frame field, and clicking buttons in the transport controls.

▶ The play range for a project isolates the portion of the project that you want to play in the Canvas. You can change the play range In and Out points by moving the playhead and pressing Option-Cmd-I (for the In point) or Option-Cmd-O (for the Out point). You can also drag a play range In or Out point in the scrubber area to move it.

▶ The spacebar is a keyboard shortcut for playing or pausing a project and will always play the project from the beginning to the end of the play range.

▶ By default, the Loop playback button in the transport controls is on so that playback will loop continuously while you work in the Canvas.

▶ Behaviors allow you to animate objects using simple graphical controls in the Dashboard. You can find behaviors in the Library pane. Behaviors are organized into folders by type, including Basic Motion behaviors and Simulation behaviors.

▶ Particle emitters allow you to create many objects (particles) from a single object (cell). Particle emitters are also organized into categories and are located in the Library.

▶ You can trim a region in the mini-Timeline by dragging the edge or by moving the playhead and pressing I to trim the beginning or O to trim the end to the playhead position.

▶ The Library contains many text behaviors that you can use to animate text. The text behaviors make text appear, disappear, or move around.

▶ You can add audio files to a project by selecting them and then dragging them to the Canvas or clicking the Import button at the top of the File Browser.

▶ Motion includes a Timing pane for viewing the Timeline, and a Project pane for viewing the objects and layers in a project.

3

Lesson Files

Lesson_03 > New Project

Master_Project > 03 Master Project start

Time

This lesson takes approximately 2 hours to complete.

Goals

Create a new project

Loop a media file

Change parameters in the Inspector

Select objects and layers on the Layers tab

Group objects to create sublayers

Replace media files

Change the order of objects on the Layers tab

Show and hide layers and objects

Crop objects in the Inspector

Change the opacity of a layer

Work with blend modes

Working with Layers in the Project Pane

Now that you've worked with the basic interface and created a motion graphics project, it's time to master layers. Understanding and organizing layers is the key to compositing, as well as to developing a solid workflow for even the most complex motion graphics projects.

In this lesson, you'll create a real-world professional project from scratch using the Project pane, the Inspector, and the Canvas. Not only will you learn how the Project pane works, but you'll also learn to plan and create a project layer by layer from the background up. The last step will be adding blend modes to polish your project with professional-looking style. Along the way, you'll also learn some time-saving and creative design tricks and tips. Sound exciting? Just wait until you see your final project!

Previewing the Finished Movie

Before you start building the project, let's take a look at the final version so you have an idea of what you're aiming for in this lesson.

The project is an introduction for a professional photographer's reel. But the photographer isn't your average amateur stringing together snapshots for a home movie. The introduction you'll be creating is the actual opening sequence for award-winning photographer Jeffrey A. Graves, who has traveled the globe, sometimes months at a time, taking photos for major companies and publications. That puts a lot more demand on the graphic designer.

The challenge is not only to show a few choice photos in an interesting manner; you also need to encompass the scope of the photographer's career—all in a mere 8 seconds.

Now that you have some perspective on the project, let's take a look.

1   Close any open Motion projects.

2   Open the Lesson_03 folder in the lower pane of the File Browser.

    NOTE ▶ The path for Lesson_03 is Desktop > MOTION_INTRO Book Files > Lesson_03.

3   Click the List view button at the top of the File Browser to see the contents of the Lesson_03 folder in List view.

    The Lesson_03 folder includes a lot of different project elements, so it will be easier to work from List view.

4   Ctrl-click the file **03_Final Project** in the lower pane of the File Browser and choose Open in Viewer from the contextual menu.

5   Click the Play button, or press the spacebar, to watch the final movie in the Viewer.

As you watch the movie, notice all of the different elements interacting with one another to create the overall composite.

6   Close the Viewer.

Creating a New Project

Now that you've seen the finished project, let's create it. In the previous lessons, you opened projects that I had prepared for you in advance. This time, you'll create a project yourself.

Setting the Project Preset

One of the first steps in creating a new project is to decide what type of project you'll be creating. You can select the type of project from the list of presets in the Preferences window. This project you're creating is the introduction for a digital video promo that will be edited in Final Cut Pro. Let's open the Preferences window and select the DV preset for the new project.

There are three simple ways to open the Motion Preferences window:

▶   Choose Motion > Preferences.

▶   Press Cmd-, (comma).

▶   Launch Motion from the Finder and choose Start a New Project from the Welcome window.

For this exercise, you'll use the most common method: You'll choose Motion from the Preferences menu.

1 Choose Motion > Preferences.

The Preferences window opens.

The Preferences window includes many different panes that you can view and modify, including General, Appearance, Project, Canvas, Output, Presets, and Gestures. Throughout this book, you will learn many different preference settings as you need them. For now, you'll focus on the presets.

2 Click the Presets icon at the top of the Preferences window to open the Presets pane.

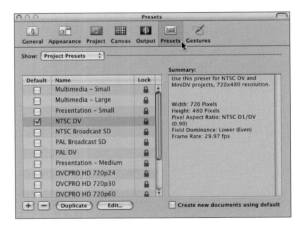

The left side of the Presets pane lists the presets available for your project. The right side shows the Summary field, where you can read a summary of the selected preset.

Motion offers more than a dozen different presets to accommodate any type of project you wish to build in Motion. These presets cover everything from multimedia to broadcast and high-definition television.

3 In the Project Presets list on the left side of the window, click the NTSC DV preset to select it and see the summary of the preset.

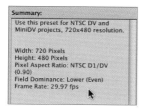

The NTSC DV summary shows that a project created using this preset will be at 720 × 480 resolution. NTSC DV is a common format for consumer video cameras and is a good resolution size for this exercise.

MORE INFO ► You can find more specific information on the various Motion presets in the Motion documentation that comes with the application.

Selecting a Default Preset

If you use the same preset in most of your projects, you can set a default preset so that all your new projects will be created with the default settings. You can always change the preset or the default when needed. Let's set NTSC DV as the default preset.

To set a default preset, you simply click the Default check box next to the desired preset. You can set only one default preset at a time.

1 On the left side of the Presets pane, click the box in the Default column next to the NTSC DV preset.

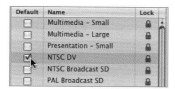

A check appears in the box to show that this preset is the default.

You can also choose to create all new documents using the default by checking the box at the bottom of the window.

2   Check the "Create new documents using default" box at the bottom right of the Presets pane, if it's not already checked.

Now when you create a new project, it will automatically use the default preset NTSC DV.

You're finished with the Presets pane for now.

3   Click the Close button (X) in the upper-left corner of the window to close it.

Opening a New Project

Now that you've selected a preset, it's time to open a new project. There are two ways to start a new project in Motion:

▶   Choose File > New.

▶   Press Cmd-N.

For this exercise, let's try the keyboard shortcut method, since it is such an easy shortcut to remember.

1   Press Cmd-N to open a new project.

An empty Canvas window opens, ready to build your project.

Now set the duration for the project and play range.

2   In the Project Duration field, type *8.00* and press Return.

3   Press Option-X to reset the play range to the entire duration of the project.

The last step is saving the project. It's always a good idea to save your project as you go. In this case, this will be the starting point for your project.

4   Choose File > Save As to open the Save As window.

5   In the Save As field, type *3-1 starting*.

6   Click the pop-up menu below the Save As field and choose My Motion
    Projects from the Recent Places list at the bottom of the menu.

7   Click the Save button at the lower right of the window to save your project
    in the My Motion Projects folder on the Desktop.

Exploring Import File Types

In the first two lessons, you imported different types of media files into your
projects. As you have already experienced, it is easy to import files by either
dragging them to the Canvas or clicking the Import button. It is also important to understand the different types of media that you can import into your
projects. Throughout this book, you'll be importing a variety of formats,
including TIFF, JPEG, and even layered Photoshop files.

Motion supports a wide variety of video, still-image, and audio files for both
multimedia and broadcast. Since it's a QuickTime standard application,
Motion supports many of the same file formats that QuickTime does.

Here is a partial list of the most popular file formats that Motion supports. You can use it as a quick reference when creating your projects.

Still-image formats:

- ▶ BMP
- ▶ JPEG
- ▶ JPEG-2
- ▶ MacPaint
- ▶ Photoshop
- ▶ PICT
- ▶ PNG
- ▶ QuickTime image files
- ▶ SGI
- ▶ TGA
- ▶ TIFF

QuickTime video codecs:

- ▶ Animation
- ▶ Apple DV/DVCPRO
- ▶ Apple DVCPRO HD
- ▶ Apple DVCPRO50
- ▶ Apple M-JPEG A and B
- ▶ Pixlet
- ▶ Uncompressed 8- and 10-bit 4:2:2

Other image formats:

- ▶ Layered Photoshop files
- ▶ PDF files

Audio formats:

- ▶ AAC (listed in the Finder with the .m4p file extension)
- ▶ AIFF
- ▶ CDDA
- ▶ MP3
- ▶ WAV

QuickTime audio codecs:

- ▶ 24-bit integer
- ▶ 32-bit floating point
- ▶ 32-bit integer
- ▶ 64-bit floating point
- ▶ ALaw 2:1
- ▶ AMR narrowband
- ▶ Apple lossless
- ▶ IMA 4:1
- ▶ MACE 3:1
- ▶ MACE 6:1
- ▶ MPEG-4 audio

Now the next time you create a project, you will know how to change the preset for the new project and what types of files you can import.

MORE INFO ▶ If you'd like more specific information about the different file formats that Motion supports, consult the Motion documentation that came with the application.

Shortcuts from the File Browser to the Project Pane

Some say that a successful project is 10 percent inspiration and 90 percent perspiration. This is equally true when building a project in Motion. Part of the perspiration comes from clicking and navigating the mouse to move from tab to tab and window to window. Fortunately, the Motion developers created some easy keyboard shortcuts to cut down the time you spend hunting and fumbling through the interface, so you can focus on the fun, creative, inspirational elements in building your project.

You've already learned that Cmd-1 opens the File Browser tab and Cmd-2 opens the Library tab of the Utility window. The Utility window has one more tab: the Inspector tab.

If Cmd-1 opens the File Browser and Cmd-2 opens the Library tab, then it would only make sense that Cmd-3 opens the Inspector tab.

Let's test this theory.

1   Press Cmd-3.

The Inspector tab opens.

The Inspector tab in the Utility window shows details about anything selected in the project. Since you have an empty project with nothing selected, the Inspector is empty. You'll work with the Inspector again shortly. For now, let's focus on the shortcuts to get there and back.

2   Press Cmd-2 to open the Library tab.

3   Press Cmd-1 to open the File Browser.

Cmd-1, Cmd-2, and Cmd-3 open and close tabs in the Utility window. Cmd-4, Cmd-5, and Cmd-6 open and close tabs in the Project pane. Let's start with Cmd-4 to see which tab it opens in the Project pane.

4   Press Cmd-4.

The Layers tab opens in the Project pane. You'll be opening and closing this tab often during this lesson.

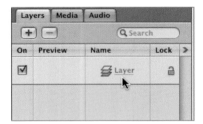

By default, all new projects include one empty layer on the Layers tab. When you add an object to your project, it will appear on that layer.

You can close a pane with the same shortcut that you used to open it.

5   Press Cmd-4 again to close the Project pane.

There are two other tabs in the Project pane next to the Layers tab. Let's take a look.

6   Press Cmd-5.

The Media tab opens in the Project pane. You'll work more with the Media tab later in this lesson.

7   Press Cmd-6 to open the Audio tab.

You'll work with the Audio tab in Lesson 9.

You can open any combination of tabs in the Utility window and Project pane. For example, you can open the Layers tab in the Project pane and the Inspector tab in the Utility window.

8   Press Cmd-4 to go back to the Layers tab.

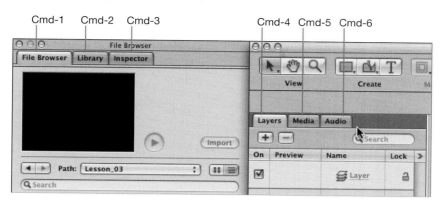

9   Press Cmd-3 to open the Inspector tab.

Now both the Layers tab and the Inspector tab are open.

10   Press Cmd-4 to close the Layers tab and the Project pane and then Cmd-1 to return to the File Browser.

Creating a Background Layer

Good—you've made it through all of the setup. Now you can move on to the first layer: the background. Whenever possible, it's a good idea to build a composite like you would a building: from the ground up. The background layer is your foundation, and it is used to add strength to your overall project. It's also useful as a guide for aligning your other objects and layers.

For this project, you'll use some of the Motion content located in the Library. Over the next series of exercises, you'll add a spinning globe and a map to the background of your project.

Selecting and Importing a Background Object

The globe you'll be using for this project is a movie file and is located in the Travel subcategory of the Content folder in the Library. Let's start by selecting the file and adding it to the Canvas.

1   Press Cmd-2 to open the Library.

2   Click the Content folder to see the Motion content.

3   In the right column in the upper pane of the Library, click the Travel folder to select the Travel subcategory of content.

NOTE ▶ You may need to drag the scroll bar on the right side of the Library window to see the Travel folder.

4   Select **Globe Corner.mov** from the lower pane of the Library.

5   Select the Canvas window; then press the spacebar to begin playback.

6   Drag and drop the **Globe Corner.mov** icon from the Library to the Canvas and release the mouse.

A huge spinning globe fills more than half of the screen in your project and then disappears.

7   Look at the Globe Corner region in the mini-Timeline.

Notice that the region is much shorter than the project duration. Our goal now is to make the movie continue for 8 seconds.

8   Drag the right edge of the Globe Corner region in the mini-Timeline to try to stretch the region and make it longer.

Unfortunately, if a media file is too short for a project, you cannot make it longer by stretching it in the mini-Timeline. You can, however, extend its length by changing the way a file ends. First, let's find the new Globe Corner object on the Layers tab.

Comparing Objects and Layers on the Layers Tab

You've added an object to your project; let's look at the changes that have occurred on the Layers tab.

First, though, what is a layer? A layer is like a vessel that contains objects in your project. Layers can contain an entire project or just part of a project. In this case, you're building the background layer for a project, so the goal is to include all of the background objects in the background layer.

The name of a layer always appears underlined. The names of the contents within a layer are not underlined and appear indented (farther to the right), in contrast to the name of the layer itself.

1   Press Cmd-4 to open the Layers tab.

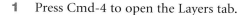

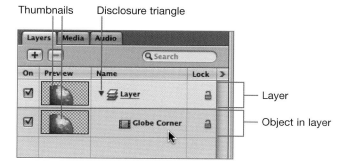

Notice how objects that are on the layers appear different from the layers themselves.

The Globe Corner movie appears below the layer, and the name *Globe Corner* is indented to the right of the underlined word *Layer* above it.

The Preview column on the Layers tab shows a thumbnail of the object. You can resize the thumbnails and the height of the rows using the Scale slider at the bottom of the Project pane.

2   At the bottom of the Layers tab, drag the Scale slider toward the right to make the thumbnail image and rows larger.

Now that you've seen how an object appears on a layer on the Layers tab, let's move on to the Media tab.

Exploring the Media Tab in the Project Pane

After you add a media file like Globe Corner to your project, you can find more information about the file on the Media tab of the Project pane. The media information is organized into columns, which you can resize, move, or hide. Let's take a look at the Globe Corner movie on the Media tab.

1   Press Cmd-5 to open the Media tab.

The Media tab opens and reveals the **Globe Corner.mov** file.

NOTE ▶ The Media tab shows all media that have been imported into a project, even if a file is no longer in the Canvas. Behaviors, filters, and other elements generated from within Motion do not appear as part of the project media.

You can resize the Project pane by dragging the right edge of the pane. Let's expand the pane to see more of the columns on the Media tab.

2   Move the pointer over the right edge of the Project pane until it changes to the Resize tool (an arrow pointing left and right).

3   Click and drag the Resize tool to the right to expand the Media view in the Project pane.

Each column reveals different information about the media file.

4   Locate the Duration column.

The original media file is only 2 seconds long, represented by 2;00, but the entire project is 8 seconds long (8;00). To make the media file last longer, you'll need to loop it. To do that, you need to go to the Inspector. First, let's finish with the Media tab.

You can move a column to a different location by dragging its header to the right or left.

5   Click the Duration column header and drag the column in front of the Kind column.

Your cursor becomes a Hand tool when you grab and move a column.

6   Press Cmd-5 to close the Media tab and the Project pane.

7   Press Cmd-5 again to reopen the Media tab.

The Media tab in the Project pane reopens to whatever size it was when you closed it.

Since you'll be opening the Media tab a lot while working in the Canvas, it's a good idea to change it to a more compact size.

8   Drag the right edge of the Project pane toward the left so that the last column visible is the Duration column.

9   Press Cmd-5 to close the Media tab.

Modifying Object Parameters in the Inspector

It's time to take a look at the Inspector tab in the Utility window. As in other Apple Pro applications, the Inspector allows you to inspect and change detailed parameters based on whatever is selected in your project. To view or change a parameter in the Inspector, all you need to do is select the object or layer you want to change in the Canvas or on the Layers tab.

The Inspector is divided into four tabs: Properties, Behaviors, Filters, and a contextual tab that changes depending on the type of element that is selected.

1   Press Cmd-3 to open the Inspector tab.

2   Click the Globe Corner object in the Canvas to select it.

The contextual tab changes to Image to show that an image has been selected.

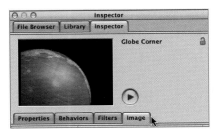

3   Click the Properties tab to view the properties of the selected object.

Changing an Object's Properties

As its name suggests, the Properties tab in the Inspector allows you to view and modify an object's properties.

Since you have selected the Globe Corner movie in the Canvas, you are currently viewing the properties for that object.

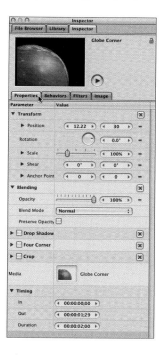

The Properties tab is organized into sections: Transform, Blending, Drop Shadow, Four Corner, Crop, and Timing. These parameters correspond to the tools that you use in the Canvas, such as the Select/Transform tool.

For this exercise, you'll work with the Transform parameters. In previous exercises, you transformed an object's scale and position in the Canvas. This time, you'll change the scale to exactly 50 percent using the Properties tab and then change the position of your object to the lower-left corner of the frame.

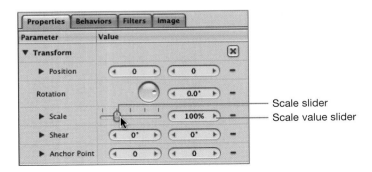

Scale slider
Scale value slider

The Scale parameter has both a slider and a value slider with incremental arrows. The Scale value slider works just like the Current Frame field does, meaning you can drag it, click the incremental arrows, or type a new amount.

1   Drag the Scale slider all the way to the left and then all the way right to adjust the size of the object from smallest to largest.

The object changes in the Canvas as you adjust the Scale parameter in the Inspector.

2   Type *50* in the Scale value slider and press Return.

The object in the Canvas changes to a 50 percent scale.

As you can see, it's easy to change an object's properties. Now let's use the Properties tab as a reference as you change an object's position in the Canvas.

3   Locate the Position parameter at the top of the Transform properties in the Inspector.

The Position parameter shows the position of the selected object in the Canvas.

4   In the Canvas, drag the Globe Corner object toward the lower-left corner of the frame.

The Position parameter changes as the object moves in the Canvas.

5   Position the Globe Corner object in the left corner of the Canvas so its position is −160 (*x*), −105 (*y*) in the Position parameter fields.

6   Press Cmd-S to save your project.

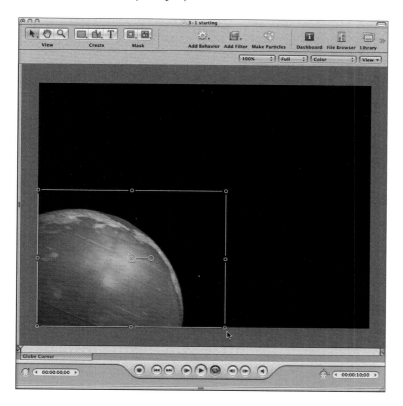

Looping a Media File in the Inspector

We've resized and placed the Globe Corner movie; now let's modify the properties of the media file itself. Remember that our goal is to make a 2-second movie play for 8 seconds. To accomplish this, we need to loop the ending of the movie.

The first step in modifying a project media file is to select the file on the Media tab of the Project pane.

1   Press Cmd-5 to open the Media tab.

2   Select the **Globe Corner.mov** media file.

    The contextual tab in the Inspector changes to a Media tab.

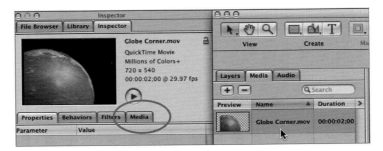

The Media tab in the Inspector lists many of the same parameters that you saw earlier in the columns of the Media tab in the Project pane.

The difference is that the Media tab in the Project pane only *shows* the information, and on the Media tab of the Inspector you can actually *change* the parameters. The Media tab in the Inspector also includes parameters that are not listed in the Project pane, such as the End Condition parameter.

MORE INFO ▶ You can find more detailed information on all of the parameters in the Inspector in the Motion documentation that came with the application.

Changing the End Condition of a Movie

The End Condition parameter controls the way that a movie file ends in your project. Currently, the **Globe Corner.mov** file ends when it reaches the last frame of media in the original file. If a piece of media ends as is, with no modification, the end condition is None.

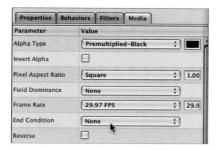

Motion provides four end conditions: None, Loop, Ping-Pong, and Hold.

Let's look at the different choices in action so we can select the best option for our project.

1   On the Media tab of the Inspector, click the End Condition pop-up menu to view the four choices.

2   Choose Loop from the End Condition pop-up menu.

You've just applied a loop to the end of the media file. Now try to extend the region in the mini-Timeline.

3   Select the Globe Corner object in the Canvas.

The Globe Corner region appears in the mini-Timeline.

4   Drag the right edge of the Globe Corner region in the mini-Timeline until the yellow tooltip shows that the Out point occurs at exactly 8 seconds (8;00).

5   Press the spacebar to play the looped Globe Corner movie in the Canvas.

The Loop end condition repeats (loops) the entire movie, so it plays from the first frame to the last frame, and then the entire movie repeats, from the first frame to the last frame, indefinitely.

Fortunately, the original movie you're working with is a complete revolution of the globe, so the looped version gives the appearance of the globe revolving over and over again, or spinning.

Let's try the other end condition options to see how they work.

6   On the Media tab of the Project pane, select the **Globe Corner.mov** file.

7   On the Media tab of the Inspector, open the End Condition pop-up menu and choose Ping-Pong. Press the spacebar to begin playback if the movie is not already playing.

The Globe Corner movie now plays forward until it reaches the last frame, then plays in reverse back to the beginning, and then plays forward again. This end condition doesn't really work for this project. The Ping-Pong effect might distract the viewer and draw attention away from the more important elements of the project.

NOTE ▶ The Ping-Pong effect is more commonly used to loop a moving pattern that doesn't have a particular start or stop point or doesn't move in a specific direction. For example, you could use the Ping-Pong end condition to show globules floating around a lava lamp. Forward or backward, the globules would just appear to float around without a real beginning or ending point.

8   From the End Condition pop-up menu, choose Hold.

This time, the movie plays once and then holds (freezes) on the last frame.

9   Choose Loop from the End Condition pop-up menu to change back to the Loop end condition.

There you have it. You've just turned a 2-second movie file into an 8-second movie in the project.

10 Press Cmd-S to save your project.

TIP▶ It's a good idea to save your projects often to protect your progress against a power outage or other unforeseen event.

Adding a Second Background Movie to the Project

The Globe Corner movie looks great now that it lasts the entire duration of the project. However, the remaining background is pretty stark. A map would nicely fill the void around the Globe Corner movie.

Let's add a map from the Motion contents in the Library. As we do, we'll use the Layers tab to observe the changes that occur.

1   Press Cmd-2 to open the Library tab, and press Cmd-5 to open the Media tab.

2   Select the Content folder in the Library.

The Content folder opens just as you left it, with the Travel subcategory still selected.

3   Select the **Map Loop.mov** icon in the lower pane of the Library.

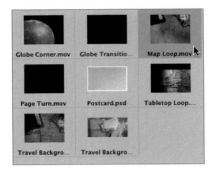

The Map Loop movie plays in the Preview area at the top of the Utility window. You can also see that the duration of the movie is 5 seconds (5;00). Let's practice all of your skills so far and add the movie to the background, loop the end condition, and extend the Out point to the end of the project.

4   Press the spacebar to begin playback, if the movie is not already playing.

5   In the Preview area, click the Apply button to add the movie to the project.

The Map Loop movie appears on the Media tab below the Globe Corner movie. Files are added to the Media tab in the order that they are added to a project, from top to bottom.

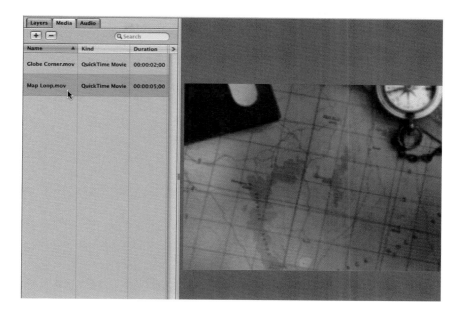

6   Select the **Map Loop.mov** file on the Media tab.

7   Press Cmd-3 to open the Inspector.

The Inspector opens just as you left it, with the Media tab selected.

8   From the End Condition pop-up menu, select Loop.

The Map Loop movie will work really well with the spinning globe, but it will look even better if we reverse the direction that the map moves in the background.

Let's reverse the direction that the looped media plays by checking the Reverse box located below the End Condition pop-up menu.

9 Check the Reverse box to reverse the Map Loop movie.

The map now plays in reverse in the Canvas.

10 Select the Map Loop object in the Canvas.

> **NOTE** ▶ If you don't see the Map Loop object, you may have stopped playback in the Canvas. Press the spacebar to begin playback, and select the Map Loop object when it appears in the Canvas.

11 Press the spacebar to stop playback.

12 Press the End key to move the playhead to the end of the project.

13 Press O to extend the Out point of the Map Loop region in the mini-Timeline to the location of the playhead.

You've successfully added and looped another movie file in the project. There's just one problem—we've lost the globe!

Changing Object Order on the Layers Tab

Files are always added to a project *above* the previous objects. This is one reason why it's good to start with the background and build upward. Since the map was added after the globe, it is currently above the globe in the Canvas and on the Layers tab. In this exercise, you'll change the order of the objects and then rename the entire layer.

To change the order of objects on the Layers tab, you simply drag an object either upward to move it above another object or downward to move it below.

Dragging an object up or down on the Layers tab can also create a new layer containing the object that is being moved. You control whether you *move* an object or *create a new layer* by aligning the position indicator with the desired icon. If you align the object with the Layer icon, you create a new layer; if you align it with an object icon, you move the object.

The Layer icon looks like a series of layers.

Layer icon

The object icon varies, depending on the type of object file. There are four object icons: Still image, Movie, Shape, and Text.

Still image

Movie

Shape (created in Motion)

Text (created in Motion)

The position indicator takes the guesswork out of moving objects within layers. As you move an object, the position indicator appears as a black line between the rows. When the position indicator is aligned with the correct icon, release the mouse to place the object.

Let's move the Map Loop object to create a new layer; then we'll move the Map Loop object within the new layer.

1   Press Cmd-4, or click the Layers tab, to open the Layers tab.

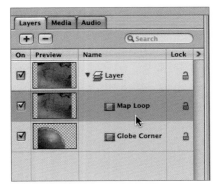

As you can see, the Map Loop object is above the Globe Corner object.

2   On the Layers tab, drag the Map Loop icon downward and to the left, below the Globe Corner icon, until the position indicator aligns with the Layer icon. When the Add symbol—a green circle with a plus sign— appears, indicating that you are adding a new layer, release the mouse.

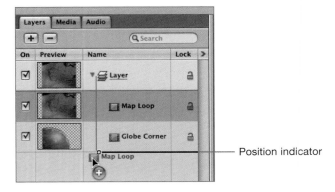

Position indicator aligned with the Layer icon, creating a new layer containing an object

A new layer containing the Map Loop object is created.

3 Press Cmd-Z to undo the last step.

Now let's move the object without creating a new layer.

4 Drag the Map Loop object below the Globe Corner object. Make sure the position indicator is aligned with the object icons; then release the mouse.

Position indicator appears to
show a move within the layer.

The map is now below the globe both on the Layers tab and in the Canvas.

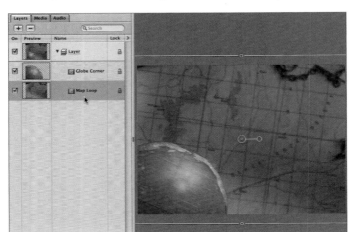

Renaming and Hiding a Layer

You've finished the background layer, so let's name it and then hide it. Naming layers as you build a project helps you keep the project organized.

By default, all layers are given the name Layer followed by a sequential number based on the number of layers with the same name in the project.

To change the name of a layer, you simply double-click the layer's Name field and type a new name.

1   On the Layers tab, double-click the Name field of the layer.

2   In the Name field, type *Background* and press Return.

The Name field changes to Background.

As you build your projects, it's a good idea to turn off layers that you aren't working on so that you can save your computer's processing power for the elements that you are currently building. You can always turn a layer back on whenever you need to see it.

The On column at the left of the Layers tab contains Activation check boxes for turning layers on and off. When a layer is active, the box appears blue with a check.

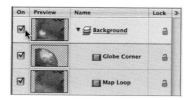

3   Click the Activation check box for the Background layer to turn the layer off.

The layer name becomes dimmed, and the Activation boxes for the objects within the layer turn gray to show that the layer they inhabit is currently off.

To save space on the Layers tab, you can close layers to hide the contents. To hide or show the contents of a layer, you click the disclosure triangle to the left of the layer's icon.

4   Click the disclosure triangle for the Background layer to hide the contents
    of the layer.

Creating a New Layer

It's time to build a new layer that will contain all of the photographs for the
project. Motion gives you three ways to create new layers:

▶   Choose Object > New Layer.

▶   Press Shift-Cmd-N.

▶   Click the Add new layer button (+) at the top of the Layers tab.

For this exercise, you'll create and name a new layer to contain the photographs.

> **NOTE** ▶ If you did not complete the previous exercises and wish to con-
> tinue the lesson, close your current project and open **3-2 Background** from
> the Lesson_03 folder.

1   Click the Add new layer button (+) to add a new layer.

    A new layer appears above the Background layer on the Layers tab.

2   Double-click the Name field of the new layer and type *Photographs*; then
    press Return.

NOTE ▶ If a layer is selected and you click the Add new layer button on the Layers tab, you'll add a new sublayer within the selected layer. If you want to create a new layer, deselect all layers and objects first.

Planning Your Workflow

Before you dive into building a project, it's a good idea to have a plan. Over the next series of exercises, you'll learn many time-saving techniques that can help you become more efficient in building complex layered projects.

The final version of the project you're creating here includes two rows of still photographs moving across the screen in opposite directions. One time-saving technique for creating this element is to use a single still object to represent all of the other photographs in the build. By duplicating one still and using it as a placeholder, you can copy, align, and group all of the still objects without using the actual media files. Then you can easily replace the media with the actual stills to complete your build.

Here's the plan to complete this project:

▶ Add one still object to the project, resize it, and move it into position.

▶ Copy the still three times and align the objects in a row at the top of the frame.

▶ Group the four stills together and copy the group to the bottom of the frame.

▶ Replace the media for the stills with the actual photographs.

▶ Clean up the alignment of the stills.

▶ Apply a Throw behavior to each row of stills to move them across the screen.

▶ Add titles.

Now that you know the plan, let's get started applying the first photograph to the project.

Importing a File to the Layers Tab

You've already learned how to import a file by dragging it to the Canvas or clicking the Import button. In this exercise, your goal is to import a file to a specific layer.

There are two ways to import to a specific layer. You can select a layer on the Layers tab and click the Import button in the File Browser, or you can drag a file from the File Browser directly to the layer in the Project pane.

Let's drag the file directly to the Photographs layer in the Project pane.

1   Press Cmd-1 to open the File Browser in the Utility window.

2   Click the disclosure triangle next to the Photographs folder in the lower pane of the File Browser to see the contents of the folder.

> **NOTE** ▶ If your files appear as icons in the File Browser, click the List view button to see the lesson files in List view.

3   Select the **Big Ben London.jpg** file to see it in the Preview area.

4   Press the down arrow key to preview the next still in the list.

5   Repeat step 4 until you see the last photo in the list, **Sunset.jpg**.

We'll use **Sunset.jpg** as the placeholder for the other photos in the Canvas.

NOTE ▶ If the Sunset.jpg file is at the top of the list of photographs, you are viewing your list in reverse alphabetical order. Click the Name header at the top of the lower pane to reverse the order.

When you drag a file from the File Browser to a layer on the Layers tab, the layer is highlighted with a black border, and an Add symbol appears to show that you are adding a file to that layer.

6   Drag the **Sunset.jpg** file from the File Browser and drop it on the Photographs layer on the Layers tab.

The Sunset file appears on the Photographs layer and in the Canvas.

7 Press Cmd-S to save your progress.

8 Press Cmd-4 to close the Layers tab.

Duplicating Objects in the Canvas

Our goal in this exercise is first to resize the Sunset object and then to dupli-cate it in the Canvas. There are three ways to duplicate a selected object in the Canvas:

▶ Choose Edit > Duplicate.

▶ Press Cmd-D.

▶ Hold down the Option key and drag the object.

Not only are you learning to duplicate objects in this lesson, but you also are learning about workflow. It's much easier to resize the object before you dupli-cate it. If you duplicate before you resize, you will have to resize both the origi-nal and the duplicate objects.

1 Press Cmd-– (hyphen) to zoom out of the Canvas by one level.

2 Press Cmd-3 to open the Inspector tab.

3 Change the Scale parameter to 27 percent.

The Sunset object shrinks to 27 percent of its original size in the Canvas.

4 Drag the Sunset object to the upper-left corner of the Canvas.

Now let's use the Option-drag method to make a duplicate object in the Canvas. To Option-drag, you hold the Option key while you drag the object.

5   Option-drag the Sunset object toward the right to make a duplicate; then release the mouse.

6 Repeat step 5 until you have a total of four Sunset objects.

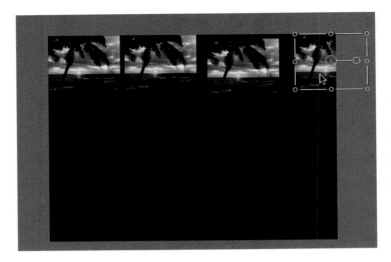

7 Press Cmd-S to save your progress.

Aligning Multiple Objects in the Canvas

You could spend a lot of time trying to align the four objects in a row, with equal space between the objects—or you could have Motion take care of the alignment for you. That's right: You can choose from the Objects menu the way you want to align selected objects, and Motion will fix the alignment for you automatically. All you have to do is select all of the objects that you want to align.

The Objects menu provides 12 alignment choices, allowing you to automatically align edges, align centers, distribute edges, or distribute centers. For this exercise, you'll align the top edges of the objects and then distribute the left edges.

First, let's look at the duplicate objects on the Layers tab.

1 Press Cmd-4 to open the Layers tab.

There are now four Sunset objects on the Photographs layer: the original
Sunset object and the three copies.

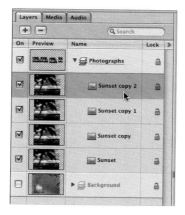

Selecting an object on the Layers tab also selects that object in the Canvas.

A shortcut for selecting a group of contiguous objects on the Layers tab is
to select the first object in a list and then Shift-click the last object.

Let's Shift-click to select all four Sunset objects on the Layers tab.

2   Select the Sunset object on the Layers tab.

3   Shift-click the Sunset copy 2 object.

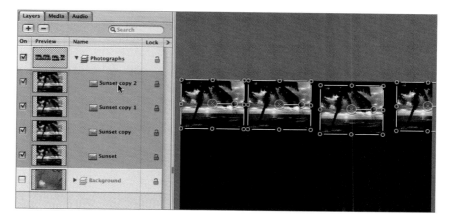

All four Sunset objects are selected both on the Layers tab and in the Canvas.

4   Choose Object > Alignment > Align Top Edges.

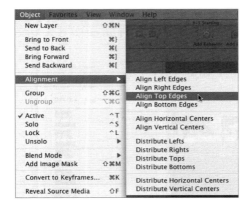

5   Choose Object > Alignment > Distribute Lefts.

Your objects are now perfectly aligned and spaced across the top of the frame.

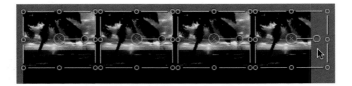

Grouping Objects into Sublayers

The next step in your workflow is to duplicate the entire row of photographs. You could just Option-drag the selected objects to duplicate them. However, you would then have a total of eight loose objects to deal with in your Photographs layer. Instead, let's group the first row of photographs. Grouping objects turns them into a sublayer, which allows you to modify all four at one time while maintaining their alignment.

There are three ways to group selected objects in Motion:

▶ Choose Object > Group.

▶ Press Shift-Cmd-G.

▶ Create a new layer and drag it onto the existing layer to create a sublayer; then move the objects onto the sublayer.

Let's try the menu method here.

1 Choose Object > Group.

> **NOTE** ▶ Make sure that all four Sunset objects are selected before you group them.

A new sublayer appears within the Photographs layer, and a single bounding box appears around all of the Sunset objects in the Canvas.

Now you have a choice of selecting an individual Sunset object or the entire sublayer. To select an individual object in the sublayer, you need to select it on the Layers tab. Clicking the objects in the Canvas without holding down the Command key will select only the group sublayer.

2 Select the Sunset object on the Layers tab to select only that object.

3 Select the sublayer that contains all four Sunset objects to select the entire layer.

Let's duplicate the entire sublayer in the Canvas and drag it to the bottom of the frame.

4 Option-drag the grouped sublayer downward in the Canvas to duplicate it.

A duplicate sublayer appears on the Photographs layer and in the Canvas.

5 Drag the duplicate layer in the Canvas to the bottom of the frame.

It's a good idea to keep the project organized as you go. Let's apply what you learned earlier in this lesson to change the names of the two sublayers to Top and Bottom, hide the contents, and then change the order of the sublayers.

6 Double-click the Layer copy Name field, type *Bottom*, and press Return.

7 Double-click the Layer Name field, type *Top*, and press Return.

8   Click the disclosure triangles on both of the sublayers to hide their contents.

9   Drag the Top sublayer above the Bottom sublayer. Use the placement indicator to make sure that you are moving it within the Photographs layer.

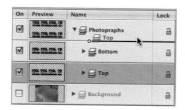

10 Press Cmd-S to save your progress.

Working with Safe Zones

If you create projects that will eventually be viewed on a television, it is very important to understand safe zones.

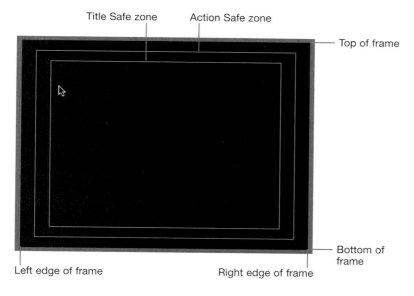

The *Title Safe zone*, sometimes referred to as the TV safe zone, is the inner blue square. Objects inside the boundaries of the zone will be visible on any television screen. You should place all text and your most important objects within the Title Safe zone. This feature is less relevant to flat-screen televisions, but it is necessary to accommodate curved-screen television sets.

The *Action Safe zone* is the outer blue square. Objects inside its boundaries will likely be seen on all televisions. If the action on the screen is a baseball player swinging the bat and the tip of the bat is within the Action Safe zone, the tip of the bat will most likely be visible on any set. If it is vital that the tip of the bat be visible to all audiences, you should align the video file so the tip of the bat is within the Title Safe zone.

You can turn the display of safe zones on or off in the View pop-up menu at the upper right of the Canvas window.

1   From the View pop-up menu on the Canvas, choose Safe Zones to turn on the safe zone guides.

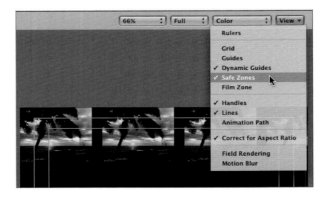

2   In the Canvas, drag the Top sublayer downward until the top of the layer is inside the Title Safe zone.

3   Drag the Bottom sublayer upward until the bottom of the layer is inside the Title Safe zone.

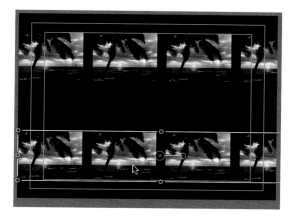

4   From the View pop-up menu, choose Safe Zones to turn off the safe zones.

5   Press Cmd-S to save your progress.

Replacing Media on the Layers Tab

Another time-saving feature in Motion is the ability to replace one file with another directly on the Layers tab. In this exercise, you'll exchange seven of the eight Sunset objects with other still images.

To replace media, you simply drag a new file from the File Browser and drop it onto the object on the Layers tab.

When you drop a new file onto an object on the Layers tab, the object's row is highlighted with a black border, and a small curved arrow appears to show you that you are replacing the contents of the file.

Let's try it.

NOTE ▶ If you did not complete the previous exercises and wish to
continue the lesson from this point, close your current project and open
3-3 Photo Groups from the Lesson_03 folder.

1   On the Layers tab, click the Top sublayer's disclosure triangle to view its
contents.

Remember: Objects on the Layers tab appear in the order in which they
were added to the project, from bottom to top. The original Sunset object
was the first object in the layer, so it is in the lowest position on the Layers
tab. You placed the original Sunset object in the upper-left corner and
then made copies one at a time, moving toward the right of the frame. To
select the objects in the Canvas from left to right, you need to select the
lowest object first and then work your way up.

2   Select the lowest object in the Top sublayer—in this case, the original
Sunset object.

The first object in the top row of pictures in the Canvas becomes selected.
We'll replace this object first.

TIP ▸ It's a good idea to select an object before you exchange media so that you can locate the selected object in the Canvas and verify that it is the object you want to change.

3 Drag the **DFB Tower01.jpg** file from the File Browser to the selected object on the Layers tab.

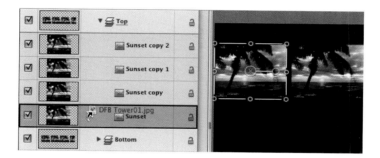

The first object in the top row of the Canvas changes to the DFB Tower01 still.

As you can see, it's quite easy to replace media files on the Layers tab.

Replacing the Remaining Objects

Now that you know how to select and replace media files on the Layers tab, you can replace the rest of the stills on your own. Follow the sequence here to complete the task. Start with the Top sublayer and then move to the Bottom sublayer. Since you can't read the names of the files in the Canvas, let's rename the objects in the sublayer based on their positions to make them easier to identify.

1   Double-click the name of the lowest object in the Top sublayer and type *Left* in the name field; then press Return.

2   Change the name of the object above Left to *Left Center*.

3   Change the name of the object above Left Center to *Right Center*.

4   Change the name of the object above Right Center to *Right*.

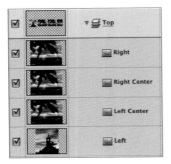

Now that you've made the objects easier to identify, let's replace their media.

5   Select the Left Center object on the Layers tab and replace it with the **South Korea 505** file.

6   Select the Right Center object on the Layers tab and replace it with the **Big Ben London** file.

7   Select the Right object on the Layers tab and replace it with the **Blue Mesa Turkey** file.

8   Click the disclosure triangle for the Bottom sublayer to view the contents.

9   Select the lowest object in the Bottom sublayer and replace it with the **Israel 110** file.

10 Rename the objects in the Bottom sublayer from the lowest to the highest to correspond with their positions in the Canvas as you did with the Top sublayer (Left, Left Center, Right Center, Right).

Now let's replace the remaining objects on the Bottom layer.

11 Select the Left Center object on the Bottom layer and replace it with the **Inverness Castle_1** file.

12 Select the Right Center object on the Bottom layer and replace it with the **Greece 176** file.

We'll leave the Right object on the Bottom layer with its original media file. You should now have eight different photographs showing in the Canvas.

13 Press Cmd-5 to view the files on the Media tab.

All of the files that you added to the project are listed in the order that you imported them, from top to bottom. The Media tab lists the objects by their filenames in the File Browser instead of by the names that you gave the objects on the Layers tab.

14 Press Cmd-4 to return to the Layers tab.

15 Press Cmd-S to save your progress.

Checking the Details

The project looks pretty good, but did you notice any problems with the image sizes?

If you look closely, you'll notice that several of the objects don't match the height of the other objects in their row. Also, the spacing between the last two objects in the bottom row is off. Finally, there's a blue line at the bottom of the Left object in the Top layer object that looks like digital noise and should be removed.

Rule #2: Pay attention to details, because if you see an imperfection in your work, others are likely to see it, too.

Attention to detail is one of the things that separates amateurs from professionals in the graphic design world, and in most other professions.

If you turn in a written document full of misspellings and grammatical errors, whoever reads it will get the impression that you didn't care enough to make it right. The same principle goes for your motion graphics projects.

Your projects are a direct representation of you and your professionalism. I'm not saying everything always has to be perfect. Sometimes, keeping things a little rough around the edges is the look you are going for. However, in most cases, if something looks off, or out of alignment, or too big or too bright, or whatever, chances are good that you won't be the only one who notices it. Take the extra time to fix the little details as you build a project so that you won't be stuck dealing with them all at the end.

Cropping Objects in the Inspector

If you're working with paper photographs in the physical world, you can use a paper cutter to clean up the edges of a photo. When you're working with digital photography, you can use the Crop tool or the Crop parameters on the Properties tab of the Inspector.

Let's start with the Left object on the Top sublayer shot and crop the lower
edge to clean it up. First, you'll need to select the Left object on the Layers tab
or in the Canvas. Let's Cmd-click the object in the Canvas to select it.

1   In the Canvas, Cmd-click the Left object on the Top sublayer to select it.

2   Press Cmd-3 to open the Inspector, or click the Inspector tab in the Utility
    window.

    The Crop parameters are toward the bottom of the Parameter list on the
    Properties tab.

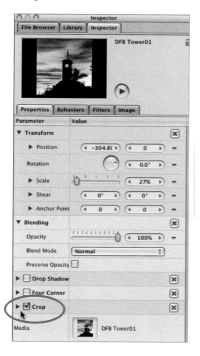

NOTE ▶ The image in the Preview area does not show the lower edge of
the image that you need to crop. Often you won't see small imperfections
around the edges of an image until it is in the Canvas.

3 Check the box next to Crop to turn on the Crop parameter.

4 Click the disclosure triangle for the Crop parameter to view the four Crop parameters.

The Crop parameters are Left, Right, Bottom, and Top.

NOTE ▶ The Crop check box must be checked for you to modify the Crop parameters.

5 In the Bottom Crop parameter's value field, click the right incremental arrow three times, or type 3 in the field and press Return.

If you click the incremental arrow, you will see the crop changes in the Canvas as you click.

You have just cropped three rows of pixels from the bottom of the DFB Tower01 object. The blue line is now gone from the image.

Before crop

After crop

The Left Center object (South Korea 505) on the Top sublayer is taller than the other objects in the same row. Let's crop the top and bottom of the object until it matches the height of the others.

6   On the Canvas, Cmd-click the Left Center object on the Top sublayer.

7   Crop the bottom of the South Korea 505 object by 37 rows of pixels and the top by 35.

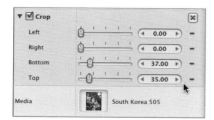

The last object to crop is the Left Center object on the Bottom sublayer.

8   Cmd-click the Left Center object (Castle) on the Bottom sublayer in the Canvas.

9   Crop the bottom and top of the Castle object until it visually matches the height of the other objects in the same group (14 rows of pixels).

You've finished the cropping; now you need to fix the alignment of the Right object in the bottom row.

10   On the Layers tab, select the Right object on the Bottom sublayer, which is the Sunset object.

You can use the Dynamic Guides to align the Right object in the bottom row with the Right object in the top row.

11   Drag the Sunset object to the right in the Canvas until the Dynamic Guides show that it is even with the other objects in the Bottom sublayer, and the left edge is aligned with the left edge of the object above it in the Top sublayer.

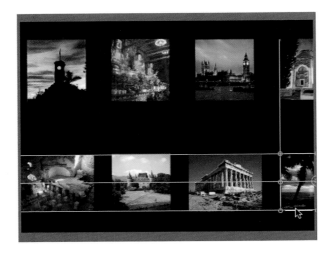

12 Press Cmd-S to save your progress.

Adding Behaviors to Layers

In the previous lesson, you added behaviors to an object and text. You can also add behaviors to a layer so that you can animate a group of objects collectively rather than each object individually.

Over the next series of exercises, you'll apply Throw behaviors to both the Top and Bottom sublayers to make them move into the frame.

First, let's move the layers into their starting positions so it will be easier to modify the Throw behaviors once they are applied.

> **NOTE ▶** If you did not complete the previous exercises and wish to continue the lesson from this point, close your current project and open **3-4 Exchange Media** from the Lesson_03 folder.

1 Press Cmd-4 to close the Layers tab, if it is still open.

Closing the Layers tab will make it easier to work in the full Canvas window.

2 Press Cmd-– (hyphen) several times until you can clearly see the frame with the rows of pictures and the gray space around the frame.

Now you'll be able to manipulate the layers more easily.

Constraining Object Movement

As you've already learned, the Shift key constrains the proportions of an object as you resize it in the Canvas or draw an object with the Create tool. The Shift key also constrains the movement of an object or layer in the Canvas. If you Shift-drag an object, you will be able to move that object only in a straight line up and down or left and right.

Let's use the Shift-drag method to move the layers into position. There's just one catch. Shift-clicking something also deselects it. So to successfully Shift-drag, you need first to start to drag in the direction that you want to go and then press and hold the Shift key. In other words, what you're actually doing is more like drag-Shift-dragging.

Our goal in this exercise is to place the top row of pictures out of the frame on the left side, and the bottom row of pictures out of the frame on the right side.

1 Drag the Top sublayer toward the left; then press the Shift key and continue dragging until the entire layer is out of the frame on the left.

2   Drag the Bottom sublayer toward the right; then press the Shift key and continue dragging until the entire layer is out of the frame on the right.

Now the layers are ready for a Throw behavior.

Dragging a Behavior to the Layers Tab

You add behaviors to layers the same way that you add behaviors to objects or text. The only difference is that for layers, you drag the behavior directly to the layer or sublayer on the Layers tab.

You've built most of this project without moving the playhead. Since you're about to add movement to the layers in the Canvas, it's a good time to start playback.

1   Press the spacebar to begin playback in the Canvas.

2   Press Cmd-4 to open the Layers tab.

3   Press Cmd-2 to open the Library tab in the Utility window.

4   From the Library, select Behaviors.

5   Select the Basic Motion subfolder to view the Basic Motion behaviors.

6   Drag the Throw behavior from the Library to the Top sublayer.

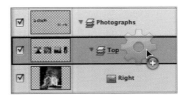

A green Add symbol appears to show you that you are adding the behavior to the sublayer.

A row called Throw appears below the Top sublayer on the Layers tab. A small Behaviors icon (gear) also appears to the right of the layer name to show that a behavior has been added to the entire layer.

7   Drag the Throw behavior from the Library to the Bottom sublayer.

Modifying Throw Behaviors in the Dashboard

Now that the Throw behaviors have been added to both the Top and Bottom sublayers, let's adjust the Throw parameters in the Dashboard.

1   On the Layers tab, select the Throw behavior on the Top sublayer.

2   Press D to open the Dashboard window.

3   Move the Dashboard window to the left of your screen so you can clearly see the Layers tab and the Canvas.

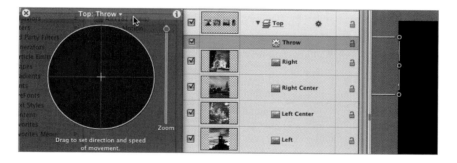

The Throw behavior should appear in the Dashboard. You can constrain the parameters in the Dashboard by holding down the Shift key as you drag the Select/Transform tool.

4   Shift-drag toward the right in the Throw Dashboard to start your layer moving in a straight line across the screen.

An arrow appears, showing you how your object will move.

5   Adjust the length of the arrow in the Dashboard so that the last picture in the top row exits the frame at the end of the play range.

Checking Timing in the Canvas

How do you know if your throw timing is perfect? Simple. Just stop playback and move the playhead to the end of the project. If the layer is where you want it at the end, the timing is good. If it's off, then make adjustments in the Dashboard while the playhead is stopped over the last frame of the project.

Let's try it.

1   Press the spacebar to stop playback.

2   Press the End key to move the playhead to the end of the project.

Where is the top row of pictures?

If it's still visible onscreen, you'll need to make the arrow longer in the Dashboard. If it's nowhere to be seen, you may have thrown it too far; in that case, you'll need to make the arrow shorter, until the bounding box around the layer is just to the left of the frame.

3   Adjust the Throw behavior in the Dashboard until the left edge of the layer appears outside the right edge of the frame.

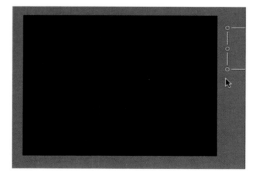

4   Press the spacebar to view the finished Throw behavior on the Top sub-layer of pictures.

The Top sublayer looks great. Now, with what you've just learned, adjust the Throw behavior on the Bottom sublayer so that the pictures move across the screen toward the left.

5   On the Layers tab, select the Throw behavior on the Bottom sublayer.

6   Shift-drag the Throw display in the Dashboard toward the left.

7   Adjust the timing by changing the length of the arrow in the Dashboard.

8   Press the spacebar to stop playback; then press the End key.

9   Fine-tune the adjustment to the arrow in the Dashboard until the Bottom sublayer is just outside frame left.

10 Press the spacebar to view both sublayers of pictures moving in opposite directions across the screen.

11 Press Cmd-S to save your progress.

Viewing the Sublayers with the Background

The project is nearly finished. All that's left is to see how it works with the background and possibly to add a few advanced touches to polish it.

We'll start by turning on the Background layer to see how our project plays against the background.

1   Click the check box next to the Background layer to turn on the layer.

2   Press the spacebar to view the project in the Canvas.

It looks pretty good, but it would be even better if the Bottom sublayer of pictures went *behind* the globe. No problem. All you need to do is move the Globe Corner movie from the Background layer to the Photographs layer.

NOTE ▶ The more elements that you add to a project, the more Motion (and your computer) have to process the project. Motion caches each frame in video memory (VRAM) as you play the revised project. After you've played through the entire revised project in the Canvas one time, you should be able to see it play in real time.

3   Click the disclosure triangle for the Background layer to view the contents of the layer.

4   Drag the Globe Corner object upward from the Background layer to the Photographs layer and release.

The Globe Corner object appears at the top of the Photographs layer.

The bottom row of pictures now moves behind the spinning globe.

Working with Opacity and Blend Modes

Now that you understand the basics of layers and sublayers and the position of objects on the Layers tab, let's look at the opacity and blend mode. *Opacity* comes from the word *opaque*, which describes a solid object that you cannot see through. If an image has 100 percent opacity, it appears solid, and you cannot see anything behind it. Opacity does not change the shape or size of an object; it changes only the level of transparency. An object with an opacity of 0 percent is completely transparent; you can completely see whatever is behind the object. If you set the opacity of an object to 50 percent, the object becomes 50 percent transparent relative to the object behind it.

Modifying Opacity in the Dashboard

Instead of showing solid photo objects moving across the screen, let's adjust the opacity so that we can see some of the map below.

You can adjust the opacity for an object or layer in the Dashboard.

1   Press the spacebar to begin playback.

2   On the Layers tab, select the Top sublayer within the Photographs layer.

3   Press D to open the Dashboard window, if it's not already open.

The Dashboard window opens, with an Opacity slider at the top.

NOTE ▸ The Opacity and Blur sliders at the bottom of the Dashboard modify the object's Drop Shadow parameters.

4 Move the Dashboard window so it's easy to see both the Dashboard and the images in the Canvas.

5 Drag the Opacity slider in the Dashboard to the left until the value reads 50%.

The Top sublayer of photographs appears transparent in the Canvas, and you can see the background through the layer.

6   Drag the sublayer's Opacity slider in the Dashboard back to 100%.

Adding Blend Modes in the Dashboard

Lowering the opacity is okay for many jobs, but this project needs to show off the photographs, not fade them out and make them look dim and lifeless. Changing the opacity is one way to combine multiple objects or layers. Another approach is to blend the objects together using *blend modes*. Blend modes use mathematical calculations to combine information from two layers. Fortunately, Motion does all of the calculating for you. All you need to do is experiment to find the blend mode that works best for you.

You need to remember four points when you work with blend modes:

▶   You can use blend modes only between layers, not from object to object within the same layer.

▶   Always add the blend mode to the highest layer—in this case, to the Top sublayer. If you add a blend mode to a layer at the bottom of the composite, such as the Background layer in this project, the layer will be blending with black instead of with other layers within the project.

▶   You can apply only one blend mode to a layer.

▶   Blend modes are processor intensive.

> **TIP** ▶ Because blend modes can be very processor intensive, it's a good idea to build your entire project first and then, at the end of your project, apply blend modes. In other words, bake the cake; then ice the cake.

Let's experiment with some of the blend modes to combine the rows of photographs with the background.

1 In the Dashboard, click the Blend Mode pop-up menu.

NOTE ▶ If the Dashboard says anything other than Group: Top, select the Top sublayer on the Layers tab to view the sublayer in the Dashboard.

The Blend Mode pop-up menu opens, displaying the Blend Mode choices.

2 Choose Subtract from the Blend Modes pop-up menu.

The Subtract mode makes the photographs look like photo negatives.

3   Choose Silhouette Luma near the bottom of the Blend Modes pop-up menu.

This option makes the photographs look like black silhouettes against the background.

These are both very cool looks, but they're not right for this project.

4   Choose Hard Light from the Blend Modes pop-up menu.

This option makes the photographs look like slides.

Hard Light is perfect! Not only do the photos maintain their brilliance and image quality, but you can also see the map moving behind them. We have a winner.

NOTE ▸ Your playback will likely be slower as you add blend modes to multiple layers. You will still be able to see the project play back; it will just play more slowly in the Canvas. The final project will always export at full speed.

5   On the Layers tab, select the Bottom sublayer and change the blend mode to Hard Light.

6   Press Cmd-S to save your project.

> **MORE INFO** ► For more detailed information about all of the blend modes, consult the Motion user manual that came with the application.

Finishing the Project

To finish this project, all we need to do is add the Photographer Title object on a new layer. I built the title as a Motion project and then exported it as a movie file.

You'll find the Photographer Title object in the Lesson_03 folder in the File Browser.

You'll apply the skills you've learned in this lesson to finish the project.

> **NOTE** ► If you did not complete the previous exercises and wish to continue the lesson from this point, close your current project and open **3-6 Blend Modes** from the Lesson_03 folder.

1   Press Shift-Cmd-A to deselect everything in the project.

2   Hide the layer contents on the Layers tab by clicking the disclosure triangle for any open layers.

3   Click the Add new layer (+) button on the Layers tab to create a new layer.

4   Change the name of the new layer to *Title*.

5 Press Cmd-1 to open the File Browser, if it's not already open.

6 Drag the **Photographer Title.mov** file from the File Browser to the Title layer on the Layers tab.

Yikes! The title has a black background and covers the entire project!

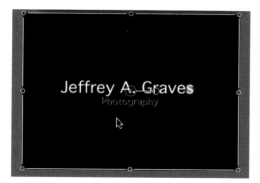

Fortunately, there is a blend mode for almost every occasion. The Screen Blend Mode will essentially remove any black pixels from the upper layer.

7 Press D to open the Dashboard, if it's not already open.

8 From the Blend Mode pop-up menu in the Dashboard, choose Screen.

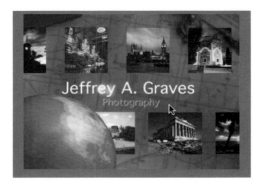

The black is screened out of the top layer, revealing the other layers below.

NOTE ▶ If your playback is very slow, it's because this project is so processor intensive. You'll learn how to render a project and export it in Lessons 10 and 11.

9   Press Cmd-S to save your final project.

Congratulations! You've finished a very complex motion graphics project.

TIP ▶ To make the photographs stand out even more against the background, select both the Top and Bottom sublayers and check the Drop Shadow box in the Dashboard.

What You've Learned

▶   You can set and change project presets on the Presets tab of the Motion Preferences window.

▶   If you set a preset default, all new projects will be created with the default settings.

▶   To extend the duration of a movie file in the mini-Timeline, you can change the file's end condition to Loop.

- ▶ You can easily navigate among the tabs in the Utility window and the Project pane by pressing the Command key plus a number that corresponds to the tab. Cmd-1 = File Browser, Cmd-2 = Library, Cmd-3 = Inspector, Cmd-4 = Layers tab, and Cmd-5 = Media tab.

- ▶ All new projects start with an empty layer on the Layers tab.

- ▶ Layers are vessels that contain objects and sublayers.

- ▶ The order, from top to bottom, in which objects and layers appear on the Layers tab corresponds to the order in which they appear in the Canvas.

- ▶ You can drag layers or objects up or down on the Layers tab to change their positions. Dragging objects outside of a layer creates a new layer containing that object.

- ▶ Grouping objects places them on a sublayer.

- ▶ To replace a file, you drag the new file from the File Browser to the object on the Layers tab.

- ▶ You can crop the edges of an object in the Dashboard or the Inspector.

- ▶ You can turn layers and objects on and off on the Layers tab by checking or unchecking the Activation check box.

- ▶ Each layer has a disclosure triangle that you can use to hide or show the contents of the layer.

- ▶ You can apply behaviors to objects, layers, and sublayers.

- ▶ Opacity refers to the amount of transparency of an object. Changing the opacity of an object or layer allows you to see through it to the objects and layers below. Opacity of 100 percent means no transparency; 50 percent opacity means 50 percent transparency; and 0 percent opacity means completely transparent.

- ▶ Blend modes represent mathematical calculations for combining layers and objects and are always applied to the upper layer.

- ▶ A layer or object can have only one blend mode applied to it.

- ▶ Blend modes can be applied to objects or sublayers, but not to objects within the same layer.

Master Project Tasks

The more you work with Motion and the more practice you get as you complete each lesson, the better you'll become with the application. To polish your skills as you work through this book, or as a refresher, you can build a Master Project. Starting with this lesson, and continuing at the end of the subsequent lessons in the book, you will have the opportunity to complete short Master Project tasks. The Master Project tasks focus on Motion features that you've just learned in the lesson. Step by step, lesson by lesson, you will add to your Master Project until it is completed at the end of the book.

In the Master Project tasks for this lesson, you will create two new layers and add objects to those layers.

Adding Layers to the Master Project

The Master Project and all Master Project files are located in the Master_Project folder within the MOTION_INTRO Book Files folder.

1   Click the Path pop-up menu in the File Browser and select MOTION_INTRO Book Files.

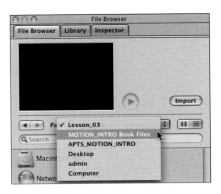

2   Double-click the Master_Project folder in the File Browser to open it.

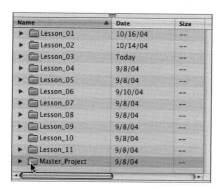

3   In the Finder, open the **Master Project_03** file.

4   Press Cmd-4 to open the Layers tab.

5   Click the Add new layer button (+) four times to create four new layers.

6   Rename the layers from top to bottom as follows:

▶   *Text*

▶   *Weather*

▶   *Leaves*

▶   *Tree*

▶   *Background*

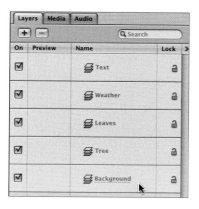

7   Drag the **IMG_2256.tif** file from the Master_Project folder in the File Browser to the Tree layer on the Layers tab.

8   Press Cmd-4 to close the Layers tab.

9   Press Cmd-3 to open the Inspector.

10 On the Properties tab of the Inspector, change the Scale parameter of the Tree image to 41 percent.

11 Choose File > Save As and save the first part of your Master Project in the My Motion Projects folder on your Desktop.

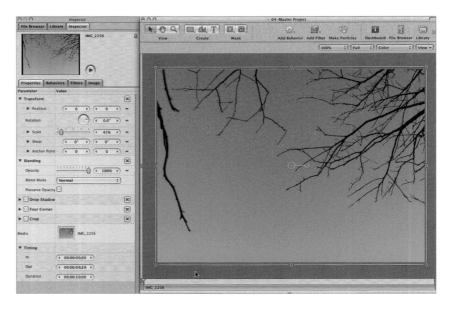

4

Working with Behaviors

Behaviors make it possible to create both basic motion effects and complex simulations involving multiple objects. They are designed to work alone or in combination with one another, to create more interesting effects.

Want to make a ball move across the screen? Just add a simple Throw behavior. Do you need the ball to bounce around the frame, repelling any objects it approaches? No problem—simply combine the Throw, Edge Collision, and Repel From behaviors. Add a little Gravity behavior, and you'll have the bouncing and repelled objects responding to gravity as nature intended. Sound like fun? In this lesson, you'll be creating those effects and a lot more.

In this lesson, you'll build a real-world project from scratch, using Basic Motion behaviors to animate product stills and text. Once you've finished with the Basic Motion behaviors, you'll move on to explore some of Motion's more advanced Simulations behaviors. Along the way, you'll also learn how to use the rulers and guides as you crop video in the Canvas and modify behaviors in the Dashboard, Inspector, and mini-Timeline.

Previewing the Finished Movie

Before you start building the first project, let's take a look at the finished video so you have an idea of what you're aiming for in this lesson. The project you'll be creating is a 6-second advertisement for Oakley watches. This short clip could be edited together with similar clips to create a looping video to play in stores that sell the Oakley watch line. This particular advertisement highlights some of the company's cool sports watches.

In the earlier lessons, you opened files in the Viewer using the contextual menu. You can also open a media file in the Viewer by double-clicking it in the File Browser.

1   Close any open Motion projects.

2   Open the Lesson_04 folder in the lower pane of the File Browser. Then double-click **Basic Behaviors Final.mov** to open it in the Viewer.

3   Press the spacebar to play the finished movie. Then close the Viewer.

All of the movement in the project was created in real time with Basic Motion behaviors. Now let's open the first project, located in the Lesson_04 folder.

4   Open the project **4-1 Basic Behaviors**.

Now save the project.

5   Choose File > Save As to open the Save As window. Name the project *4 - Basic Behaviors*. Change the path to the My Motion Projects folder on your Desktop. Then click Save.

Positioning an Object in the Canvas

In the next series of exercises, you'll crop and position a video clip directly in the Canvas. Your goal in the first part of the exercises is to move the surfing man to the left half of the frame. The video file you'll be working with is called surf_1_SD_jpg.mov and is located in the Lesson_04 folder.

1   Press the spacebar to begin playback in the Canvas.

2   Select surf_1_SD_jpg.mov in the File Browser; then click the Import button to import the movie into the project.

A video clip of a surfing man fills the Canvas screen.

3   Press Cmd--(minus) to zoom out of the Canvas one level for a better view of the bounding box around the surf_1_SD object in the Canvas.

You could now try to place the surfer visually, or you could use some handy tools that Motion provides to help you work with more precision.

Working with the Grid, Rulers, and Guides

The Motion Canvas includes three visual tools to help you move, crop, and align objects. They are a grid, rulers, and guides, and they can be turned on and off in the View pop-up menu in the Canvas. You can use these tools one at a time or all together.

Let's start with the grid.

1   From the View pop-up menu, choose Grid.

A grid appears over the frame in the Canvas. You can use this grid to align objects.

To place something in an exact location, you can use the rulers.

2   From the View pop-up menu, choose Rulers.

Rulers appear on the left and top of the frame in the Canvas.

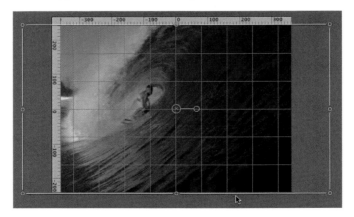

You can use the rulers alone or together with guides. Guides are horizontal and vertical yellow lines that mark positions you select on the rulers.

3 Choose Guides from the View pop-up menu to turn on the guides in the Canvas.

You won't see any guides until you create them.

Creating and Deleting Guides

The ruler across the top of the Canvas measures the horizontal values of the Canvas and creates horizontal guides. The ruler on the left edge of the Canvas measures the vertical values of the Canvas and creates vertical guides.

To create guides, you click the appropriate ruler and drag the guide into position. Let's use the guides to mark the vertical center of the frame.

The coordinates for the center of the frame are always 0,0. The first 0 represents the coordinate on the horizontal ruler, or the *x*-coordinate. The second 0 represents the coordinate on the vertical ruler, or the *y*-coordinate. Therefore, the coordinates for the frame's center are 0,0. If the center of an object is aligned with the center of the frame, the object's coordinates are also 0,0.

1 Click the vertical ruler to create a guide; then drag the guide to the center (0) of the horizontal ruler.

As you drag a guide, a small value window appears to show the current position.

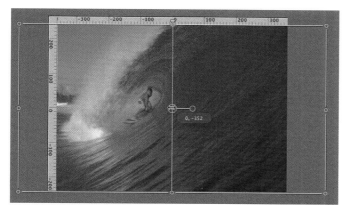

x-coordinate = 0

2   Drag the horizontal ruler to create another guide and mark the vertical center (0) of the frame.

y-coordinate = 0

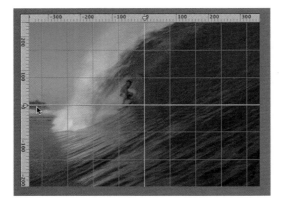

To delete a guide, you simply drag it to the upper-left corner of the rulers until it is no longer visible. When you release the mouse, the guide vanishes in a puff of smoke. Really.

We need only the vertical guide to divide the frame down the middle, so let's delete the horizontal guide.

3   Drag the horizontal guide upward until it's no longer visible in the frame. Release the mouse.

Puff.

Now that you have a guide to work with, you can turn off the grid.

NOTE ▶ The grid does not need to be turned on for you to create guides. However, you do need the rulers to create guides.

4   From the View pop-up menu, choose Grid to turn off the grid in the Canvas.

Moving an Object into Position

The next step is to move the video object toward the left so that the surfer remains in the left half of the frame for the entire clip.

1   Press Cmd-3 to open the Inspector.

2   Click the Properties tab, if it's not already selected, so that you can view the new position of the object in the Canvas.

3   Press the spacebar to start playback, if the video is not already playing.

4   Drag the video object toward the left so that the surfer remains on the left half of the screen for the clip's entire duration.

Toward the end of the clip, the front tip of the surfboard should be in the lower-left corner of the frame.

5   On the Properties tab of the Inspector, check the Position coordinates. The final coordinates should be approximately –135,0 (where –135 is the x-coordinate, and 0 is the y-coordinate).

6   Click the disclosure triangle for the Position parameter to view the x- and y-coordinates.

It's a good idea to save the project before moving on.

7   Press Cmd-S to save your progress.

Cropping an Object in the Canvas

In the previous lesson, you cropped images using the Crop parameters in the Inspector. In this exercise, you'll use the Crop tool to crop a video clip directly in the Canvas.

Your goal is to crop off any excess video from the right side of the image.

There are three ways to change the Select/Transform tool to the Crop tool:

▶   Ctrl-click the image and select Crop from the contextual menu.

▶   Choose the Crop tool from the View drop-down menu in the toolbar.

▶   Press Tab.

The Tab key toggles through the various transform modes: Select/Transform, Anchor Point, Shear, Drop Shadow, Four Corner, and Crop.

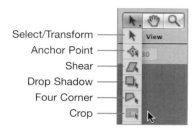

Since the Tab shortcut lets us easily toggle through the tools without using the mouse, let's try it.

You'll know that the Crop tool is active when the leftmost tool in the toolbar is a cropping tool and the crop handles in the corners of the bounding box look like the corners of a picture frame.

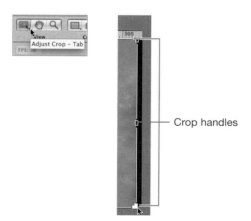

The crop handles turn white when selected. If you drag the object instead of the crop handle, you'll drag the entire object instead of cropping it.

1   Press Tab five times to change from the Select/Transform tool to the Crop tool.

2 Move the arrow pointer over the crop handle at the center of the right edge of the object.

The crop handle turns white.

3 Drag the right center crop handle toward the center of the frame. Use the vertical yellow guide to align the cropped edge.

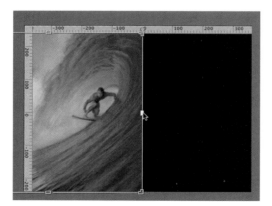

4 Press Tab once, or press Shift-S, to go back to the Select/Transform tool.

Locking an Object on the Layers Tab

It's a good idea to lock your objects or layers if they have been precisely aligned. If you lock an object or layer, it can't be modified until you unlock it. This prevents accidental moving, dragging, cropping, deletion, and other hazards known to happen in an active Canvas.

Motion provides three ways to lock an object:

▶ Choose Object > Lock.

▶ Press Ctrl-L.

▶ Click the Lock button next to the object on the Layers tab.

Let's try the last method: using the Lock button on the Layers tab. The Lock button looks like a padlock; it appears open when the layer is unlocked and closed when the layer is locked. All new objects and layers start as unlocked by default.

Unlocked (default)

Locked

1 Press Cmd-4 to open the Layers tab in the Project pane.

2 Click the Lock button next to the surf_1_SD object to lock it.

   If you select a locked item in the Canvas, you'll see a red line around the object to show that it is locked.

3 Click the surf_1_SD object in the Canvas to select it.

A red line appears around the object in the Canvas to show that it is locked, and diagonal lines appear across the object's region in the mini-Timeline.

4   Press Cmd-4 to close the Layers tab.

5   Press Cmd-S to save your progress.

Congratulations! You've positioned, cropped, and locked the video clip. Now it's time to add the first watch image.

Adding a Second Object

The next step in building the product spot is to add the product. You'll be working with two different watch images in this project. You'll start by adding the Detonator watch to the Canvas. Your goal in this exercise is apply what you've just learned to add the watch image, resize it in the Canvas, and then move it into position in the Canvas.

1   Press Cmd-1 to open the File Browser in the Utility window.

2   Change the File Browser to List view, if that view is not already set.

The names of the files are long in this project, so it's a good idea to resize the Name column in the lower pane so that you can read the entire name of the file.

To make a column wider or narrower, simply drag the edge of the header right or left.

3   Drag the right edge of the Name column header toward the right until you can read the full names of all the files.

Now locate the **detonator_stealth_trans.psd** file.

4   Drag **detonator_stealth_trans.psd** from the File Browser and drop it on the center of the Canvas.

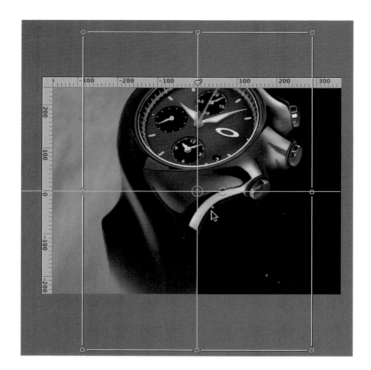

A huge watch fills most of the Canvas. The image is twice the size that we need, so let's change the scale to 50 percent.

TIP ▶ If you're working with important files such as product shots, you should export them from the original software—for instance, from Photoshop—at twice the image size that you will actually need them in the project. That way, once you import them into Motion, you'll be able to zoom in on the object and still maintain good image quality and detail. If your image is too large, it's easy to make it smaller. If your image is too small, however, and you try to make it larger, you'll lose resolution and quality in the process.

5   Press Cmd-3 to change to the Inspector tab.

6 Shift-drag the handle in the upper-right corner of the watch's bounding box toward the center until the scale is 50%.

Now that the scale is set, let's change the watch's position. First, you'll need to set a horizontal guide to mark the *y*-coordinate, where you'll align the face of the watch.

7 Drag the horizontal ruler downward to create a guide; then drag the guide down to exactly −105. Use the small window display to determine when the guide is in the correct position.

8 Drag the watch toward the right until the center of the watch face is at the intersection of the two yellow alignment guides.

The watch's coordinates in the Position parameter should be approximately 0,−184. (The coordinates don't need to be exact and probably won't be.)

9   Press Cmd-S to save your progress.

Your precision alignment duties are through for now, so you can turn off the rulers and guides.

10   Turn off the rulers and guides from the View pop-up menu in the Canvas.

Establishing a Project Feel

Your goal is to tastefully show off the watch by moving it into the right half of the frame.

That brings up another rule.

Rule #3: Decide on an overall look and feel for your project; then choose behaviors and effects that fit your plan.

Once again, this may seem obvious, but to many it's not. Motion puts a lot of professional motion graphics tools and effects at your fingertips. The trick is knowing which ones to use for a particular project and which ones to save for another time. In other words, just because you *can* do something doesn't mean that you *should*.

In this project, you're creating a point-of-purchase product spot (an advertisement that plays in stores that sell the product) for a high-end—yet cool—manufacturer. Most companies have an image they want to project, and when you create an advertising piece, you should try to project the company's style. The goal of the product spot you are creating is to highlight several stylish action watches in a cool action environment.

Everything is carefully planned, including the video clip. The surfer is in control, confident, and stable on his surfboard as he catches the wave wearing his Oakley watch. The watch also needs to be solid, stable, and confident as it glides across the right side of the screen. Remember: The idea is to attract attention to the watch.

> **NOTE ►** If you didn't complete the previous exercises and wish to continue with the lesson from this point, close any open Motion projects and open **4-2 surf&watch** from the folder 04_backup projects in the Lesson_04 folder.

Working with Basic Behaviors

The project is coming along nicely. You have your first two objects in place. Finally, you get to dive into the fun stuff: Basic Motion behaviors! Sure, you've already worked with a few of the Basic Motion behaviors in the previous lessons, but practice makes perfect. In the next series of exercises, you'll add four different Basic Motion behaviors to the watch to bring it to life in the Canvas.

The Basic Motion behaviors are the most common behaviors used in motion graphics and are conveniently located in the Library.

One point to remember about Basic Motion behaviors is that by default, they last the length of the object they are applied to. You can, however, edit their length in the mini-Timeline. You'll try that feature later in this lesson. For now, let's add some behaviors.

1   Press the spacebar to begin playback, if your project is not already playing.

2   Select the Detonator watch in the Canvas.

A bounding box appears around the object in the Canvas, and a blue region appears in the mini-Timeline.

3   Press Cmd-2 to open the Library.

4   Click the Behaviors icon; then select the Basic Motion subfolder to view the Basic Motion behaviors.

Let's start with a Throw behavior to get the watch moving.

5   Drag the Throw behavior icon from the File Browser to the watch object in the Canvas.

6   Press D to open the Dashboard, if it's not already open.

Let's throw the watch toward the upper-right corner of the frame.

7 Drag the center of the Throw behavior toward the upper right in the Dashboard.

NOTE ▶ The Zoom slider on the Dashboard allows you to zoom in for more refined motion changes.

8 Adjust the arrow length in the Dashboard so that the watch gets near the upper-right corner of the frame but doesn't quite reach it.

NOTE ▶ The longer the arrow in the Dashboard, the faster and farther the object will move. The shorter the arrow, the slower the object will move and the less distance it will travel.

9 Press D to cycle from the Throw Dashboard to the detonator_stealth_trans Dashboard. Notice that the purple Throw region in the mini-Timeline is the same length as the detonator_stealth_trans region.

10 Press Cmd-S to save your progress.

Adding the Grow/Shrink Behavior

The Grow/Shrink behavior either makes your object grow larger over time or shrink smaller. The object always starts at its original size at the first frame of the behavior. One way to show off a product is to have it slowly get larger to reveal more details. Also, when objects grow larger, they appear to be moving closer; when objects shrink, they appear to be moving away.

The Grow/Shrink element in the Dashboard consists of two square regions. The first square, with a dotted line, represents the object's original size. The second square, with a solid line, represents the relative growth rate. If you drag the edges of the solid square inward, the object will shrink; if you drag the edges outward, the object will grow.

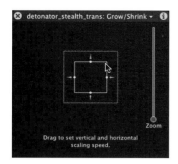   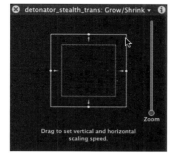

Shrink   Grow

Let's add a Grow/Shrink behavior and make the watch grow as it moves.

1   Drag the Grow/Shrink behavior from the File Browser and drop it on the watch object. Make sure playback is active as you apply and adjust the behaviors in the Dashboard.

2   In the Dashboard, drag the Zoom slider to the lowest position (zoomed all the way in). Then slowly drag the edges of the square outward. You don't want the watch to grow too big, or the effect may become annoying.

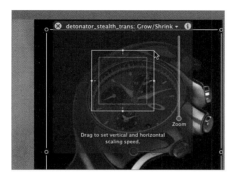

Changing Behaviors in the Inspector

The Dashboard offers by far the easiest way to adjust Basic Motion behaviors. However, sometimes you may want to change behavior parameters to a specific amount. In that case, you can turn to the detailed behavior parameters on the Behaviors tab of the Inspector.

The Behaviors tab includes parameters for all behaviors applied to the selected object. Since this object includes both Throw and Grow/Shrink behaviors, the Behaviors tab includes parameters for both, from bottom to top in the order they were applied.

Let's take a look at the Grow/Shrink behavior parameters and adjust the growth rate to a specific amount.

1   Press Cmd-3 to open the Inspector.

    Since you are working with a behavior, the Behaviors tab is automatically selected in the Inspector.

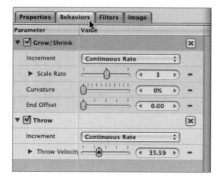

    For this exercise, let's focus on the Scale Rate parameter, which defines the speed and magnitude of the growth over time.

2   Drag the Scale Rate slider all the way to the right to see a scale rate of 100.

    The watch becomes very big, very fast—too big and too fast!
    Let's try something more subtle.

3   Type *7* in the Scale Rate field and press Return.

The watch grows slowly, just enough to catch your attention without screaming *Look at the big watch!*

MORE INFO ▶ You can find detailed information on all of the behavior parameters in the Motion documentation that came with the application.

Trimming an Object and Behaviors

Basic Motion behaviors remain the length of the object they are applied to, even if you change the object's length in the mini-Timeline. The watch is looking great, but we need to make room for a second watch. To do that, let's change the length of the first watch and its behaviors.

The project's duration is 5;26, which is the exact length of the video clip. That's only four frames short of 6 seconds, so let's show the first watch for 3 seconds and 15 frames (half of 1 second), or 3;15.

1   Press the spacebar to stop playback.

2   Type *3.15* in the current frame field and press Return. Remember to type a period between seconds and frames in the timecode field.

3   Press Shift-Cmd-A to deselect everything in the Canvas.

4   Select the watch in the Canvas.

The detonator_stealth_trans region appears in the mini-Timeline.

5   Press O to set the Out point (end) of the object to the playhead position (3;15).

The region changes length in the mini-Timeline and ends at the playhead position.

6   Press D to cycle through the Dashboard from the object to the behaviors.

Notice that the purple behavior regions in the mini-Timeline are now shorter, to match the length of the object.

Now let's set the play range Out point to 3;15 so we can finish adding the other behaviors to the watch.

7   Press Option-Cmd-O to change the play range Out point.

8   Press the spacebar to see the project with the shortened watch duration.

The watch now moves and grows faster because the action takes place in half of the original time.

9   Press Cmd-S to save your progress.

Adding Spin and Fade Behaviors

The first watch is almost complete. All it needs is a nice spin and a fade in and out. Why a spin? One of the oldest tricks in filming product shots is to slowly spin or rotate the object as the camera creeps in (slowly zooms closer). Spin doesn't mean spin around like a top. What you're trying to achieve is more like a bride showing off her gown with a slow quarter turn to the right or a new car on a turntable in the showroom.

The Spin behavior in the Dashboard consists of a circle divided into quarters; it works somewhat like the circle for the Throw behavior. The object always starts at the top center of the circle; then you drag an arrow from the starting point to any other point on the circle to create the spin. If the arrow moves clockwise, the object spins clockwise the same distance as the arrow. If the arrow moves counterclockwise, the object spins counterclockwise the same distance as the arrow.

 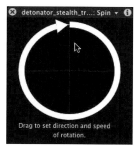

Half spin clockwise (180°)   Full spin clockwise (360°)

Let's use the Spin behavior to add a quarter spin clockwise (90 degrees) to the watch.

1   Press Cmd-2 to open the Library tab.

2   Press the spacebar to begin playback, if your project is not already playing.

3   Drag the Spin behavior from the File Browser and drop it on the watch object in the Canvas.

4   Press D to open the Dashboard, if it's not already open.

5   Drag the arrow in the Spin Dashboard clockwise one-quarter spin (90°).

The combination of throw, grow, and spin have created a nice arcing movement toward the right that draws attention to the watch in a classy "check out the cool watch" way.

NOTE ▶ The spin amount is often described in clock time to make it easy to understand, such as the 3 o'clock position for 90 degrees and the 6 o'clock position for 180 degrees.

The last Basic Motion behavior that you'll add to the watch is Fade In/Fade Out, which you have already used in previous lessons.

6   Drag the Fade In/Fade Out behavior from the File Browser and drop it on the watch in the Canvas.

The watch fades in at the beginning and then out at the end. Perfect!

7   Press Cmd-S to save your progress.

Copying an Object and Its Behaviors

The Detonator watch is finished. Now it's time to add a second watch. You could start from scratch with the second watch and follow all of the previous exercises to add the watch and behaviors to the project. Or you could save a lot of time and energy by duplicating the first watch with all of its behaviors and then replacing the object on the Layers tab.

In the next series of exercises, you'll work on the Layers tab to duplicate the Detonator watch and then replace the second watch object with the Time Bomb watch.

NOTE ▶ If you have not completed the previous exercises and wish to continue with the lesson from this point, close any open Motion projects and open **4-3 behaviors** from the folder 04_backup projects in the Lesson_04 folder.

1   Press Cmd-4 to open the Layers tab in the Project pane.

2   Press Cmd-1 to open the File Browser tab in the Utility window.

3 Click the disclosure triangle next to the detonator_stealth_trans object to show the behaviors associated with the object, if they aren't already visible.

The behaviors are listed below the object in the order in which they were applied, from bottom to top.

4 Select the detonator_stealth_trans object on the Layers tab.

5 Ctrl-click the selected object to open a contextual menu that lists options that you can apply to the selected object.

A copy of the detonator_stealth_trans object appears above the original object.

Replacing the Duplicate Object on the Layers Tab

You've duplicated the watch; now you'll replace the object. The object you'll use for the second watch is the **time_bomb_trans.psd** file in the Lesson_04 contents.

1   Drag the **time_bomb_trans.psd** file from the File Browser to the detonator_stealth_trans copy object on the Layers tab and release the mouse.

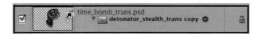

The Time Bomb watch overlaps the Detonator watch in the Canvas. The watches move in sync, doing the exact same thing at the same time.

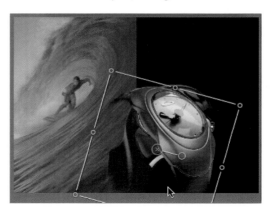

NOTE ▶ When you replace a duplicated object with a new media file, the object's content changes, but the object's name remains the same.

2   On the Layers tab, change the name of the detonator_stealth_trans copy object to time_bomb.

3   Press Cmd-S to save your progress.

Moving an Object in the Mini-Timeline

The project lasts almost 6 seconds—plenty of time to show both watches one at a time. Let's start the project with the Detonator watch and then fade in the Time Bomb watch for the second half of the spot. In this exercise, you'll reset the project play range and move the time_bomb object in the mini-Timeline.

1   On the Layers tab, select the time_bomb object, if it's not already selected.

2   Press Cmd-4 to close the Layers tab and the Project pane.

3   Press Option-X to reset the project play range to include the full duration of the project (5;26).

4   Drag the time_bomb region in the mini-Timeline toward the project Out point until the Out point of the time_bomb region aligns with the end of the project (5;25).

NOTE ▶ The duration of the project is 5;26, but the last frame is actually 5;25 because the first frame of the project is set to 00, not 01, in the project preferences.

The moving watches now play in the Canvas one at a time.

Adjusting Behaviors in the Dashboard

The timing is good—both watches are moving. But there's just one problem: The watches are moving in exactly the same way. The motion looks repetitive and becomes distracting. That's definitely not our goal. Let's adjust the behaviors on the Time Bomb watch so that it moves in the opposite direction of the Detonator watch. You'll be using skills you've already learned in this lesson to perfect your watch movements.

1   Press D to open the Dashboard, if it's not already open.

2   In the Canvas, select the Time Bomb watch, if it's not already selected.

3   Press D four times to toggle through all of the behaviors in the Dashboard.

This is one method for viewing the different behaviors applied to an object.

Switching Dashboards Using the Title Bar Pop-up Menu

The Dashboard includes a pop-up menu that allows you to select all behaviors and effects applied to an object. To open this menu, you simply click the downward-pointing arrow next to the object name in the Dashboard title bar.

1   Click the downward-pointing arrow in the Dashboard title bar to open the pop-up menu.

2   Choose Throw from the pop-up menu to open the Throw Dashboard.

Let's move the Time Bomb watch downward and to the left, to contrast it with the Detonator watch, which moves upward and to the right.

3   Drag the Throw arrow downward and to the left.

4   Open the pop-up menu in the title bar again and choose time_bomb to view the object in the Dashboard and mini-Timeline.

Moving an Object and Behaviors in the Canvas

The Time Bomb watch looks good moving in the opposite direction of the Detonator; however, it's now moving into the left half of the frame. Let's move the entire object and all its behaviors to the right of the frame, so the watch will move toward the center. To move it, you simply drag the object to the desired position in the frame.

1   Press Cmd--(minus) to zoom out one level if your project currently fills the Canvas.

2   In the Canvas, drag the time_bomb object to the middle-right side of the frame.

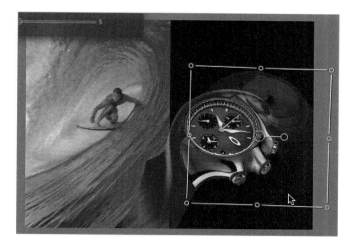

3   Press Cmd-S to save your progress.

Project Task

Now it's your turn to add your own design creativity to the watch behaviors. Take a few minutes to adjust the various behaviors in the Dashboard until the watches move exactly the way you want. Experiment, have fun, and adjust to taste. Be sure to save your work when you're finished.

Adding Text Behaviors

The last step in this project is to add a title. The look and feel of a title should fit with the look and feel of the overall project. In this case, the title should be interesting yet tasteful, with some movement that complements the other movement in the project.

Your goal in the next series of exercises is to create a title and add behaviors to it, and then change the color of the title to fit the project.

First you need to create the title using the Text tool.

> **NOTE** ▶ If you have not completed the previous exercises and wish to continue with the lesson from this point, close any open Motion projects and open **4-4 copy** from the folder 04_backup projects in the Lesson_04 folder.

1   Press the spacebar to pause playback if the project is playing. Then press T to select the Text tool.

2   Click the Text tool near the upper center of the frame.

TIP It's a good idea to create text over a solid color or empty space in the frame so it's easy to see. You can always move the text object later.

3   Type *Time   Oakley* with four spaces between the words.

4   Press the Esc key to change from the Text tool to the Select/Transform tool.

5   Move the text object to the middle of the frame so that the word *Time* is in the left half of the frame and *Oakley* is in the right half.

Trimming Text in the Mini-Timeline

The text object starts at the beginning of the project and lasts for the project's entire duration. If you remove the text from the beginning of the project, however, and let it enter later, you'll allow the viewer's attention to focus on the first watch and then on the text as it appears. Let's trim the In point of the text object so that it starts at 2 seconds (2;00).

1   In the mini-Timeline, move the playhead to 2;00.

2   Press I to change the In point of the region to the playhead position (2;00).

The In point at the beginning of the Time Oakley region in the mini-Timeline changes to the playhead position.

Adding Behaviors from the Toolbar

The Add Behavior button in the toolbar allows you to apply a behavior to the selected object from a pop-up menu. Let's try this method to add a Behind Camera zoom to the text object.

1   Click the downward-pointing arrow on the Add Behavior button in the toolbar to open the Behaviors pop-up menu.

The behaviors in the pop-up menu are organized into categories just like those of the behaviors in the File Browser.

When you choose a category from the pop-up menu list, a submenu of choices appears for the selected category.

2   From the Behavior pop-up menu, choose Text-Zoom > Behind Camera.

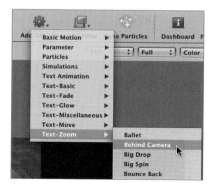

3   Watch the project in the Canvas to see the Behind Camera text behavior in action. The Behind Camera effect makes the text appear to zoom onto the screen from behind the camera. Then press the spacebar to stop playback.

Changing Behavior Length in the Mini-Timeline

You can make a behavior faster or slower by changing the Out point of the behavior in the mini-Timeline. If you stretch the purple behavior region longer in the mini-Timeline, the behavior will be slower and last longer. If you make the purple behavior region shorter in the mini-Timeline, the behavior will be faster and last a shorter amount of time.

The default duration for the Behind Camera zoom is 2 seconds. Let's drag the Out point of the Behind Camera zoom toward the left to shorten it by half of a second (15 frames). The new duration will be 1 second, 15 frames, or 1;15.

As you drag an In or Out point in the mini-Timeline, a yellow tooltip appears to show you the amount of change in duration.

1   In the mini-Timeline, drag the Out point for the Behind Camera region until the tooltip shows that the new duration is 1;15.

2   Watch the faster Behind Camera behavior in the Canvas.

The behavior seems a little too fast. Let's extend the behavior in the other direction by a full second (30 frames)—that is, the new duration will be 2 seconds, 15 frames (2;15).

3   In the mini-Timeline, drag the Out point of the Behind Camera region until the tooltip shows that the new duration is 2;15.

4   Watch the extended behavior in the Canvas.

That looks much better. I like the slower pace of the effect.

5   Press Cmd-S to save your progress.

Adding Throw and Fade Behaviors to Text

This project is nearly complete. The last steps are to add Throw and Fade behaviors to the text. In this exercise, you'll apply the skills that you have already learned to add and adjust two more Basic Motion behaviors to the text.

1   Start playback and select the text object, if it's not already selected.

2   Click the Add Behavior button in the toolbar to open the pop-up menu.

3   Select Basic Motion > Throw from the pop-up menu.

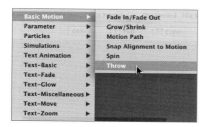

4   Press D to open the Throw Dashboard, if it's not already open.

5   Shift-drag an arrow upward in the Throw Dashboard to move the text upward in a straight line.

6   Adjust the length of the arrow (the speed and distance) in the Dashboard so that the text ends near the top of the frame.

The last behavior you'll add is the Fade.

7   Add the Fade In/Fade Out behavior to the text object.

By default, the Fade In/Fade Out behavior is set to a 20-frame fade-in and fade-out. The fade-out is okay, but the fade-in interferes with the Behind

Camera zoom behavior. Let's change the fade-in on the Dashboard to 0 frames.

8   In the Dashboard, drag the fade-in portion of the interface toward the left until the left edge is a straight vertical line.

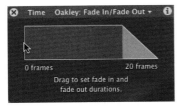

9   Watch the finished project in the Canvas.

10   Press Cmd-S to save your progress.

Congratulations! You've finished the Basic Motion behaviors project. In the next lesson, you'll apply filters to the project to polish it up. However, right now, let's take a look at some advanced simulation behaviors.

Preparing for the Next Project

Before you move on to the next part of the lesson, let's close the Basic Motion project and open **4-6 Simulations**. This is a new project that demonstrates some of Motion's Simulations behaviors.

1   Choose File > Close to close the current project.

2   Choose File > Open and select **4-6 Simulations** from the Lesson_04 folder.

Working with Simulations Behaviors

You just created a professional-looking project from scratch using many different Basic Motion behaviors. Now let's have a little fun experimenting with a few of the Simulations behaviors.

The Simulations behaviors simulate movement based on laws of physics and geometry. Fortunately, you don't have to be a scientist or math whiz to apply them. All you need is Motion, a mouse, and a little imagination.

1   Press the spacebar to play the **4-6 Simulations** project in the Canvas.

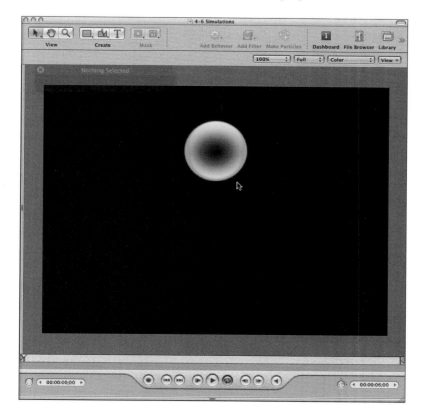

Not very exciting, is it? In fact, all you have is a static AquaBall object on an empty background. The AquaBall comes from the Motion contents in the Library.

In the real world, a ball or bubble or any object on Earth cannot hover in the air because of the law of gravity. Gravity pulls all objects toward the ground. Let's apply the Gravity behavior to the AquaBall to see what happens.

Since you'll be applying some new behaviors, you should select the behaviors in the Library so that you can preview each behavior before you apply it.

2   Press Cmd-2 to open the Library tab in the Utility window.

3   Select Behaviors and then the Simulations subfolder to view the Simulations behaviors in the File Browser.

4   Click the Gravity behavior to select it.

The selected behavior is demonstrated in the Preview area, accompanied by a brief description.

5   In the Canvas, click the AquaBall to select it.

6   In the Preview area of the Library, click the Apply button to apply the selected behavior to the selected object.

The Gravity behavior pulls the AquaBall off the screen.

You can adjust the acceleration of the gravity in the Dashboard.

7   Press D to open the Dashboard, if it's not already open.

8   In the Gravity Dashboard, drag the Acceleration slider to the right until the amount is 50.

The AquaBall falls faster.

Applying a Throw Behavior

Currently, the AquaBall drops straight down. That's okay. But what happens if you add the Throw behavior? Normally, the Throw behavior makes an object move in a straight line. With Gravity and Throw behaviors combined, the object will still attempt to move in one direction, but the movement will be affected by gravity, creating an arc.

1   Click the Add Behavior button in the toolbar and select Throw from the Basic Motion category.

2   In the Throw Dashboard, drag an arrow toward the upper right so the AquaBall moves upward in an arcing movement and then falls off the bottom of the frame.

Adding an Edge Collision Behavior

The AquaBall has come to life, but it would be a lot more fun if it bounced around the frame. In Lesson 2, you added an Edge Collision behavior to the yellow circle to make it bounce off the frame. Let's add an Edge Collision behavior to the AquaBall to make it bounce around the frame in this project.

1   Drag the Edge Collision behavior from the Library to the AquaBall in the Canvas.

The AquaBall bounces off the bottom of the frame.

2   Experiment with different behaviors in the Dashboard to create your own unique bouncing AquaBall effect.

3 Choose File > Save As and save your Simulations project in the My Motion Projects folder on the Desktop.

4 Choose File > Close when you are finished with the project.

Working with the Repel From Behavior

The last Simulations behavior that you'll experiment with in this lesson is the Repel From behavior. Simulations behaviors include Attract and Repel behaviors that either move objects toward each other or cause them to move away from each other. The Repel From behavior is applied to an object or objects; then you specify what the objects are repelled from.

Let's open the project **4-7 Repel From** to see this Simulations behavior in action.

1 Choose File > Open and select **4-7 Repel From** in the Lesson_04 folder.

2 Play the project in the Canvas to see the effect.

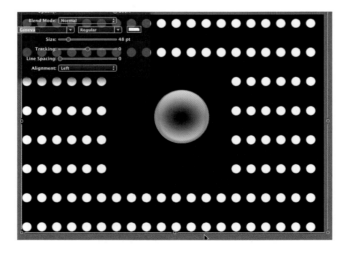

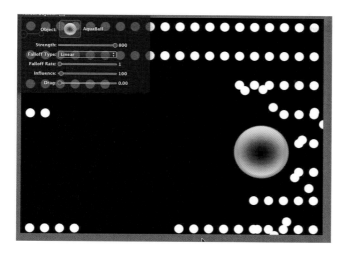

As the AquaBall bounces around the frame, the small white circles move away from the AquaBall.

NOTE ▶ This project was really easy to create. The AquaBall is just an object with Throw and Edge Collision behaviors. The small circles are actually bullet points (Option-8) that I created as one piece of text using the Text tool.

Now it's your turn.

Resetting Parameters in the Inspector

The secret to making the Repel From behavior work is experimenting with the parameters until you get the desired result. Let's re-create the effect we just saw by setting the Repel From parameters from scratch.

First, let's reset the current parameters in the Inspector. To reset parameters, you click the Reset button (X) in the Inspector.

To open the Inspector from the Dashboard, Motion gives you a really handy shortcut. All you need to do is click the Inspector button, which looks like a white circle with an *i* in the center.

1   In the upper-right corner of the Dashboard, click the Inspector button.

The Inspector tab opens in the Utility window with the Behaviors tab showing.

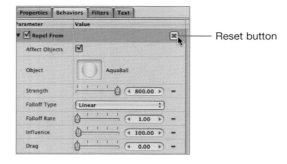

2   Click the Reset button.

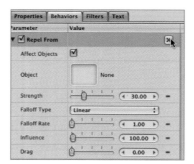

The parameters are reset to the default values.

3   Play the project in the Canvas.

The AquaBall bounces around behind the white circles.

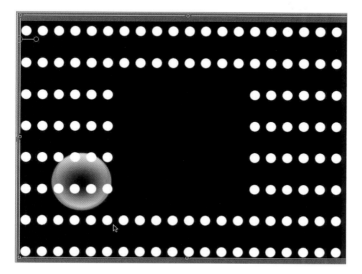

Setting Repel From Parameters in the Inspector

To make the Repel From behavior work, you need to designate the object that you want other objects to be repelled from.

All you need to do to designate an object is to drag the object from the Layers tab to the Object well. The Object well is the empty square next to the Object parameter.

1   Press Cmd-4 to open the Layers tab.

2   Drag the AquaBall object from the Layers tab to the Object well in the Inspector.

Object well

The AquaBall appears inside the Object well.

3 Watch the project in the Canvas with the default Repel From settings.

The default settings don't make the white circles repel enough to be effective. You need to increase the strength of the repellency.

4 In the Inspector, drag the Strength slider for the Repel From parameters all the way to the right to change the Strength value to 100.

5 Watch the project in the Canvas again.

The effect is better, but the repellency still isn't strong enough. So what do you do when you've reached the maximum value on the slider and still need more strength? Easy—just type in the value you want.

6 Click the Strength value field and type *800*; then press Return.

There you have it. You've re-created the Repel From behavior settings.

NOTE ▶ Parameter values in the Dashboard are fixed, so if you want to exceed the initial parameter values, you need to type a new value in the parameter field in the Inspector.

7 Experiment with the different Repel From parameters to create your own repellency effect.

8 When you've finished, save your project in the My Projects folder.

What You've Learned

▶ You can use the grid, rulers, and guides in the Canvas to align objects precisely in the Canvas.

▶ The grid, rulers, and guides can be turned on and off from the View pop-up menu in the Canvas.

▶ Coordinates come in pairs that consist of x and y values. The horizontal coordinates in the Canvas are the x-coordinates and correspond to the horizontal ruler. The vertical coordinates in the Canvas are the y-coordinates and correspond to the vertical ruler.

▶ The Crop tool is used to crop the edges of an object in the Canvas.

▶ The Tab key toggles through six different tools, including Crop and Select/Transform.

▶ You can lock an object or layer on the Layers tab to prevent it from being accidentally moved or modified.

▶ You can modify behavior parameters in both the Dashboard and the Behaviors tab in the Inspector.

▶ Basic Motion behaviors initially match the duration of the object they are applied to. You can change the duration of a behavior by changing the region length in the mini-Timeline.

▶ If you change the In and Out points of an object in the mini-Timeline, the Basic Motion behaviors applied to that object will change their duration to match the object.

▶ Duplicating an object also duplicates all behaviors, and their settings, applied to that object.

▶ Moving an object in the mini-Timeline also moves all of the behaviors applied to that object.

▶ The Add Behavior pop-up menu in the toolbar allows you to add a behavior to the selected object without going to the File Browser.

▶ You can use the pop-up menu in the Dashboard title bar to display the Dashboard for another behavior or effect applied to the selected object.

▶ The Dashboard includes an Inspector button, which automatically opens the Inspector for the current behavior or object.

▶ To reset behavior parameters to the default values, you can click the Reset button next to the name of the behavior in the Inspector.

▶ Simulations behaviors are based on laws of physics and geometry and include Gravity, Edge Collision, and Repel From.

▶ To use the Repel From behavior, you need to drag from the Layers tab to the Object well in the Inspector the object that you want other objects to be repelled from.

Master Project Tasks

If you enjoyed working with behaviors, you'll like the next exercise in the Master Project. In this exercise, you'll resize the tree object and then add two different leaf objects to the project. Once the leaves are in place, you'll apply a series of behaviors to make one leaf break away and fall against the second, causing it to fall downward and exit at the bottom of the frame. The purpose of these Master Project tasks is to hone your skills by applying them to a project. I'll give you some guidelines, but you will need to solve the problems and complete each task on your own. To help you with your challenge, I've included a finished movie and a finished Master Project file for each lesson for you to use as a guide.

Let's start by opening your Master Project in the My Motion Projects folder. If you didn't complete the Master Project tasks in the previous lesson, you can open **04 Master Project start** in the Master_Project folder.

1   Open your Master Project or the **04 Master Project start** project.

2   In the File Browser, navigate to the Master_Project folder in your MOTION_INTRO Book Files folder. Then double-click the Master_Project folder to open it in the File Browser.

3   Select the **04 MP finished.mov** file in the File Browser to preview the finished Master Project task.

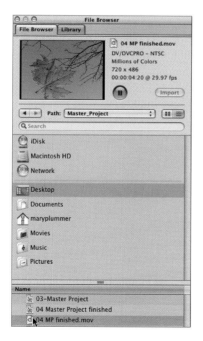

4   On the Layers tab, select the tree object (IMG_2256).

5 On the Properties tab of the Inspector, change the IMG_2256 scale to 63% and the Position value to –78.96,27.47.

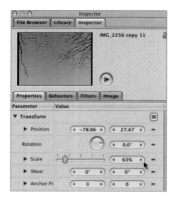

Next you need to find two different leaf objects from the Content folder in the Library.

6 Select the Seasons subfolder in the Library's Content folder.

7 Drag the Maple Leaf Orange and Maple Leaf Yellow files from the File Browser to the Leaves layer on the Layers tab.

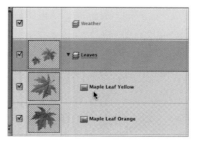

8 Adjust the leaves to the following sizes and positions:

Orange Leaf: Scale = 100%, Position = –78.96,0

Yellow Leaf: Scale = 163%, Position = 241.25,161.36

NOTE ▶ Set the initial Scale and Position values for the leaves with the playhead stopped on the first frame of the project.

9 Set the play range Out point to 4;15.

10 Experiment with different combinations of behaviors to move the yellow leaf toward the orange leaf, causing both to fall out of the frame.

There are many different behavior combinations that will achieve your goal. If you get stuck, you can open the **04 Master Project Finished** project to see which behaviors I used to create the falling leaves effect.

You can also use the following image to get some ideas.

Good luck, and have fun! Don't forget to save your project when you finish.

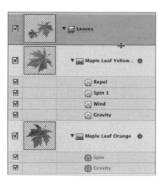

5

Lesson Files

Time

This lesson takes approximately 1 hour to complete.

Goals

Preview filters in the Library

Apply filters to objects and layers

Use the color picker to select a specific color

Modify filters in the Dashboard

Copy and paste filters

Work with Keying filters and masks

Create an image mask

Working with Filters and Masks

Filters are a motion graphics artist's secret weapon for enhancing, fixing, and finishing a project. They are usually the last step in the creative process of building a graphics composite. Think of filters as the icing on the cake. Sometimes the icing is subtle and delicate, other times it's heavy with sprinkles, and occasionally it's used to glue layers of cake together or to cover an imperfection. In all cases, the icing is applied *after* the cake is baked. The same goes for filters. They can be used subtly, heavily, as decoration, or to hide or fix imperfections in the project, and they usually are applied after the project has been built.

In the previous lessons, you spent most of your time on one project. We're going to do things a little differently in this lesson. Since you already know how to build a project, here we'll look at five different projects that have already been built except for the finishing touches. Each project shows you a different real-world use of filters; you'll apply and manipulate these filters to complete the projects. With five projects to practice with, you'll not only sharpen your skills, but also learn some new techniques for working with filters, keying, and masks to add to your growing arsenal of Motion tools and graphic design tricks.

Previewing the Finished Oakley Movie

In Lesson 4, you built a point-of-purchase spot for Oakley brand watches. The project looks good, but with the addition of some filters it can look stylish and great! When you are competing with other graphic designers for clients, there will be a lot of competition from *good* projects—it's the *great* projects that clients will remember and that keep your career on the upswing.

Let's take a look at the finished Oakley project with the filters already applied so that you can see what you are aiming for in this project.

You'll find the Oakley Finished project in a subfolder titled Oakley in the Lesson_05 folder.

Since you'll be working with five different projects in five different subfolders, it's a good idea to set the File Browser to List view to make finding and working with all of the projects easier.

1   In the File Browser, open the Lesson_05 folder.

2   Click the List view button to switch the File Browser to List view, if this view is not already active.

3   In the lower pane of the File Browser, click the disclosure triangle for the Oakley subfolder to view the contents.

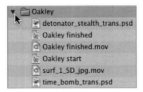

4   Double-click the **Oakley finished.mov** file to open the finished movie in the Viewer. Then press the spacebar to play the finished movie.

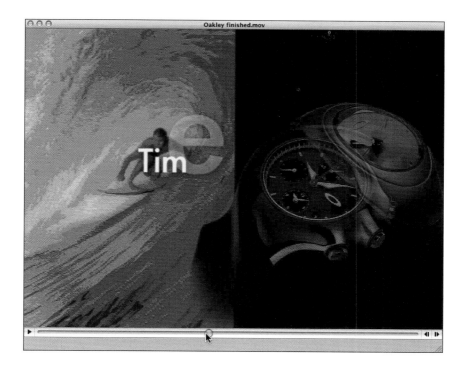

As you watch the finished movie, notice the color that has been added to the text and watches and the cool Posterize filter that has been applied to the Surf video clip to stylize the look.

5   Close the Viewer window.

Opening the Oakley Project

Now that you've seen how filters can enhance the look and feel of a project, it's your turn to begin working with filters to improve the project. First, let's open the **Oakley start** project using a contextual menu in the File Browser.

1   In the Oakley subfolder, Ctrl-click the **Oakley start** project and select Reveal in Finder from the contextual menu.

The Finder opens with the **Oakley start** project already selected.

2   Double-click the **Oakley start** project in the Finder to open the project in Motion.

The **Oakley start** project opens with all of the contents and behaviors that you applied in Lesson 4.

3   Choose File > Save As and save the **Oakley start** project in the My Motion Projects folder on the Desktop.

Previewing Filters in the Library

Working with filters is very similar to working with behaviors. You can organize filters in the Library, demonstrate them in the Preview area, add them to both objects and layers, and modify them in either the Dashboard or the Inspector. The main difference between behaviors and filters is that behaviors are used to animate (move) objects and layers, and filters are used to change the way objects and layers look.

Motion comes with 100 filters that are organized into categories: Blur, Border, Color Correction, Distortion, Glow, Keying, Matte, Sharpen, Stylize, Tiling, Time, and Video. Throughout this lesson, you'll work with a variety of filters to achieve different goals, from colorizing to keying out a background and adding a border.

The Filter icon in Motion looks like a movie file's icon with a transparent filter applied above it.

Filter icon

Let's go to the Library in the Utility window to see the different categories of filters and preview a few to see what they look like.

1   Press Cmd-2 to open the Library tab in the Utility window.

2   In the Library, click Filters to view the different categories of filters.

3   Click the Stylize category folder to view the Stylize filters in the lower pane of the File Browser.

Filters in the Stylize category are used to add a stylized look to your project. They are fun to experiment with and can either add to or detract from a project depending on the overall look and feel you are trying to achieve. Often, Stylize filters are applied to Motion graphics projects to make video images match the stylized look of a company's print artwork and logo.

4   Click the List view button in the Library to change the lower pane of the Library, if it's not already in List view.

> **NOTE ▸** The File Browser and Library are separate tabs and therefore
> have separate view buttons. Changing the File Browser to List view has no
> effect on the view settings in the Library, and vice versa.

5   Select the first filter listed in the lower pane to see it in the Preview area.

6   Press the down arrow key to preview the next Stylize filter in the list.

7   Continue pressing the down arrow key until you've previewed all of the
    Stylize filters.

    Notice that each filter is demonstrated in the Preview area using the same
    dolphin shot to show how the same image differs with each filter.

Now that you've previewed the various filters in the Stylize category, let's apply
one to the Oakley project.

Applying a Filter to an Object

In the next series of exercises, you'll apply a filter to the Surf movie in the
Oakley project to stylize the look. As with behaviors, there are many methods
for applying filters to objects in Motion. Let's start with the simple drag-and-
drop method.

First, you'll need to unlock the surf_1_SD_jpg object on the Layers tab.

Unlocking an Object on the Layers Tab

In Lesson 4, you locked the surf_1_SD_jpg object in the project to prevent accidental movement or modification of the object. Locking an object also prevents the application of any filters, which happens to be your goal in this exercise. Let's unlock the object in the Layers tab so that you can apply a filter.

1   Press Cmd-4 to open the Layers tab.

2   On the Layers tab, click the Lock button next to the surf_1_SD_jpg file to unlock it.

3   Click the surf_1_SD_jpg object on the Layers tab to select it.

4   Press Cmd-4 to close the Layers tab.

Dragging a Filter to an Object in the Canvas

In the previous lessons, you've gained a lot of experience dragging things from the File Browser and Library to the Canvas. In this exercise, you'll drag the Posterize filter from the Library to the Canvas and then drop it on the surf_1_SD_jpg object to apply the filter.

When you selected the surf_1_SD_jpg object on the Layers tab, you also selected the same object in the Canvas.

1   In the Library, locate and select the Posterize filter.

2   Drag the Posterize filter from the Library to the Canvas and drop it on the surf_1_SD_jpg object.

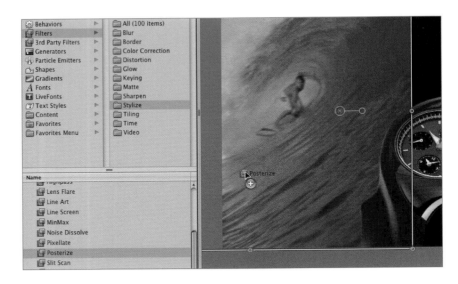

A purple Posterize region appears in the mini-Timeline, and the surf_1_SD_jpg movie displays an impressionistic, posterized look in the Canvas.

3   Press the spacebar to watch the project with the Posterize filter applied to the video clip.

NOTE ▸ Your project in the Canvas may play more slowly than it normally does because your computer has to process the filter along with the rest of the project. As the playhead moves through the project, your computer processes and then remembers (caches in video RAM) each frame sequentially. Once all of the frames have been processed and stored in memory, the project will play faster and more smoothly, depending on your processor speed, graphics card, and available video RAM. You'll learn more about managing projects and media in Lesson 10.

4   Press Cmd-S to save your progress.

Working with the Colorize Filter

You've applied a Stylize filter to the video clip to give it a posterized look. Now it's time to add a little color to the watches to make them jibe better with the new look of the project. Filters that modify color are located in the Color Correction category of filters in the Library. Let's apply the Colorize filter to the Detonator watch. Your goal in the next few exercises is to add a touch of blue color to the Detonator watch that matches the colors in the posterized Surf movie.

First, you need to select the Detonator watch object in the Canvas.

1   Press the spacebar to begin playback, if the project is not already playing.

2   Click the detonator_stealth_trans object (the first watch) in the Canvas to select it.

A bounding box appears around the object in the Canvas to show that it has been selected.

3   In the Library, click the Color Correction category folder to view the Color Correction filters.

4   Select the Colorize filter to view it in the Preview area.

The Preview area shows a demonstration of the Colorize filter applied to the dolphin (preview) image.

The Colorize filter allows you to remap (substitute) black and white brightness values with colors that you choose. In this case, you'll choose a blue color once the filter has been applied.

5   In the Preview area, click the Apply button to apply the Colorize filter to the selected object in the Canvas.

The Detonator watch changes to a sepia color, which is the default for the Colorize filter.

Modifying a Filter in the Dashboard

Now that you've applied the Colorize filter, let's modify the color in the Dashboard. First, you'll need to open the Colorize Dashboard. Then, you'll click the Remap White To color well and select a new color from the Colors window.

1   Press D to open the Colorize Dashboard, if it's not already open.

2   Click the Remap White To color well to open the Colors window.

Whatever color you choose in the Colors window will be applied to the white (lightest) areas of the original watch image.

The current, default sepia color appears as the selected color in the Colors window.

3   Select any shade of blue from the color wheel in the Colors window.

The Detonator watch changes to the same shade of blue.

4   Drag the Select/Transform tool across the color wheel to change the selected color.

The Detonator watch changes dynamically to match the selected color in the Colors window.

5   Select a shade of blue that you think works well with the posterized Surf video.

NOTE ▶ When selecting colors on the color wheel, keep in mind that colors toward the center of the wheel are lighter and less saturated (less intense), and colors toward the outer edges of the wheel are more saturated.

6   Press Cmd-S to save your progress.

Selecting a Specific Color with the Color Picker

I'm sure that you selected a great shade of blue for the Detonator watch, or perhaps you selected an entirely different color. Whatever you selected, you're going to need to change it. The client wants you to match the Detonator watch to an exact color in the posterized Surf video clip. Now is as good a time as any to get used to the idea of meeting and exceeding the expectations of your clients. In this case, your client doesn't want a color that looks similar to the video; the client wants an *exact* match.

You could spend an hour trying different selections on the color wheel, or you could find a match instantly with the color picker.

Color picker

The color picker is the little magnifying glass located near the upper left of the Colors window. When you click the color picker, your cursor turns into a Color Picker tool so that you can select any color on your computer screen, including a color in the Surf video clip in the Canvas. Seeing is believing, so let's give it a try.

> **TIP** ▶ You can use the color picker while the playhead is moving; however, sometimes you can more easily pick the specific color you want if you stop playback.

1   Click the color picker in the Colors window to activate the Color Picker tool.

Your cursor changes to the Color Picker tool, which looks like a magnifying glass.

2   Move the Color Picker tool over the Surf video clip on the left side of the Canvas and click any color to select it.

The selected color field in the Colors window shows the color you selected with the color picker.

Your goal is to pick the dark blue color from the video clip.

It's difficult to grab the color from the video clip while the playhead is moving. Let's try again, only this time you'll pause the playhead first.

3   Press the spacebar to stop playback.

4   Move the playhead in the scrubber area to 1;06, which is a frame with plenty of dark blue to select with the color picker.

5 Use the Color Picker tool to select the dark blue color from the posterized Surf video in the Canvas.

Congratulations. You picked the exact color that the client wanted. Unfortunately, it's really, really dark. It's so dark that you can barely see any details in the watch. The client definitely won't be happy about that.

Adjusting Color Brightness and Intensity

Relax. The Colors window includes a slider to lighten or darken the selected color. The higher the slider position, the lighter the color; the lower the slider, the darker the color. Let's try it.

1   On the right side of the Colors window, drag the slider upward to the highest position.

The selected color lightens significantly. Now all you need to do is lower the intensity of the color in the Colorize Dashboard.

2   Close the Colors window.

The Colorize Dashboard includes an Intensity slider to adjust the intensity (saturation) of the selected color. The default intensity setting is the highest level (1.0), or fully saturated. The lowest intensity setting (0) means that there is no color. Let's split the difference and reduce the intensity to 0.50, which is half of the current intensity level.

3   Drag the intensity slider toward the left until the intensity level is 0.50 on the Colorize Dashboard.

The intensity of the color on the Detonator watch in the Canvas changes as you move the slider.

4   Press the spacebar to play the project with the newly colorized Detonator watch.

The colorized watch looks terrific, as if you'd planned to make it that color all along.

5   Press Cmd-S to save your progress.

Copying and Pasting Filters

Now that you've brilliantly colored (pun intended) the Detonator watch, it's time to add a splash of color to the Time Bomb watch. Instead of starting from scratch, you can copy and paste the Colorize filter that you've already adjusted. The easiest place to copy and paste filters is on the Layers tab.

You can copy and paste filters using the Edit menu, shortcut keys, or contextual menus. Let's use contextual menus on the Layers tab to copy the Colorize filter on the detonator_stealth_trans object and paste it onto the time_bomb object.

1   Press Cmd-4 to open the Layers tab in the Project pane.

2   Drag the right edge of the Project pane toward the right to extend the Layers tab until you can clearly see the filenames of the objects.

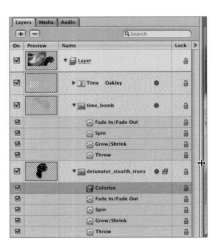

The Colorize filter is located below the detonator_stealth_trans object on the Layers tab.

3   On the Layers tab, Ctrl-click the Colorize filter to open the contextual menu for that particular filter.

4   Select Copy from the contextual menu to copy the filter.

You have copied the filter and its settings into memory.

5   On the Layers tab, Ctrl-click the time_bomb object and select Paste from the contextual menu.

A filter named Colorize copy appears on the Layers tab below the time_bomb object.

6   Press Cmd-4 to close the Layers tab.

7   Press Cmd-S to save your progress.

Evaluating the Colorized Objects

You've successfully colorized both of the watches in your project. The only problem now is that they are both the exact same color. Why is that a problem? Remember that your goal is to attract attention to the watches. If you view the current project, your eyes will probably be attracted to the first watch—but when the second watch appears with the same color, your attention is likely to shift to anything moving that is a lighter color than the watches.

This feels like a good time for another rule.

Rule #4: Too much of anything, including a specific color, will tend to lose attention rather than gain it. Okay; this rule may not be as obvious as the others. I'll give you two analogies to help make my point.

Have you ever walked into a room that had signs plastered all over the walls? Because there were so many, your mind likely registered them more as decoration or clutter than signs, and you didn't read them all. On the other hand, when you walk into a room with only one or two signs on the walls, they likely catch your attention and register as important enough to read, even if they aren't meant for you. What's the moral of this story? Less is more.

Here's another example. Have you ever been to a national park with gorgeous mountain scenery? When you see the first mountain, your attention is transfixed by the majestic beauty of it all. Three hours later, after you've seen the tenth majestic view, your attention is more likely to be drawn to a squirrel, a butterfly, or a poorly dressed tourist—anything different. Why? It's not because you don't appreciate beauty; it's because the novelty of the scenery has worn off and your mind tends to look for something new and different.

One of the most important skills in creating effective motion graphics is focusing attention where you want it to go. The first blue watch in your composite works because of the way it moves and uses color. The second watch, on the other hand, feels redundant and almost camouflaged because it's the same color as the first watch.

One way to catch attention and keep it on the second watch is to use a complementary color.

Choosing Complementary Colors

Your goal in this exercise is to select a *complementary color* for the second watch object. What is a complementary color? Complementary colors come in pairs that are located directly across from each other on the color wheel. All complementary color pairs contain one primary and one secondary color.

Together, each primary pair uses all three primary colors, yet the two elements contrast because they share no common color. At the most basic level, complementary color pairs are red and green, yellow and purple, and blue and orange.

How do you find a complementary color? Easy—all you need is the color wheel. If you draw a straight line from your selected color through the center of the color wheel, the color you arrive at on the opposite side is the complementary color. The complementary color for blue is orange, but depending on the shade of blue that you select, it may be closer to yellow.

Let's change the color of the Time Bomb watch to a yellow color that is complementary to the blue color of the Detonator watch.

1   In the time_bomb Colorize Dashboard, click the Remap White To color well to open the Colors window.

2   Locate the currently selected blue color (dot) on the color wheel.

3   Click the opposite position on the color wheel, to select the complementary yellow color.

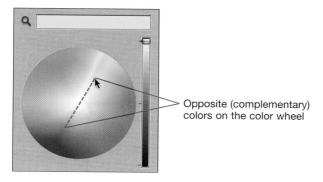

Opposite (complementary) colors on the color wheel

Complementary color for Detonator watch blue

The time_bomb object changes to a yellow color.

The complementary yellow color would also work nicely for the text in this project.

Saving a Color Swatch in the Colors Window

In the decorating world, a swatch is a sample piece cut from a material such as fabric or carpeting. The nice thing about a swatch is that you can carry it with you to match other objects. You can also save swatches of color in the Colors window so that you can keep them and apply them to other objects or projects.

To save a color in the Colors window, you simply drag a color chip from the color bar at the top of the window to the white swatches at the bottom of the window.

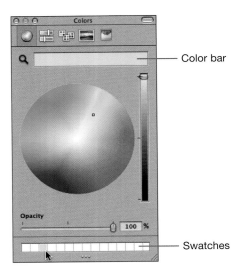

Let's create a swatch using the selected yellow color so that you can reuse the swatch in the next exercise to change the text color.

1   In the Colors window, click inside the color bar to grab a color chip.

2   Drag the color chip to one of the empty white swatches at the bottom of the Colors window and release the mouse. It doesn't matter which swatch you place the color chip on as long as it doesn't already contain a color.

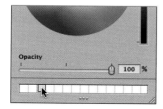

A yellow swatch appears at the bottom of the Colors window.

3   Close the Colors window.

4   Press Cmd-S to save your progress.

Applying a Color Swatch to an Object

The last step in the Oakley project is to change the color of the text. Your goal in this exercise is to use the color swatch that you created in the previous exercise to change the color of the text. The text object and the second watch both appear in the project at about the same time. If they are the same yellow color, your eyes will notice both, and you'll likely take the time to read the text and admire the second watch. That will make the client very happy.

1   Press Shift-Cmd-A to deselect all objects in the project.

2   Press the spacebar to play the project, if it's not already playing.

3   In the Canvas, click the Time Oakley text object to select it.

4   In the Text Dashboard, click the color well to open the Colors window for the text object.

5   Click the yellow color swatch at the bottom of the Colors window to make it the selected color.

The text object in the Canvas changes to the yellow swatch color.

6   Close the Colors window.

7   Close the Dashboard.

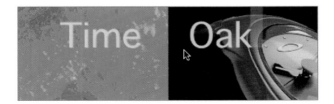

8   Press Cmd-S to save your project.

Viewing a Project in Full Screen Mode

Congratulations! You've completed a stylish-looking product spot. Wouldn't it be nice to be able to see it on the full screen? No problem. Motion includes a Full Screen mode for viewing projects. There are two ways to activate Full Screen mode:

▶   Choose View > Full Screen Mode.

▶   Press F8.

Since you'll probably want to use the Full Screen mode often while you build your projects, let's use the simple keystroke method.

1   Press Shift-Z to fit your project to the Canvas window.

2   Press F8 to switch to Full Screen mode.

3   Press the spacebar to play or pause your project.

4   Watch the final spot in Full Screen mode.

As you watch the finished spot, think about how you created it from scratch. Notice how nicely the complementary yellow color works with the blue color.

5   Press F8 again to go back to the Motion interface.

6   Choose File > Close to close the **Oakley** project.

Working with Keying Filters

In the previous exercises, you worked with filters to add color and stylize objects in the Canvas. Other filters are used for more practical purposes.

The Keying filters are used to change an image area that is of uniform color or brightness into a transparent alpha channel based on the same shape as the selected area. For example, the TV weathercaster stands in front of a large green or blue screen to do a weather report. The green or blue background can be removed using Keying filters and replaced with the image of a computerized map.

Motion includes five Keying filters: Blue Green Screen, Color Key, Lumakey, Primatte RT, and Spill Suppressor.

Your goal in the next series of exercises is to add moving clouds to a still image with a solid blue sky. To accomplish this, you'll use the Primatte RT filter to remove the blue sky from the image and then add clouds to the background from the Motion Library Content folder.

Opening the Clouds Project

First, you'll need to open the **Greece Clouds start** project located in the Lesson_05 folder in the File Browser. The project already contains two layers. The first layer contains a photograph of the Parthenon. The second layer is an empty background layer where you'll add the moving clouds.

1   In the lower pane of the File Browser, click the disclosure triangle on the Oakley folder to hide the contents.

2   Click the disclosure triangle on the Clouds folder to reveal the contents.

3   Ctrl-click the **Greece Clouds start** project and select Reveal in Finder from the contextual menu.

4   Double-click the **Greece Clouds start** project in the Finder to open the project.

An image of Greek ruins appears in the Canvas.

Notice that the sky is a fairly uniform blue color without any clouds.

Applying the Primatte RT Filter

The Library tab in the Utility window is a great place to look for filters when you're not sure exactly what you want to use. Not only can you browse through the filter categories, but you can also see the filters in the Preview area, which helps you choose the right one.

The Primatte RT filter is a high-quality Keying filter that renders the blue or green areas of an image transparent, allowing the background images to show through.

If you already know what filter you want to apply, you can choose it from the Add Filter pop-up menu in the Canvas. The Add Filter pop-up menu applies filters to selected objects or layers.

Let's use the Add Filter pop-up menu to apply the Primatte RT filter to the Greece image in the Canvas.

1   Click the Greece image in the Canvas to select it.

2   At the top of the Canvas, open the Add Filter pop-up menu and choose Keying > Primatte RT.

The Primatte RT filter works instantly, removing all of the blue background from the image. The black (empty) background shows through the transparent areas that the Primatte RT filter creates.

Let's save the project before you modify it further.

3   Choose File > Save As and save the **Greece Clouds start** project in the My Motion Projects folder on the Desktop.

Evaluating the Primatte RT Filter in the Dashboard

Before you add a background image to the project, let's look at the Primatte RT Dashboard to see what just happened.

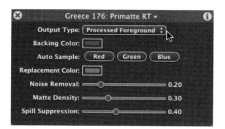

The top portion of the Primatte RT Dashboard includes a pop-up menu for changing the type of output in the Canvas and a color well to show you the color that the filter rendered transparent.

Let's look at the Output Type pop-up in the Primatte RT Dashboard to see the various elements that make the finished view: Foreground, Background, Processed Foreground, and Matte.

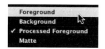

1   In the Primatte RT Dashboard, open the Output Type pop-up menu and choose Foreground from the menu.

The output (image in the Canvas) changes to reveal the original image.

2   Open the Output Type pop-up menu again and choose Background.

The entire Canvas turns black, indicating there is no background content.

3 Open the Output Type pop-up menu again; this time choose Processed Foreground.

The processed foreground is the finished image that combines the foreground and background images.

4 Open the Output Type pop-up menu and choose Matte.

The Matte view reveals the image transparency in black and white. The black areas of the matte indicate 100 percent transparency; the white areas of the matte indicate 0 percent transparency; the gray areas in the matte indicate partial transparency. A clean matte has only black and white, with no gray areas of partial transparency.

5 Change the output type back to Processed Foreground.

Let's add a background to see how the Parthenon looks with clouds behind it.

Adding a Background to the Image

Now that you've used the Primatte RT filter to remove the original blue background in the Greece image, let's add some clouds to the project. These will become the new background for the image.

To make sure that the new object goes to the background, we need to select the Background layer on the Layers tab.

1 Press Cmd-4 to open the Layers tab.

2 On the Layers tab, select the Background layer.

Switching to the Library from the Canvas

You've become quite a master at using the keyboard shortcuts to move among the tabs in the Utility window and Project pane. Let's look at another way to switch the Utility window to the Library tab, without using the keyboard.

If you look at the top-right corner of the Canvas window, you'll see a set of three icons: Dashboard, File Browser, and Library. These icons show or hide the corresponding tab or window.

1 Click the Switch to Library Tab icon to switch the Utility window to the Library tab.

If you click the switch icon for a tab that is already open, the entire window will close.

2 Click the Switch to Library Tab icon again to close the Utility window.

3 Click the Switch to Library Tab icon again to open the Utility window with the Library tab active.

Applying a File from the Library to a Layer

Now that you've opened and reopened the Library, let's look into the Library and find a shot of clouds in the Content folder.

1   In the Library, click the Content folder to view the various content categories.

2   Type *clouds* in the refine search field to narrow the search to files that include *clouds* in the name.

One file, named Clouds.mov, appears in the lower pane of the Library.

3   Select the Clouds.mov file in the Library to see it in the Preview area.

4   Click the Apply button to apply Clouds.mov to the selected layer in the project.

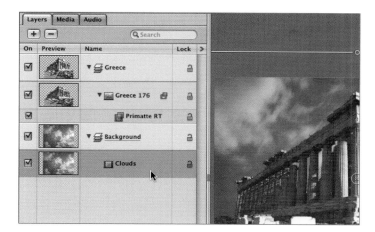

The Clouds.mov image appears in the Background layer on the Layers tab and in the background of the image in the Canvas.

5   Press the spacebar to play the project in the Canvas.

The Greece image looks much more interesting with the moving clouds background.

Cleaning Up the Matte in the Dashboard

You're almost finished with this project. The only thing you still need to do is clean up the matte. Did you notice the clouds on the rocks and on the left side of the pillars? Remember the image in the Canvas when you chose Matte in the Output Type pop-up menu? There were several areas that were gray instead of black or white. The gray areas in the matte are the same areas where you see the clouds spilling through the foreground.

Let's make a few adjustments in the Dashboard to clean up the matte and the overall image.

1 On the Layers tab, select the Primatte RT filter.

2 In the Primatte RT Dashboard, select Matte from the Output Type pop-up menu.

The Primatte RT parameters in the Dashboard are the same as the parameters in the Inspector and include three sliders: Noise Removal, Matte Density, and Spill Suppression.

Noise Removal and Matte Density work together to clean up any parts of the matte that are partially transparent. The Spill Suppression parameter introduces an opposite color to the edges of the matte to de-emphasize the edges of the matte. Since the original color was blue, the spill suppressor will introduce the opposite color: yellow.

The goal is to remove as much of the gray area (partial transparency) from the matte as possible. A little gray in the sky area won't be a problem because both the image and the background have sky colors that will work.

The best way to learn how to use the parameters on this filter is to practice with them; however, it can take a long time to get the settings just right. For now, I'll give you a set of parameters to use to achieve a good result. You can experiment more with the various parameters after this lesson.

3 Adjust the parameters in the Primatte RT Dashboard as follows:

▶ Noise Removal: 0.02

▶ Matte Density: 0.26

▶ Spill Suppression: 0.19

4   On the Primatte RT Dashboard, change the output type back to Processed Foreground.

The image looks great, except for the clouds showing through the rock in the lower center of the frame.

Cropping an Image to Hide the Background

To solve the problem of the clouds showing through the rock, you can simply crop the Clouds image.

1   On the Layers tab, select the Clouds object.

2   Press Cmd-3 to open the Inspector tab in the Utility window.

3   On the Inspector tab, select the Crop check box to activate the Crop parameters for the Clouds object.

Next, let's crop the bottom of the Clouds object until the lower edge is just above the rock.

4　Drag the Bottom Crop slider all the way to the right to crop the bottom of the Clouds object to a value of 200.

The slider is limited to a value of 200, which is not quite enough. You need to crop the bottom a little bit more than that amount to remove the entire rock. To crop a higher value, you can type a number in the value slider.

5　Type *210* in the Bottom Crop value slider and press Return.

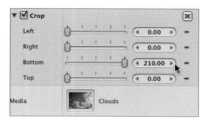

The Clouds image in the Canvas has been cropped so the clouds no longer show through the rock in the lower portion of the frame.

6　Close the current project.

Congratulations. You just "pulled a key," which is shoptalk for keying an image. Keying an image means to remove a particular color, such as blue or green.

It takes years to master the art of keying, and most professional compositors spend hours combining various key filters and tweaking parameters to perfect an image.

MORE INFO ▶ You can read more specific information about working with the Keying filters in the Motion documentation that comes with the application.

Creating a Mask Shape in the Canvas

In the last project, you learned how to use the Keying filters to create transparent areas (an alpha channel) in an image. You can also create a transparent area in an object or layer with a *mask*. Masks are used to hide portions of a selected object or layer; the area inside the mask remains visible. You can create masks using the Mask tools in the toolbar.

There are two types of Mask tools in the toolbar. The shapes-based Mask tools create masks in the form of shapes and consist of the Rectangle Mask tool and the Circle Mask tool. The free-form Mask tools create free-form masks and consist of the Bezier Mask tool and the BSpline Mask tool.

For this part of the lesson, we'll focus on a simple circle-shaped mask to gain a better understanding of how masks work. The project you'll be working on is a short piece of animation about a toy fish named Poly (for polygon) who comes to life thanks to a magical AquaBall and, of course, Motion. Poly was created in Lightwave by my friend Annie Zadie, who is a digital artist specializing in 3D modeling and animation.

NOTE ▶ Lightwave is a 3D modeling and animation application by NewTek.

Opening and Saving the Project

Since this is the third project in this lesson, you shouldn't have any trouble finding and opening the project from the File Browser. This project is located in the
Fish folder, and the project that you need to open is called **Fish Mask start**.

1   In the File Browser, click the disclosure triangle for the Fish folder to view
    the contents.

2   Open the **Fish Mask start** project from the Finder.

3   Press the spacebar to play the project in the Canvas.

4   Choose File > Save As and save the **Fish Mask start** project in the My
    Motion Projects folder on the Desktop.

Viewing the Project Elements on the Layers Tab

Before we get started creating a mask, let's look at the various elements that are
used in this project. Except for Poly the 3D fish, all of the media used to create
this project came from the Motion Content folder in the Library.

1   Press Cmd-4 to open the Layers tab.

The project is organized into two layers. The top layer is the Scene layer, and the lower layer is the Background layer.

You can see that the Background layer has been turned off because the Activation check box is unchecked.

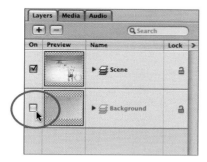

2   Click the disclosure triangle for the Scene layer to view the contents of the layer.

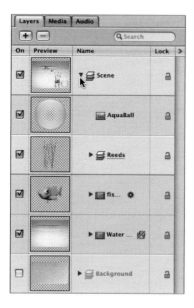

The Scene layer is composed of four elements. The elements are organized from top to bottom in the same order as they appear in the Canvas.

The first element is the AquaBall object. This object was placed on top so that Poly could swim behind it to give the scene the illusion of depth. No behaviors or filters were applied to the AquaBall object.

The next element is a grouped sublayer of reeds.

3   Click the disclosure triangle for the Reeds sublayer to view the contents.

This sublayer was created with one Grass Reed object from the Motion Content folder in the Library. I duplicated the original object six times and modified the size and position of each copy to make them look more realistic. Then I selected all seven Grass Reed objects and grouped them together to create a grouped sublayer.

There are no behaviors or filters applied to the Reeds sublayer.

4   Click the disclosure triangle for the Reeds sublayer to hide the contents.

The Reeds sublayer is also above Poly in the composite so that she can swim behind them.

The next element down is Poly the fish. Her object is called fish_animation90 because she is composed of 90 frames of animation (3 seconds' worth).

The Behaviors icon on the right of the fish_animation90 object shows that at least one behavior is applied to this object.

Enabling and Disabling Filters and Behaviors

The little gear icon on the Layers tab is actually an enable/disable behaviors control to enable or disable the behaviors applied to an object. If you click the enable/disable behaviors control for the fish_animation90 object, a red line appears over the button to show that all behaviors applied to that object have been disabled.

Let's disable the behaviors for the fish_animation90 object to see how this affects the project.

1   Click the Behaviors enable button for the fish_animation90 object to disable the behaviors.

2   Press the spacebar to view the project in the Canvas, if the project is not already playing.

The fish disappears altogether because the object starts outside the frame; with the behaviors disabled, she never actually enters the frame.

3   Click the Behaviors enable button again to reenable the behaviors.

4   Click the disclosure triangle for the fish_animation90 object to view the various behaviors applied to the object.

I used a combination of three behaviors to make Poly swim across the screen. The Throw behavior and Grow/Shrink behavior were combined to make her slowly grow as she moves across the frame. The Random Motion behavior is a Simulations behavior that creates a random pattern in the motion path. The Throw behavior moves objects in a straight line. The Throw behavior combined with the Random Motion behavior creates a more random-looking, natural movement.

Notice the purple Activation check boxes next to each behavior. You can use the Activation check boxes to turn individual behaviors on or off, just as you can use the Activation check boxes to turn individual objects or layers on or off.

NOTE ▶ Any element that has been turned off (using the Activation check boxes) will not be rendered in the final output of a project.

5   Click the disclosure triangle for the fish_animation90 object to hide the behaviors.

The last and lowest element in the Scene layer is the Water Bubbles-Large object.

Notice that the enable/disable filters control has a red line through it, which means there is a filter applied to the Water Bubbles-Large object and it has been disabled.

6   Click the Filter enable button to enable the applied filter on the Water Bubbles-Large object.

The water in the Canvas changes to a cartoonish blue to go with the rest of the scene. What filter do you think was used to colorize the water?

7 Click the disclosure triangle on the Water Bubbles-Large object to view the applied filter.

Sure enough, I used the Colorize filter.

As you can see, this project was created using all of the skills that you have learned so far in this book. Now all you need to do is apply a mask.

First, you'll need to select the entire Scene layer.

8 Click the disclosure triangle for the Scene layer to hide all the contents.

9 On the Layers tab, select the Scene layer.

10 Press Cmd-4 to close the Layers tab.

Creating a Circle Mask

Your goal is to draw a circle mask that includes only part of the scene. You'll use this type of mask because a circle mask acts like a boat's porthole, showing only part of the scene.

The Circle Mask tool works the same as the Circle tool that you used to create a circle. The only difference is that instead of creating a circle object, you are creating a circle mask.

By default, the Rectangle Mask tool is visible in the toolbar. To reveal the
Circle Mask tool, you click and hold down the Rectangle Mask tool in the toolbar. The Rectangle Mask tool looks like a light square within a darker square.

1   In the toolbar, click and hold down the Rectangle Mask tool to reveal the
pop-up menu that also contains the Circle Mask tool.

2   Select the Circle Mask tool from the pop-up menu.

3   With the Circle Mask tool, drag a circle in the lower-right corner of the
frame in the Canvas window.

4   Release the mouse to create the mask.

Anything within the circle mask remains visible. Anything outside of the
mask is now transparent. The black space that appears around the circle is
the part of the image that was masked out and made transparent. Any
image in the background of (below) this layer in the project would become
visible around the circle mask.

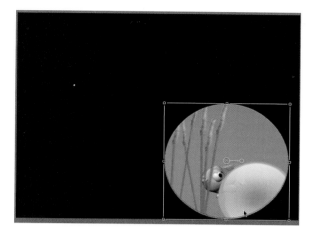

Once you create a mask, you can move it, or animate it with behaviors to reveal different portions of the frame.

5 Press the spacebar to start playback, if the project is not already playing.

6 Drag the circle mask to the center of the frame to view only that portion of the frame.

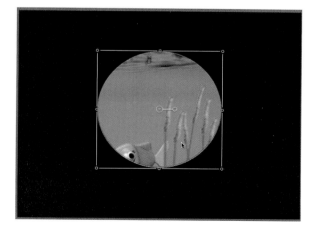

7 Experiment with the circle mask by moving it to different locations on the frame. You can resize the mask if you want by dragging the corners.

Modifying a Mask in the Dashboard

Once you have created a mask, you can adjust it in the Dashboard. Mask controls include the Mask Blend Mode pop-up menu, the Invert Mask check box, and the Feather slider.

Let's open the Circle Mask Dashboard and test the Invert Mask and Feather controls.

1   Press D to open the Dashboard, if it's not already open.

2   Select the Invert Mask check box to invert the mask.

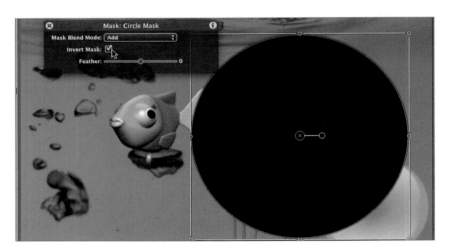

The circle mask inverts, revealing the entire image except for the masked area.

3   Select the Invert Mask check box again to uncheck it.

4   Drag the Feather slider toward the right to feather the edge of the circle mask outward, making it larger.

5   Drag the Feather slider toward the left to feather the edge of the circle mask inward, making it smaller.

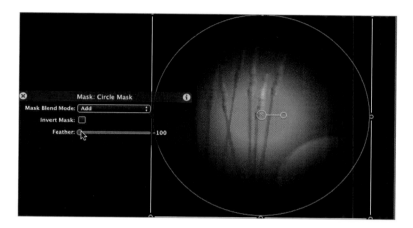

6   Drag the Feather slider back to the center until the value is 0, so there is no feathering.

Adding a Background to the Masked Area

Now that you've created and placed the circle mask, it's time to add a background. A Background layer already exists on the Layers tab; it is just turned off.

1   Press Cmd-4 to open the Layers tab.

2   On the Layers tab, select the Activation check box for the Background layer to turn this layer on.

The Background layer appears in the Canvas. This background image was created using the Postcard image from the Motion Content folder in the Library.

There you have it: a finished circle mask fish animation project complete with background.

3   Press Cmd-S to save your project.

4   Choose File > Close to close the project.

Creating an Image Mask

In the previous exercises, you created transparent areas (an alpha channel) using Keying filters and a mask, which you created with the Circle Mask tool. Another way you can create transparency in an object is by using an image mask. An image mask creates transparency in an object by using the alpha channel from another object, such as a shape, a text object, a still image, or a movie.

In this exercise, you'll apply an image mask to the Surf video clips to create a puzzle look for the image. This technique is common in commercials and music videos.

Opening and Saving the Project

For this project, you'll be working from the Puzzle subfolder located in the Lesson_05 folder. Let's open the starting project and then look at the finished movie.

1   Open the **block puzzle start** project, located in the Puzzle subfolder for Lesson_05.

The project opens; it looks like white rectangle shapes on a black background in the Canvas.

2   In the File Browser, double-click the **block puzzle.mov** file, which is located in the Puzzle subfolder.

The block puzzle movie opens in the Viewer.

3   Play the movie in the Viewer to see the finished version.

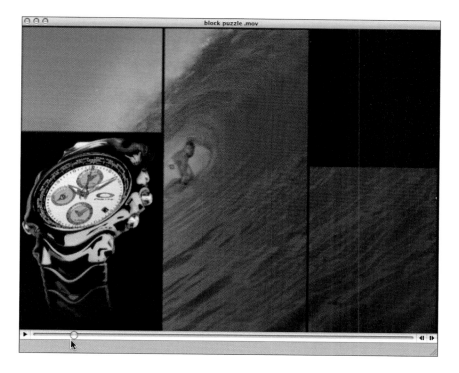

As you can see, the Surf video clips are visible only on the rectangle shapes. It's a really cool effect, created using an image mask.

4   Close the Viewer.

5   Press the spacebar to play the **block puzzle start** project in the Canvas.

A series of blocks appear and disappear on the Canvas. This effect was designed by creating shapes with the Rectangle tool and then varying the In and Out points for each shape in the mini-Timeline.

Analyzing the Mask

Let's take a look at the layer you'll be using as the image mask. We'll look on the Layers tab to see how the mask was built.

1   Press Cmd-4 to view the Layers tab.

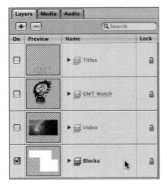

The project has four elements: Titles, GMT Watch, Video, and Blocks.

2   On the Layers tab, click the disclosure triangle for the Blocks layer to display the contents of the layer.

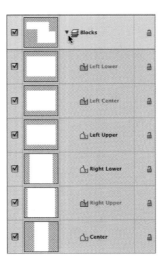

The Blocks layer contains six shapes named after their positions in the project.

3   Click the disclosure triangle for the Blocks layer again to hide the contents of the layer.

Now that you've seen how the mask was created, let's apply it to the video layer.

Analyzing the Video Layer

For the start version of this project, the Video, GMT Watch, and Titles layers have all been turned off. Let's turn on the Video layer to see what it looks like before we apply the mask.

1   On the Layers tab, select the Activation check box for the Video layer to turn the layer on.

The Video layer appears in the Canvas.

2   Press the spacebar to play the Video layer in the Canvas.

The Video layer includes two video clips, both of which have Fade In/Fade Out behaviors applied to them. The second video clip starts later in the mini-Timeline, so it doesn't appear until the second half of the project.

Applying an Image Mask to a Layer

The goal in this exercise is to use the Blocks layer as an image mask for the Video layer. The black areas between the white blocks in the Canvas are transparent areas, or the alpha channel for the Blocks layer. Using an image mask, you can apply the same alpha channel information to the Video layer. Then the Video layer will have the same black transparent areas as the Blocks layer.

You apply an image mask to a layer in either of two ways:

▶ Choose Object > Add Image Mask.

▶ Press Shift-Cmd-M.

Let's use the Object menu method.

1 Press D to open the Dashboard, if it's not already open.

2 On the Layers tab, select the Video layer.

3 Choose Object > Add Image Mask.

An image mask appears in the Video layer on the Layers tab, and the Image Mask Dashboard appears in the Canvas.

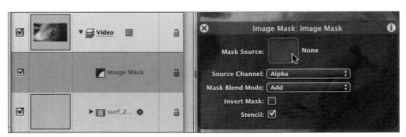

Now that you've applied the image mask, you need to assign a source object as the mask. You can assign a mask source on the Layers tab, the Inspector, or the Dashboard by dragging the source object to the image mask. Let's use the Mask Source well in the Image Mask Dashboard.

4 On the Layers tab, drag the Blocks layer to the Canvas and drop it in the Mask Source well on the Image Mask Dashboard.

The Video image now has the same alpha channel (transparency) as the Blocks layer.

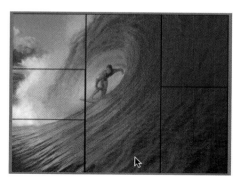

5 Press Cmd-S to save your progress.

Finishing the Project

The video looks great with the image mask applied. All you need to do to complete the project is turn on the Titles and GMT Watch layers. The GMT Watch and Titles layers are the highest layers of the project, so they will appear above the Video layer in the Canvas. I applied a Soft Light blend mode to the GMT Watch layer so it will feel like part of the video clips instead of an object sitting on top of the video clips.

1   On the Layers tab, select the Activation check boxes for the Titles and GMT Watch layers to turn them on.

2   Press Cmd-4 to close the Layers tab.

3   Play the finished project in the Canvas.

As you can see, image masks are another means of adding style and variety to your projects.

4   Press Cmd-S to save your project.

5   Choose File > Close to close the project.

Creating a News Bumper with Filters

The last exercise in this lesson is a news bumper for Hurricane Frances. It incorporates many of the skills that you've learned so far. When breaking news occurs, such as elections, wars, scandals, riots, wildfires, or hurricanes, the television stations create motion graphics *bumpers* to attract attention to the story.

I live in Orlando, Florida, so I recently had the unique experience of three hurricanes and hundreds of news bumpers about the hurricanes in a very brief span of time. While I was trapped inside a boarded-up house watching countless hours of hurricane updates, I got the inspiration to re-create a hurricane bumper for this book as a real-world example of filters in Motion.

This project includes actual Hurricane Frances footage that I shot with a digital camera and mini-DV camcorder. It's not the most exciting footage, but with filters you can make almost anything look more ominous and news bumper–worthy.

Your goal in this exercise is to use filters to colorize and add a border to some of the images. Then you'll apply an image mask to the center video image.

Opening and Saving the Project

Let's open the **Frances start** project in the Finder and view the finished movie. The **Frances start** project is located in the Frances subfolder of the Lesson_05 folder.

1 In the File Browser, click the Frances subfolder's disclosure triangle to show the contents.

2 Open the **Frances start** project in the Finder.

3 Choose File > Save As and save the **Frances start** project in the My Motion Projects folder on the Desktop.

4 In the File Browser, double-click the **Frances final.mov** file to open it in the Viewer.

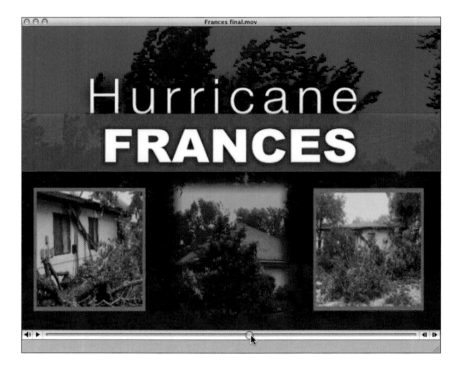

5 Play the finished movie in the Viewer.

This example is actually tame compared with some of the hurricane bumpers that aired in the Southeast during the hurricanes.

6   Close the Viewer.

7   Press the spacebar to play the **Frances Start** project.

This is the entire project without any filters.

Applying a Simple Border Filter

Now you've seen the project with and without filters. You'll start without filters on the movie and then add them.

Let's apply a Simple Border filter to the two still images in the **Frances Start** file. Your goal in this exercise is to add a Simple Border filter to one image, adjust the parameters in the Dashboard, and then copy and paste the filter to a second image.

1   Press the spacebar to pause playback, if the project is already playing.

2 Move the playhead to 3;15 for a clear view of both still images in the Canvas.

3 Press Cmd-4 to open the Layers tab.

The project has been organized into four layers: Titles, Center Square, Stills, and Background.

4 On the Layers tab, click the disclosure triangle for the Stills layer to show the contents of the layer.

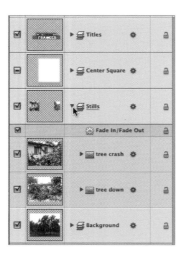

The Stills layer contains two images: tree crash and tree down.

Let's add a border to the tree crash object.

5   On the Layers tab, select the tree crash object.

6   Press Cmd-4 to hide the Layers tab.

The tree crash object is selected in the Canvas.

7   In the toolbar, open the Add Filter pop-up menu and choose Border > Simple Border.

A simple border of a thin black line appears around the selected object.

Modifying the Border in the Dashboard

The Simple Border filter has Width and Color parameters that can be modified in either the Inspector or the Dashboard.

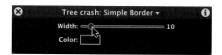

1   Press D to open the Dashboard, if it's not already open.

2   In the Simple Border Dashboard, drag the Width slider toward the right to increase the width of the border to 40.

The black border around the selected object in the Canvas becomes wider.

3   In the Simple Border Dashboard, click the Color well to open the Colors window.

The Colors window opens with a solid black color wheel.

4   Drag the slider on the right side of the Colors window to the middle position to raise the brightness of the black and set a medium gray border.

The color of the border on the selected object changes to gray. If you raise the slider to the highest position, you will get white, as illustrated within the slider.

5   Close the Colors window.

6   Press Cmd-S to save your progress.

Copying and Pasting a Border on the Layers Tab

You've finished the first Simple Border filter. Now you can copy it from the first object and paste it on the second object in the Stills layer.

1   Press Cmd-4 to open the Layers tab.

2   On the Layers tab, Ctrl-click the Simple Border filter applied to the tree crash object and select Copy from the contextual menu.

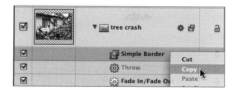

3   On the Layers tab, Ctrl-click the tree down object and select Paste from the contextual menu.

A filter called Simple Border copy appears on the Layers tab below the tree down object.

Both of the still objects in the Canvas now have gray borders.

Applying an Image Mask to the Project

The next step toward finishing this project is to have a video image appear in the lower center of the project, instead of the white rectangle.

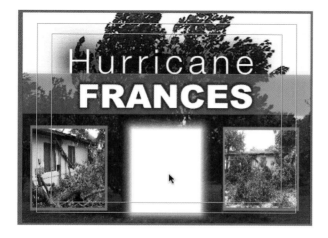

The video image and mask object are located in the Center Square layer of in the Layers tab.

1   Press Cmd-4 to open the Layers tab.

2   On the Layers tab, click the disclosure triangle for the Center Square layer to show the contents of the layer.

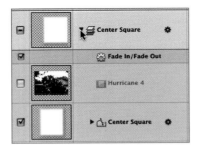

First, you need to turn on the Hurricane 4 video object.

3   On the Center Square layer of the Layers tab, select the Activation check box for the Hurricane 4 video object to turn it on.

4   On the Layers tab, select the Hurricane 4 object.

5   Choose Object > Add Image Mask to apply an image mask to the selected object.

Now all you need to do is assign the Center Square layer as the mask source.

6   Drag the Center Square layer from the Layers tab to the Mask Source well in the Image Mask Dashboard.

7   Press the spacebar to play the project to see the Hurricane 4 video image
     mapped with the Center Square object.

8   Press Cmd-S to save your progress.

Colorizing the Background

The last step in this project is to add some color to the Background layer. You
can also colorize the Center Square and Stills layers to give the project a more
consistent look. Let's start with the Background layer.

1   On the Layers tab, click the disclosure triangle for all the layers to hide all
     the contents.

2   Select the Background layer and apply a Colorize filter from the Add
     Filters pop-up menu.

     NOTE ▶ The Colorize filter is located in the Color Correction category
     of filters.

3   Click the Remap White To color well in the Colorize Dashboard to open the Colors window.

4   Select a blue color from the color wheel, or choose another color if you wish.

Let's create a swatch of the color you selected so that you can use the same color another time.

5   In the Colors window, drag a chip from the color bar to the swatches area at the bottom of the window.

6   On the Layers tab, copy the Colorize filter from the Background layer and paste it on the Center Square layer.

The Colorize filter looks a little too intense on the Center Square layer.

7   In the Colorize Dashboard, lower the Intensity slider to 0.50 to reduce the amount of color on the layer.

8   Copy the Colorize filter on the Center Square layer and paste it on the Stills layer.

9   In the Colorize Dashboard, lower the intensity of the Colorize filter on the Stills layer to 0.25.

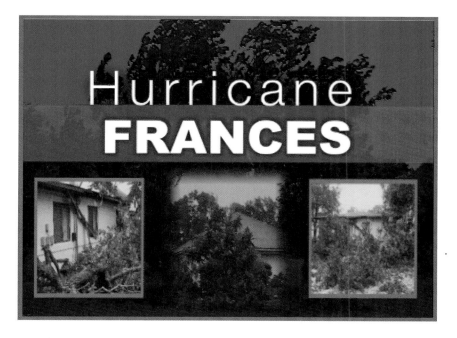

Congratulations! You have completed five out of five projects and learned how to apply and modify filters in Motion.

What You've Learned

► Motion comes with 100 filters, which are organized into categories: Blur, Border, Color Correction, Distortion, Glow, Keying, Matte, Sharpen, Stylize, Tiling, Time, and Video.

► You can view the effects of the various filters in the Preview area of the Library.

► You can apply a filter to an object by using the drag-and-drop method, by selecting the object and clicking the Apply button in the Library, or by using the Add Filters pop-up menu in the toolbar.

▶ The Color Picker tool in the Colors window allows you to select a specific color from anywhere on the computer screen.

▶ You can use the slider in the Colors window to lighten or darken the selected color.

▶ To save the selected color in the Colors window, you can drag a chip from the color bar to the swatches area.

▶ Complementary colors, which are opposite colors on the color wheel, can be used to attract attention.

▶ You can copy and paste filters on the Layers tab using the Edit menu, keyboard shortcuts, or a contextual menu.

▶ Keying filters are used to remove uniform color or brightness from an image to create transparency. The transparent part of an image is called the alpha channel.

▶ You can also create transparency on an object or layer by using masks. Masks can be created with Mask tools or applied as image masks.

▶ The Simple Border filter can be applied to an object to add a border. You can then modify the width and color of the border in the Inspector or Dashboard.

Master Project Tasks

Now it's your turn to apply your new skills with filters to the Master Project. Your goal is to make the sky behind the tree fade to black and then to fade in a cloud background movie. To accomplish this, you'll first need to duplicate the image in the Tree layer and move it in the mini-Timeline. Next, you'll add a Primatte RT filter to the copied image and remove the blue sky. Then you'll add a Clouds background movie to the Background layer and apply a Fade In/Fade Out behavior. Along the way, you'll practice other skills that you've learned in previous lessons.

Let's start by opening your Master Project in the My Motion Projects folder. If you didn't complete the Master Project tasks in the previous lesson, you can open **05 Master Project start** in the Master_Project folder.

1   Open your Master Project or the **05 Master Project start** project.

2   In the File Browser, navigate to the Master_Project folder in your MOTION_INTRO Book Files folder. Then double-click the Master_Project folder to open it in the File Browser.

3   Select the **05 MP finished.mov** file in the File Browser to preview the finished Master Project task.

4   On the Layers tab, select the tree object (IMG_2256).

5   Ctrl-click the tree object and select Duplicate from the contextual menu.

6   Move the playhead to 4;00.

7   In the mini-Timeline, drag the duplicate object (IMG_2256 copy) to the right so the object starts at the playhead position (4;00).

8   Press Shift-O to move the playhead to the Out point of the selected object.

9   Press Option-Cmd-O to set the play range Out point at the playhead position (8;16).

10   On the Layers tab, select the Tree layer.

11   Press O to extend the entire Tree layer to the playhead position.

12   On the Layers tab, select the original tree object (IMG_2256).

13   Move the playhead to 4;16 and press O to change the Out point of the first tree object to 4;16.

14   On the Layers tab, select the tree object copy (IMG_2256 copy) and apply the Primatte RT filter.

15   Find the Clouds.mov object in the Content folder of the Library.

16   Drag the Clouds.mov object from the Library to the Background layer on the Layers tab.

17   Move the Clouds region in the mini-Timeline so that it starts at 6;00.

18   Add a Fade In/Fade Out behavior to the Clouds object.

19 Move the playhead to 5;00 and adjust the Primatte RT parameters on the Dashboard as follows:

▶ Noise Removal: 0.06

▶ Matte Density: 0.12

▶ Spill Suppression: 0.50

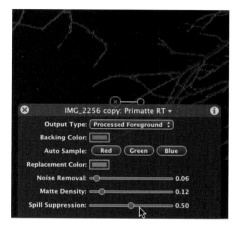

You can tweak the parameters to whatever settings you prefer.

20 Apply a Fade In/Fade Out behavior to the original tree object (IMG_2256).

21 Adjust the Fade In/Fade Out Dashboard so that the fade-in lasts 0 frames. In other words, there is no fade-in at the beginning.

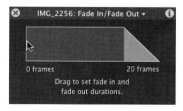

22 Save your Master Project in the My Motion Projects folder.

6

Lesson Files

Time

This lesson takes approximately 1 hour and 30 minutes to complete.

Goals

Apply a particle emitter from the Library

Modify a particle emitter

Create a particle system

Apply behaviors to particles

Limit the birthrate and initial number of particles

Save a customized particle emitter as a Favorite

Lesson 6
Working with Particles

You've already learned how to apply behaviors and filters to individual objects in Motion. You can also create and animate large numbers of objects quickly and easily using Motion's powerful Particle feature.

One of the best ways to understand how particles work is to use them, experiment with them, and see them in action.

Motion comes with more than 100 prebuilt particle emitters to choose from in the Library, or you can make your own using virtually any object, including text. Particles come in all shapes and sizes and have many uses.

This lesson includes five examples of particles, starting with a simple visual effect from the Library and working up to a complex particle system with behaviors that you build from scratch.

Opening the Oakley Project

First, let's open the **6-1 Oakley** project located in the Lesson_06 folder. Once the project is open, take a moment to review the various elements on the Layers tab.

1   Close any open Motion projects.

2   In the File Browser, open the Lesson_06 folder; then open the **6-1 Oakley** project.

This is a copy of the Oakley project that you finished in the previous lesson.

3   Play the Oakley project once to remind yourself what it looks like.

4   Press Cmd-4 to open the Layers tab in the Project pane.

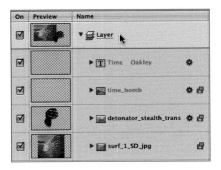

The project includes one layer and four objects within the layer: the Time Oakley text, time_bomb, detonator_stealth_trans, and surf_1_SD_jpg.

5   Press Cmd-4 to close the Layers tab.

6   Choose File > Save As and save your project in the My Motion Projects folder on the Desktop.

Previewing Particles in the Library

Particles have hundreds of uses and, like filters, can enhance the look, feel, and production values of your project. The difference is that filters are effects that you apply to objects or layers to change the way they look; particles are objects that you apply to a project to change the look of the project. For example, you can use particles to create a subtle background, or flashy pyrotechnic effects with fireworks, smoke, and explosions. For this first exercise, let's try something moderately flashy and add some sparkles to the Oakley project.

Sparkles where? At the beginning of the Oakley project, the Detonator watch makes its debut with a slow, uneventful fade-in. Let's enhance the Detonator watch's introduction so that the watch instead appears magically in a surprise burst of colorful sparkles. Sound difficult? Actually, you can apply this effect in three easy steps: Find the emitter, apply the emitter, and modify the emitter.

Particle emitters are like specialized mass-production factories that use an object as a reproduction mold and then create replicas in mass quantities in whatever size, shape, and color you choose. The factory is the particle emitter, and the replicas that it mass-produces are the particle cells.

You'll learn more specifics about emitters later in this lesson. For now, let's find the right particle emitter for this job. Since the goal is to add sparkles, let's focus the search on the Sparkles category in the Library.

1   Press Cmd-2 to open the Library.

2   Click the List view button to switch the Library to List view, if this view is not already active.

3   In the Library, click Particle Emitters to view the various categories of filters. Then click the Sparkles category folder to view the Sparkles emitters in the lower pane of the Library.

Particle emitters in the Sparkles category are used to add sparkle-type effects to your project.

4 Select the first Sparkles particle emitter listed in the lower pane to see it in the Preview area.

5 Press the down arrow key to preview the next Sparkles emitter in the list. Continue pressing the down arrow key until you've previewed all of the Sparkles emitters.

Now that you've previewed the various particle emitters in the Sparkles category, let's apply one to the Oakley project.

Dragging a Particle Emitter to the Canvas

In the next series of exercises, you'll apply a particle emitter to the beginning of the Oakley project to add a burst of sparkles as the Detonator watch fades in. As with behaviors and filters, there are many methods for applying particle emitters to a Motion project. Let's start with the simple drag-and-drop method.

In this exercise, you'll drag the Surprise Shimmer particle emitter from the Library to the Canvas and drop it on the lower center of the Canvas where the Detonator watch first appears.

1 Press the spacebar to begin playback, if the project is not already playing.

2 In the Library, locate and select the Surprise Shimmer particle emitter.

3   Drag the Surprise Shimmer emitter from the Library to the Canvas and
drop it on the lower center of the frame.

A small burst of yellow, white, and blue sparkles appears above the
Detonator watch at the beginning of the project. Not only do they add an
exciting effect to introduce the first watch—but they also happen to be the
right color scheme for this project. What luck!

4   Press Cmd-S to save your progress.

Analyzing a Particle Emitter on the Layers Tab

Let's go back to the Layers tab and see what elements have been added to the project to create the Surprise Shimmer effect.

1 Press Cmd-4 to open the Layers tab.

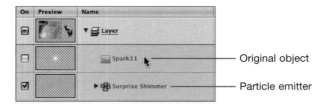

Notice that there are two new elements in the project: the Spark11 object and the Surprise Shimmer particle emitter.

The Spark11 object is the original object that was used as a mold for the particle emitter. Since it is used only as a mold, the object is turned off on the Layers tab.

Let's look inside the particle emitter.

2 Click the disclosure triangle for the Surprise Shimmer emitter to view the particle cell.

The cell, named Blur 11 copy, represents all of the particles created by the emitter. In the factory analogy, the cell represents the replicas of the original object that are mass-produced by the emitter.

Now let's look inside the cell.

3 Click the disclosure triangle for Blur 11 copy to view the contents.

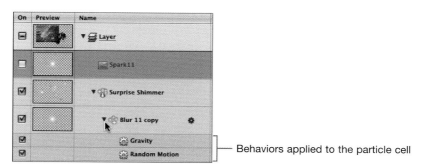

Behaviors applied to the particle cell

Two behaviors are applied to the particle cell. Applying behaviors to a particle cell actually applies those behaviors to each individual particle.

The Random Motion behavior causes the individual sparks to move about randomly. The Gravity behavior restricts the motion of the individual sparks.

Now let's try another example.

Using Particles for Visual Effects

Another use for particles is to create visual effects to make something look more realistic. As a motion graphics artist, you're not only responsible for making the project elements interact within the frame; you also need to create a sense of reality within the context of the project. For example, in an animated movie it's understood that everything happening to the characters isn't really taking place. However, within the animated world, the rules of the physical world still apply. Gravity still works, characters bump into things, and if the characters fall in the water, there should be a splash. Whether you're adding realism to a fictitious world or fiction to a real world, particles can be very useful for everything from explosions and tornadoes to clouds of dust responding to impact.

In the next series of exercises, you'll use particles to apply a little realism to a fictitious world.

Opening the Bounce Project

First, let's close the current project and open the **6-2 Bounce** project.

1 Choose File > Close to close the **6-1 Oakley** project.

2 Choose File > Open and select the **6-2 Bounce** project from the Lesson_06 folder. Then click the Open button to open the project.

3 Choose File > Save As and save your project in the My Motion Projects folder on the Desktop. Then press the spacebar to begin playback.

This simple project is a ball bouncing on a surface and then falling into a hole. Your goal is to apply Drop Impact particles each time the ball hits the floor, to make the action seem more realistic.

Analyzing the Project on the Layers Tab

Let's look at the elements of this project before we add the particles.

1 Press Cmd-4 to open the Layers tab.

The **6-2 Bounce** project includes one layer with two objects. The first is a Rectangle object, created with the Rectangle tool and positioned at the bottom of the frame to visually represent a hard surface that will cause the ball to bounce on impact. The second object is the AquaBall with Throw, Gravity, and Edge Collision behaviors applied to create the illusion of a ball bouncing.

2 Press Cmd-4 again to close the Layers tab.

Creating an Object at the Playhead Position

Before you add Drop Impact particles to the project, it's a good idea to understand your goal. The reality that you are trying to sell in this project is that the AquaBall is actually falling and that an actual impact occurs when the AquaBall bounces off the floor. Adding Drop Impact particles at the precise time and location of the impact will help you create this illusion of reality.

Normally, every object that you add to the Canvas automatically starts in the first frame at the beginning of the mini-Timeline. You can change the Project preferences, however, so that objects start at the current playhead position. Let's do that now so we can create the Dust Impact particles at the playhead position.

1   Choose Motion > Preferences.

The Preferences window opens.

2   In the Preferences window, click the Project icon to view the Project preferences.

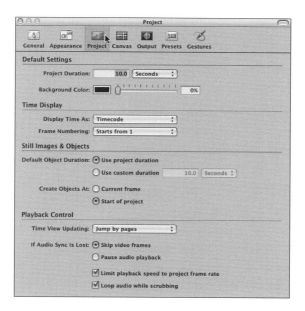

Project preferences are separated into four sections: Default Settings, Time Display, Still Images & Objects, and Playback Control.

The Default Settings preferences consist of the Project Duration (10.0 seconds) and Background Color (black) settings. You can change these default settings by typing a new duration or clicking the color well and selecting a new color.

The Time Display settings consist of a Display Time As pop-up menu for choosing Timecode or Frames, and a Frame Numbering pop-up menu to start numbering frames from 1 or 0.

The Still Images & Objects settings consist of Default Object Duration options so you can use the project duration or a custom duration amount, and Create Objects At options so you can create objects at the start of the project or at the current frame.

The Playback Control settings consist of Time View Updating and audio sync and playback speed options. You'll learn more about the Playback Control settings in Lesson 9.

3   In the Still Images & Objects section of the Project preferences window, change the Create Objects At option to Current frame, if that option isn't already selected.

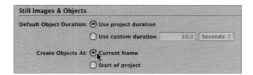

NOTE ▶ The Create Objects At: Current frame option works only for objects created while the playhead is paused. If the playhead is moving, the objects will automatically begin at the start of the project. The Create Objects At: Current frame option is the default setting for Motion.

4   Close the Project preferences window.

Applying Drop Impact Particles

You've changed the Project preferences to create new objects at the playhead position. Now it is time to move the playhead to the precise location where you want the Drop Impact particles to start in the project.

1   Press the spacebar to pause playback, if the project is currently playing.

2   Press the Home key to move the playhead to the first frame of the project.

3   Press and hold down the right arrow key to move the playhead forward one frame at a time until the AquaBall touches the Rectangle object at the bottom of the frame (2;15).

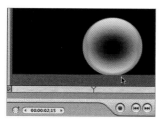

This is the precise frame in which the first impact event occurs.

4   Press Cmd-2 to open the Library tab in the Utility window, if it is not already showing.

5   In the Library, select the Nature category of particle emitters.

The Nature category of particle emitters includes acts of nature such as Clouds, Fire Flies, Fog, Rain, and Snow. For this exercise you'll apply the Drop Impact particle emitter to the Canvas.

6   Drag the Drop Impact particle emitter from the Library to the Canvas and drop it on the Canvas below the AquaBall. Use the Dynamic Guides to center the Drop Impact emitter at the bottom of the frame below the AquaBall.

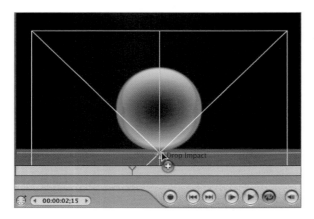

A puff of animated dust appears in the Canvas where the AquaBall touches the Rectangle object.

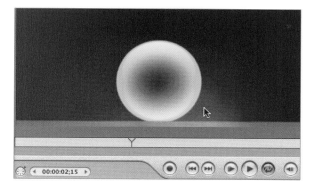

7   Press the spacebar to play the project and see the Drop Impact particles in action.

Amazing isn't it? It almost makes you want to fetch a dust mop—or sneeze. With a simple drag-and-drop particle maneuver, you created the realistic illusion of a ball bouncing on a dusty floor.

Analyzing the Drop Impact Particle System

Now that you've applied the Drop Impact particle emitter to the project, let's take a look at the changes on the Layers tab.

1   Press Cmd-4 to open the Layers tab.

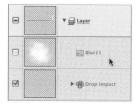

Two new elements appear on the Layers tab. The first element is the Blur11 object, which is the original object used as a mold by the emitter.

The second element is the Drop Impact particle emitter that manufactures mass quantities of Blur 11 particles.

2   Click the disclosure triangle for the Drop Impact emitter to show the contents.

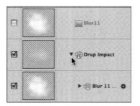

The Drop Impact particle emitter contains the Blur 11 cell that represents all of the particles.

3   Click the disclosure triangle for the Blur 11 cell to see the behaviors that have been applied to the individual particles.

The Blur 11 cell has Random Motion and Gravity behaviors applied to it so that each individual particle moves randomly, within the limitations of gravity. Without the Gravity behavior, the particles would move all over the frame, destroying the illusion of a drop impact.

4   Press Cmd-4 to close the Layers tab. Then press Cmd-S to save your progress.

Applying Another Drop Impact to the Project

The Gravity behavior applied to the AquaBall object affects the height that the ball bounces. Without gravity applied to the ball, it would bounce off the bottom edge all the way to the top edge of the frame and then back again and again, like an object moving in a vacuum with no gravitational limits on its movement. With gravity, the ball bounces about half of the distance and velocity that it originally dropped, and then half of the distance and velocity of the first bounce for the second bounce. What does this have to do with particles? The first drop impact produced a large plume of dust particles. If the ball falls half of the distance for the second impact, the dust plume should be about half the size of the original.

Let's apply the second Drop Impact particle emitter and then resize it in the Canvas.

1   Press the spacebar to pause playback.

2   Move the playhead to the frame where the AquaBall touches the Rectangle object the second time (6;15).

3   Drag the Drop Impact particle emitter from the Library to the Canvas and drop it on the bottom of the frame so that the center is aligned with the center of the AquaBall.

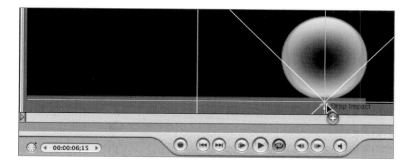

4   Press Cmd-S to save your progress.

You've successfully applied the second Drop Impact particle emitter to your project. The next step is to resize it in the Canvas.

Resizing a Particle Emitter in the Canvas

You can move and resize a particle emitter in the Canvas the same way that you move and resize an object. For this exercise, you'll use the Select/Transform tool to change the size of the second Drop Impact emitter.

1   Move the playhead to 6;15, if that is not already the current frame.

2   In the Canvas, click the dust to select the second Drop Impact emitter.

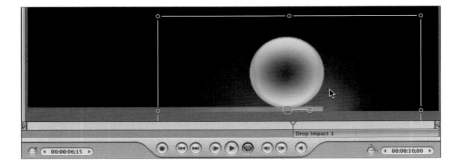

A bounding box appears in the Canvas showing the selected emitter, and a Drop Impact 1 region appears at the playhead position in the mini-Timeline.

Let's zoom out of the Canvas for a better view of the entire bounding box.

3   Press Cmd-– (hyphen) to zoom out of the Canvas one level.

Scaling an Object Toward Its Center

In previous lessons, you learned to resize an object with the Select/Transform tool by dragging the corner handles of the bounding box. You also learned that if you hold down the Shift key and drag a corner of the bounding box, you constrain the proportions of the object as you resize it. You can also resize, constrain proportions, *and* maintain an object's center position at the same time. All you need to do is hold down the Option key in addition to the Shift key as you drag the corner of the bounding box. Let's try it.

1   Press and hold down the Shift and Option keys; then drag the lower-right corner of the Drop Impact 1 bounding box to resize it to 50 percent of its original size.

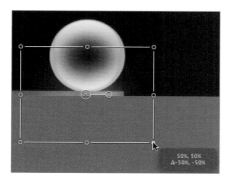

Resizing the emitter in the Canvas changes the size of the space the particles occupy in the Canvas, not the size of the particles themselves. You'll change the size of the particles in the next exercise.

2   Press the spacebar to see the finished **6-2 Bounce** project with the Drop Impact particle emitters applied to it.

Notice the large plume of dust on the first bounce, and the smaller plume of dust on the second bounce.

3   Press Cmd-S to save your project. Then close the **6-2 Bounce** project.

Now you know how to apply realistic visual effects using Motion particle emitters.

Resetting Project Preferences

Before moving on to the next project, it's a good idea to reset the Project preferences so that new objects appear at the start of the project. That way, you can focus on creating and modifying particles and won't have to think about where the playhead is located.

1   Press Cmd-, (comma) or choose Motion > Preferences to open the Preferences window.

2   In the Preferences window, in the Still Images & Objects area, change the Create Objects At setting to Start of project.

3   Press Cmd-W or click the Close button (X) to close the Project preferences window.

Creating a Particle System

In the previous exercises, you used some of Motion's particle emitters that come with the application. In the next series of exercises, you'll create your own particle emitter; then you'll apply behaviors to the particle cell and modify the particles in the Dashboard and the Inspector. Your goal is to turn a single object—the AquaBall—into dozens of bouncing balls in a variety of sizes and colors.

Opening the AquaBall Particles Project

First, let's open the **6-3 AquaBall Particles** project from the Lesson_06 folder.

1   Choose File > Open. Select the **6-3 AquaBall Particles** project in the Finder.

2   Click the Open button or press Return to open the project.

An empty project opens with the Layers tab showing in the Project pane.

3   Choose File > Save As and save your project to the My Motion Projects folder on the Desktop.

Adding the Original Object to the Canvas

All particle systems require at least one original object that acts as the mold for the particle emitter to mass-produce. For this exercise, you'll add the AquaBall to the Canvas so that it can be used as the original object for the particle system. The AquaBall is located in the Content folder in the Library.

1 Press Cmd-2 to open the Library tab, if it's not already open. Then press Cmd-4 to open the Layers tab.

2 In the Library, select the Content folder; then select the All subfolder to view all of the Content files that come with Motion.

The AquaBall.png file appears near the top of the files list (alphabetically).

3 Drag AquaBall.png from the Library and drop it in the center of the Canvas.

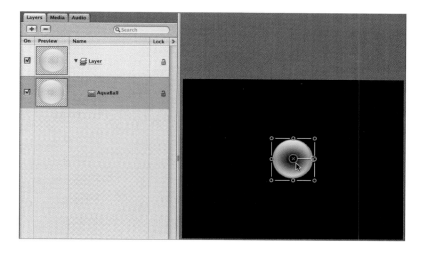

The AquaBall appears as an object in the Canvas and on the Layers tab.

Creating Particles from an Object

Motion's powerful particle engine allows you to make virtually any object into particles, including the AquaBall. There are two simple methods for creating a particle emitter from the selected object:

▶ Press E (for emitter).

▶ Click the Make Particles button in the toolbar.

Let's create some particles.

1 Press the spacebar to play the project in the Canvas.

It's easier to see the particles in action if the project is playing.

2 In the Canvas, click the AquaBall object to select it, if it is not already selected.

3 On the toolbar, click the Make Particles button to create AquaBall particles.

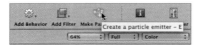

Whoa! That was easy. The frame fills with AquaBalls, all flowing from the center of the frame, and an emitter appears on the Layers tab with the AquaBall as the cell.

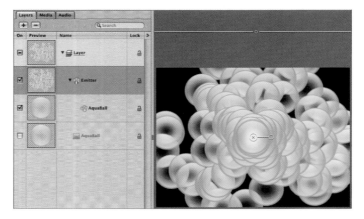

The emitter appears at the same coordinates as the original object. In this case, the original object was in the center of the frame, so the emitter is also in the center of the frame.

4   Press Cmd-4 to close the Layers tab.

5   Press Cmd-S to save your progress.

Modifying the Particle Emitter in the Dashboard

You've created particles with a simple click of the Make Particles button; now let's take a look at the Emitter Dashboard and make a few adjustments. To understand the emitter parameters, you need to understand that particles are considered living objects within your project. They are born and have a pre-determined life span; you can control their "birthrate" and when they "die." Let's take a look.

1   Press D to open the Emitter Dashboard.

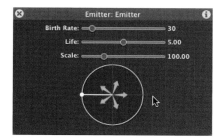

The Emitter Dashboard includes six parameters that you can adjust. You control three of the parameters by sliders. You control the other three by dragging the parameters within the Emission Control display.

The Birth Rate slider adjusts how many particles are born (created) every second.

The Life slider adjusts how many seconds the particles live.

The Scale slider adjusts the scale (size) of the particles, based on the size of the original object. If the scale is 100 percent, the particles are the same size as the original object. If the scale is 50 percent, the particles are half the size of the original object.

The Emission Control display in the lower half of the Emitter Dashboard allows you to manipulate three particle system parameters: Emission Range, Emission Angle, and Speed.

2   On the Emitter Dashboard, drag the Birth Rate slider toward the left until the Birth Rate value is 5.

There are now only five AquaBall particles born every second. The default number of particles born per second is 30. Now let's adjust the Life parameter.

3   On the Emitter Dashboard, drag the Life slider toward the left to around 2 seconds.

The AquaBall particles now disappear 2 seconds after they are born, which makes them look like they are popping before they reach the edges of the frame.

Let's extend the particles' lives so that the AquaBalls can reach beyond the edges of the frame and we don't have to witness their demise.

4   Drag the Life slider to around 4 seconds.

The AquaBalls move in all directions from the center of the frame and have enough time to exit the frame before they reach the end of their lives.

5   Drag the Scale slider toward the left to change the scale of the particles to around 50, which is 50 percent of the original object's size.

NOTE ▶ The precision of the Dashboard sliders is limited, so you may not be able to set the exact number you are aiming for. For example, 51 may be as close to 50 percent as you can get in the Dashboard. To set exact parameter values, you'll need to change the parameters in the Inspector.

Now let's take a closer look at the Emission Control parameters.

Working with the Emission Control Parameters

What is emission control, anyway? A particle emitter works like a deluxe massage-style showerhead. If you've ever used one of those, you know that you can adjust the rate and angle, or shape, of the water flow by turning the dial around the nozzle of the showerhead. The same principle applies to an emitter. You can use the Emission Control display to adjust the range, angle, and speed of the flow of particles from the emitter.

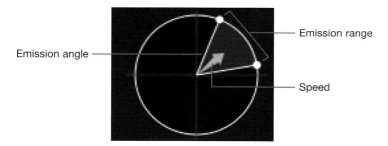

You can adjust the Emission Control parameters similar to the way you adjust the Throw parameters in the Dashboard. Let's start by adjusting the emission range.

The emission range for the flow of particles functions like the flow settings on a massage showerhead. In spray mode, the showerhead sprays a steady flow of water from the entire diameter of the showerhead (360 degrees). If you adjust the dial on the showerhead, you can change the flow of water to the deep massage mode that focuses the water to a narrow stream from one particular spot on the nozzle.

You change the emission range by dragging the two points on the outer ring of the graphical control. The wider the range, the wider the flow of particles. The narrower the range, the more focused the flow of particles. By default, the particle flow is the full 360-degree range, which means that particles flow outward in all directions from the emitter. The number of arrows visible within the control decreases as you decrease the emission range.

Let's adjust the emission range to narrow the flow of AquaBall particles to a single stream flowing toward the right.

1   Drag the points on the outer ring toward the right center edge of the ring to restrict the flow of particles to a single stream flowing toward the right.

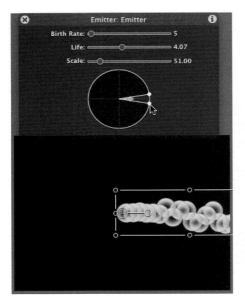

The number of arrows in the Emission Control display is determined by the angle of the emission range. Since the emission range is limited to a single stream of particles, only one arrow appears in the graphical display. The length of the arrow or arrows in the Emission Control display determines the speed of the particle flow. The longer the arrow, the faster the particles move. Let's speed up the flow of particles.

2   Drag the arrow toward the edge of the outer ring in the graphical control to make the arrow longer and the speed of the particles faster.

Adjusting the angle that the arrow or arrows are pointing modifies the angle of the particle flow.

Let's move the angle of the particles counterclockwise so the particles flow toward the upper right of the frame.

3   Drag the arrow counterclockwise until the particles flow toward the upper-right corner of the frame.

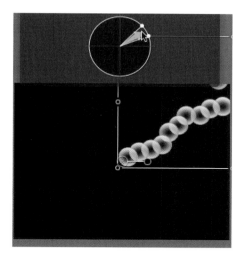

4   Press Cmd-S to save your progress.

Now that you've modified the particle emitter in the Dashboard, let's look at some of the parameters in the Inspector.

Viewing the Emitter and Particle Cell Tabs in the Inspector

The Inspector includes a wide range of parameters for modifying the particle emitter as well as individual particles. If you are using only one object in the emitter, the particle cell controls and emitter controls are combined on one tab. If the emitter has multiple cells, then you'll need to control each cell on the Particle Cell tab. Let's take a look at the various tabs in the Inspector.

You determine the tabs that you view in the Inspector by the elements that you select on the Layers tab. Let's select the Emitter object and then the AquaBall particle cell on the Layers tab to see the difference in the Inspector.

1   Press Cmd-4 to open the Layers tab in the Project pane.

2   Press Cmd-3 to open the Inspector in the Utility window.

3   On the Layers tab, select the Emitter object.

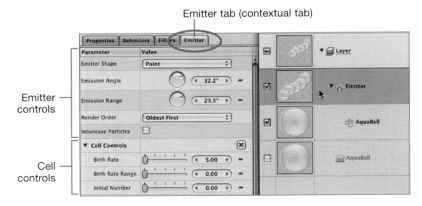

Particle emitter and particle cell controls

The contextual tab in the Inspector changes to Emitter; the Emitter tab includes both emitter and cell parameter controls. The cell parameters start with a Birth Rate slider; if you scroll downward, you'll see that the last parameter is the Random Seed generator.

4   On the Layers tab, select the AquaBall particle cell.

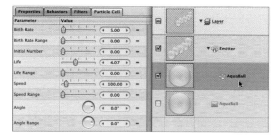

The contextual tab in the Inspector changes to Particle Cell, which includes parameters only for the selected particle cell.

The Particle Cell parameters start with a Birth Rate slider and end with the Random Seed generator, the same as the cell controls on the Emitter tab.

Because the cell controls are the same on the Emitter and Particle Cell tabs, let's work with the Emitter tab, which includes both the Emitter and Particle Cell parameters.

5 On the Layers tab, select the Emitter object.

The contextual tab changes back to Emitter.

6 Press Cmd-4 to close the Layers tab.

Modifying Particle System Parameters in the Inspector

The emitter and cell parameters can look pretty intimidating or confusing at first glance. However, once you know how the controls work, you'll be able to modify any particle system with relative ease.

Analyzing Emitter Parameters

Let's start at the top of the Emitter tab with the five emitter parameters: Emitter Shape, Emission Angle, Emission Range, Render Order, and Interleave Particles.

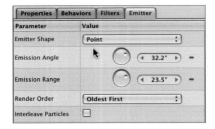

▶ Emitter Shape pop-up menu — Allows you to change the way that the particles are dispersed. You'll adjust this parameter later in the lesson.

▶ Emission Angle and Emission Range parameters — These are the same as the controls in the Emitter Dashboard. You can modify both of these parameters in the Inspector with either a dial or a value slider.

▶ Render Order pop-up — Allows you to determine whether the oldest particles are first or last in the Canvas. What does that mean? Imagine looking down at a stack of particles. If the oldest particle is first, it is at the bottom of the stack, and the newer particles appear above the older particles. In other words, the first particle is at the bottom of the stack and is the farthest in the background on the Canvas. If the oldest particle is last, it appears at the top of the stack, and the newer particles are born below the older particles. So the newer particles move farther away, toward the background, while the older particles stay in the foreground.

▶ Interleave Particles check box — Pertains to particle systems with multiple particle cells. If you check the box, the various particles will blend together when they overlap. If the box is unchecked, the particles do not blend together.

Since you already modified the Emission Angle and Emission Range parameters in the Dashboard, let's move on to the cell controls.

Working with the Cell Controls

Cell controls modify the individual particles and are fairly self-explanatory. The main concept to understand in working with cell controls is that there are absolute values and range values for almost every parameter. For example, the Scale parameter sets an absolute scale (size) value for each particle. The Scale Range parameter allows you to set a variable range for the size of the particles. If the Scale value is 100 percent, the particles are all the size of the original object. If you then set the Scale Range to 20 percent, the particles will vary in size within a range of 20 percent larger or smaller than the original object.

Let's try modifying the Scale and Scale Range parameters.

1 On the Emitter tab, scroll down to view the parameters at the bottom of the tab.

The Scale and Scale Range parameters are located near the bottom of the Emitter tab.

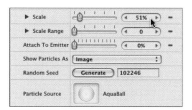

Notice that the Scale parameter is set to 51 percent because it correlates to the Scale parameter in the Emitter Dashboard.

2   Click the left incremental arrow on the Scale value slider to lower the scale to exactly 50 percent.

The Scale value changes to 50 percent in both the Inspector and the Dashboard.

Now let's change the Scale Range to 20 percent so that particles will be created in a range of sizes from 20 percent larger to 20 percent smaller than 50 percent of the original object.

3   Type *20* in the Scale Range value field and press Return to set the scale range to 20.

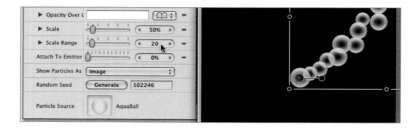

The AquaBall particles now appear in a variety of sizes within the specified range.

As you can see, the absolute value and range parameters aren't too intimidating once you understand how they work.

Moving a Particle Emitter in the Canvas

Let's take a moment to move the entire particle emitter outside of the frame so that the particles will look like they are floating into the frame, rather than appearing out of nowhere.

You can move an emitter in the Canvas the same way that you move an object. All you need to do is select the emitter with the Select/Transform tool and drag it to the new location.

First, let's zoom out of the Canvas so that we can see the empty space around the frame.

1   Press Cmd-– (hyphen) to zoom out of the Canvas one level.

2   Drag the Emitter object downward and to the left until the particles are all born outside of the frame.

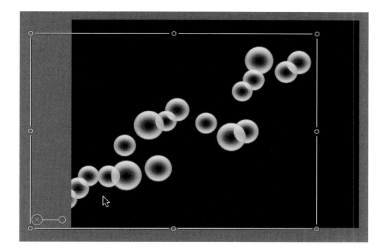

3   Play the project in the Canvas, if it is not already playing, to see how the move affects the overall look of the project.

Changing the Life Parameter in the Inspector

Did you notice that the particles are now vanishing (dying) before they exit the upper-right corner of the frame? That is because moving the emitter toward the left extended the distance that the particles now have to travel before they can exit the upper-right corner of the frame. No problem. All you need to do is extend the Life parameter to give them time to make the entire journey. Let's change the Life parameter in the Inspector.

1   In the Inspector, drag the Life slider toward the right to change the value to 5 (5 seconds).

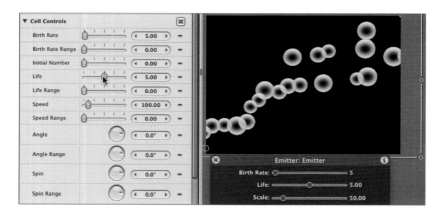

The Life value in the Emitter Dashboard changes to 5.00 to reflect the change in the Inspector, and the particles now live long enough to safely exit the upper-right corner of the frame.

Now let's change the speed range for the particles so that some of the particles move faster than others.

2   Drag the Speed Range slider to 10.00 so that the particles will travel within a range of 10 percent faster or slower than the original speed.

The particles travel at different speeds toward their final destiny beyond the upper-right corner of the frame.

The Angle and Spin parameters adjust the angle of the particles and how much they spin during their short but interesting lives. You'll work with those parameters later in this lesson.

3   Press Cmd-S to save your progress.

Working with Particle Color Modes

You've modified a few of the cell parameters that affect the life and movement of the particles; now let's look at the Color Mode parameters.

The Color Mode pop-up menu has five options:

►   Original — The default setting; the particles maintain the color of the original object they are derived from.

►   Solid — Allows you to tint the particles with a solid color that you select from the Colors window.

►   Over Life — Tints the color of the particles based on their age. A gradient control defines the range of color that each particle assumes as it ages.

►   Pick From Range — Tints the particles randomly with a range of possible colors that you select in a gradient control.

►   Take Image Color — Bases the color of the particle on the color of the image in the position at which the particle was originally generated.

Let's experiment with the Pick From Range mode to select a range of colors for the particles.

1   On the Emitter tab in the Inspector, open the Color Mode pop-up menu and choose Pick From Range.

The colors of the particles in the Canvas vary from red to blue, and a Color Range gradient appears on the Emitter tab.

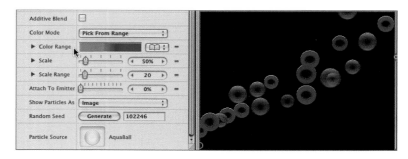

NOTE ▶ You may need to scroll down to the bottom of the Emitter tab to see the Color Mode parameter and the Color Range gradient.

To edit the Color Range gradient, you first need to click the disclosure triangle on the Color Range parameter.

2   Click the Color Range disclosure triangle to view the Gradient Editor.

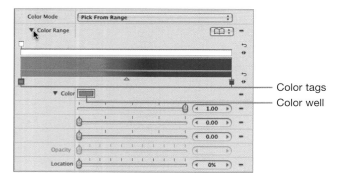

Gradient Editor

The Gradient Editor controls include square color tags that can be used to change the selected color in the Color well.

3   On the Gradient Editor, click the red color tag (a small red square) to select that color in the Color well.

4   Click the Color well to open the Colors window.

5   In the Colors window, select a yellow color.

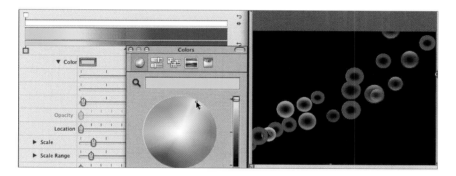

The Gradient Editor instantly updates to a new yellow-to-blue gradient, and the particles in the Canvas are now a range of colors that match the gradient.

As you can see, it's easy to change the color tint of the particles in the Inspector.

You'll work more with gradients in the next lesson.

6   Close the Colors window; then press Cmd-S to save your progress.

Applying Behaviors to Particles

You've created particles and adjusted their parameters, including their color, in the Inspector. Let's see what happens when you apply behaviors.

You can apply behaviors to either the particle emitter or the particle cell. Behaviors applied to the emitter affect the emitter—or where the particles are born. Behaviors applied to the particle cell are in turn applied to each individual particle. Let's apply the Edge Collision behavior to the particle cell so that the particles bounce off the edges of the frame.

1   Press Cmd-4 to open the Layers tab.

2   On the Layers tab, select the AquaBall particle cell.

3   On the toolbar at the top of the Canvas, click the Add Behavior pop-up menu and choose Simulations > Edge Collision.

The particles bounce off the edges of the upper-right corner, but they don't get very far before they die.

Let's extend the Life parameter of the particles in the Particle Cell Dashboard to 10 seconds.

4   Press D to change from the Edge Collision Dashboard to the Particle Cell Dashboard.

5   On the Particle Cell Dashboard, drag the Life slider all the way to the right to extend the particles' lives for the full duration of the project (10 seconds).

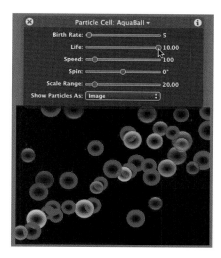

6   Press Cmd-S to save the finished AquaBall Particles project.

7   Close the current project.

Congratulations! You've just created a particle system from scratch. Now let's create some particles with a little more personality.

Limiting the Number of Particles in a System

Over the next series of exercises, you'll create a school of fish from a single fish object. Then you'll apply an Attracted To behavior to the fish so that they follow an object around the screen.

Opening the Fish School Project

First, let's open the **6-4 Fish School** project, located in the Lesson_06 folder.

1   Choose File > Open and select **6-4 Fish School** from the Lesson_06 folder.

Ϝ   The project opens with a single fish in the center of the Canvas.

2   Choose File > Save As and save the project in the My Motion Projects folder on the Desktop.

Creating Particles from the Selected Object

Particles don't necessarily have to spray, sparkle, explode, or continually flow out of the emitter. You can set the initial number of particles and limit the Birth Rate parameter so that new particles are not born every second. That way, you have the benefit of turning one object into many, without a steady flow of new particles. This technique is commonly used for emulating nature—for creating a flock of birds, leaves on a tree, or even a school of fish, for example.

In this part of the exercise, your goal is to create a school of fish. A school of fish is not a shower of fish or an explosion of fish. Therefore, the creatures shouldn't be sprayed out of the emitter like the AquaBall particles were. Instead, you'll modify the emitter parameters to start with an initial number of fish. You'll also need to control the fish population in this exercise by setting the Birth Rate to 0. Let's try it.

1   Click the fish object in the center of the frame to select it.

2   Press the spacebar to begin playback, if the project is not already playing.

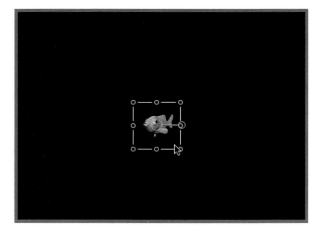

3   Press E to create a particle emitter from the selected object.

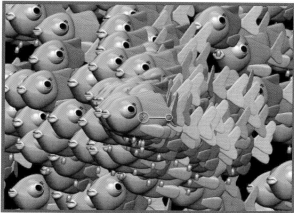

The frame fills with fish. What did I say about controlling the fish population? Let's modify the Birth Rate and Initial Number parameters in the Inspector.

4   Press Cmd-3 to open the Inspector.

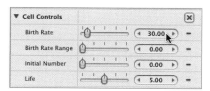

The Inspector opens with the Emitter tab selected.

5   On the Emitter tab in the Inspector, drag the Birth Rate slider all the way to the left to change the value to 0.

The fish vanish from the Canvas. Now let's change the Initial Number parameter to 20 to create a school of 20 fish.

6   On the Emitter tab, type *20* in the Initial Number value field and press Return.

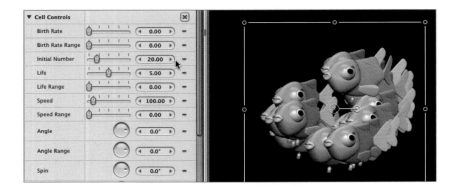

Twenty fish appear in the center of the Canvas and move away from each other as the project plays.

Controlling the Particle Movement

Okay; so you created a school of exactly 20 fish. Now you need to limit their movement so that they stay together in a cluster rather than drift apart. How far and fast particles move away from each other is determined by the Speed parameter. The higher the speed value, the faster and farther apart the particles move. The lower the speed value, the slower and less scattered the particles move. Your goal in this exercise is to stop the particles—the fish—from moving apart completely. That means that you need to set the speed value to 0.

1   On the Emitter tab, drag the Speed slider all the way to the left until the value is 0.

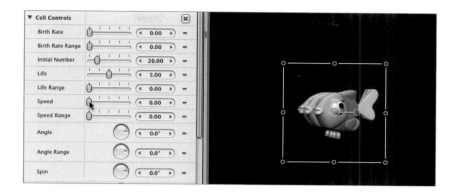

You restricted the movement, but now you've created a 20-fish pileup in the middle of the Canvas. I may not be an expert in aquatic life, but I'm pretty sure fish don't travel around in neat stacks. We're going to need to give them some distance.

2   Press Cmd-S to save your progress.

Changing the Emitter Shape

So how do you spread out your particles? All you need to do is change the emitter shape. The Emitter Shape parameter includes a pop-up menu with six choices:

▶   Point — Emits particles that emerge from a single point in the center of the emitter. This is the default setting and is why all the fish are stacked in the same spot in the frame.

▶   Line — Emits particles that emerge in a line. You can specify the coordinates of where the line begins and ends.

▶   Circle — Emits particles that emerge from the edge of a radius around the center of the emitter. You can adjust the diameter of the circle to make it larger or smaller.

▶   Filled Circle — Emits particles that emerge from a circle around the center of the emitter. You can adjust the radius of the filled circle to make it larger or smaller.

▶ Geometry — Emits particles that emerge in whatever shape you add to the Shape Source well.

▶ Image — Emits particles that emerge from an area defined by an image you add to the Image Source well.

Let's experiment with some of the Emitter Shape options and find the one that works best for our school of fish.

1 On the Emitter tab, click the Emitter Shape pop-up menu and select Line.

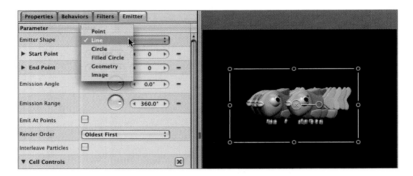

The fish appear dispersed in a line on the Canvas. This may work for a fish parade, but it still doesn't look very natural. Let's try another setting.

2 From the Emitter Shape pop-up menu, choose Circle.

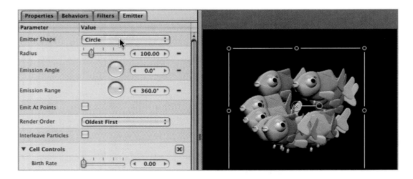

It's better, but why would the fish leave a hole in the middle of their formation? Are they mourning a fallen comrade? I don't think so. Next!

3 From the Emitter Shape pop-up menu, choose Filled Circle.

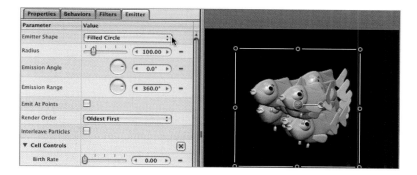

We have a winner. The emitter shape is fine, but it could be even better if the fish were clustered a little differently.

Changing the Random Seed

The Motion Particle generator creates particles using random sequences of values based on the other parameters applied to the particle. Each set of random values selected by the generator has a number called the *random seed*. If you don't like the random pattern or behavior that has been applied to the particles, you can click the Generate button to create a different random seed number. The new number will change the behavior pattern to a different variation. The Generate button is located near the bottom of the Emitter tab.

The Random Seed value is located in the field to the right of the Generate button. When you click the Generate button, the Random Seed number changes in the field, and the random behavior of the particles changes to reflect a new random sequence of values. Changing the random seed does not change absolute values that you have applied to the particles. However, it does change the range values and any parameters that rely on randomly generated numbers.

Let's change the random seed for the particles until you like the way the school of fish looks.

1   On the Emitter tab, for the Random Seed parameter, click the Generate button to change the random seed.

The Random Seed number changes, and so does the pattern of fish on the Canvas.

2   Click the Generate button until you get a pattern that you like.

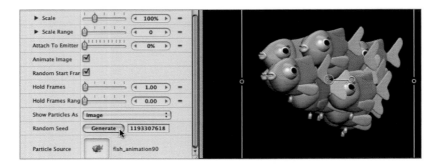

You can use any random seed that you wish, or you can use the same number that I am using (1193307618).

3   Press Cmd-S to save your progress.

Adding a Scale Range to the Particles

You've created the school of fish particles. Now let's change the Scale and Scale Range parameters to give the fish a range of sizes.

1   On the Emitter tab, in the Scale value field, type *50* and press Return to change the scale of all the fish to 50 percent of the original object size.

2   In the Scale Range value field, type *30* and press Return to change the scale
of the fish to a range of 30 percent larger to 30 percent smaller than the
original object.

Now the fish come in a variety of sizes. Let's extend their lives to last the
entire duration of the project.

3   On the Emitter tab, change the Life value to 10.00 (10 seconds).

4   Press Cmd-S to save your progress.

Attracting the Particles to Another Object

The school of fish looks pretty good. All you need to do now is give them
something to do. When I first introduced you to Poly the animated fish, I
mentioned that she was a toy fish that was brought to life by a magical
AquaBall. Well, apparently, there were a lot of toy fish, and they're all searching
for the magical AquaBall. Okay, so I made up the story—just go with it for this
exercise. Look at it this way: Wouldn't it be cool if you could get your school of
particle fish to chase an AquaBall across the frame?

To save time, I've already applied a moving AquaBall to the project; all you
need to do is turn on the AquaBall object on the Layers tab and then apply an
Attracted To behavior to the particles.

Let's try it. First let's move the school of fish to the lower-right corner of the frame so they will have plenty of room to chase the AquaBall.

1 In the Canvas, drag the particle emitter to the lower-right corner of the frame.

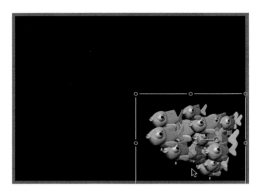

2 Press Cmd-4 to open the Layers tab.

3 On the Layers tab, click the Activation check box for the AquaBall object to turn it on.

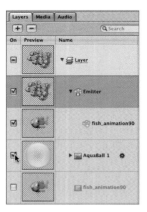

4   Press the spacebar to play the project, if it is not already playing.

An AquaBall moves across the screen, and the fish ignore it.

5   On the Layers tab, select the fish_animation90 particle cell.

6   On the toolbar, open the Add Behavior pop-up menu and select
Simulations > Attracted To.

The Attracted To behavior is applied to the particle cell (individual particles), and the Behaviors tab becomes active in the Inspector.

Now you need to assign an object for the fish to be attracted to: the
AquaBall. Notice the Attracted To behavior parameters on the Behaviors
tab in the Inspector?

7   Drag the AquaBall 1 object from the Layers tab to the Attracted To behavior on the Behaviors tab of the Inspector, and drop it in the Object well.

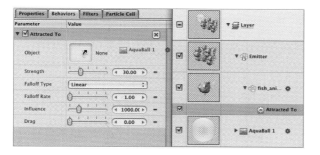

8   On the Layers tab, select the Emitter object. Then press Cmd-3 to open the
Inspector, if it's not already open.

9   Experiment with the various Attracted To parameters on the Behaviors tab of the Inspector to create an interesting attraction between the fish and the AquaBall.

I used the settings shown in the following figure for my final project.

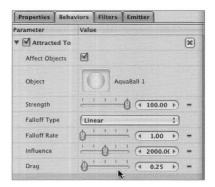

Feel free to use your own settings, or try mine to see what it looks like.

10 Press Cmd-S to save your progress.

Replacing a Particle Object

The particle systems you can create are limited only by your imagination. You can even replace the original object in a particle system to change the actual particles.

Let's change the original object in this particle system. What object should we use? Hmmm. Since you've been working so closely with the AquaBall, why not create a school of eager young AquaBalls chasing after their leader, or mother, or the Grand Poo-Ball….

Anyway, you can replace the original object on the Layers tab the same way that you replaced the objects in previous exercises. All you need to do is drag the AquaBall object from the Library to the original object on the Layers tab.

The original object in this scenario is fish_animation90, which is also the lowest element on the Layers tab.

1   Press Cmd-2 to open the Library.

2   Drag the AquaBall.png file from the Library and drop it on the fish_animation90 object on the Layers tab.

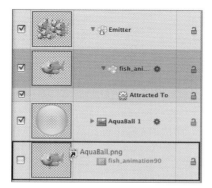

The particles in the Canvas become a school of AquaBalls that are attracted to the larger AquaBall object.

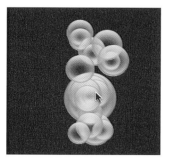

3   Press Cmd-S to save the finished project.

4   Close the current project.

Changing Behaviors over the Life of the Particles

You can not only apply behaviors to particles, but also modify the behaviors so that they change over the life of the particles. In this exercise, you'll modify the scale and color of a particle system over the life of the particles. The last project in this lesson is called Tree Growth, and it uses many of the skills that you've learned so far to create a particle system that changes over the life of the particles.

The goal in this project is to show the life cycle of the leaves on a tree. First, you'll turn a leaf object into 100 leaves; then you'll apply behaviors so that the leaves grow, change color, and then fall off the tree. Let's start by opening the project.

Opening the Tree Growth Project

1   Choose File > Open and select the **6-5 Tree Growth** project from the Lesson_06 folder.

2   Choose File > Save As and save the project in the My Motion Projects folder on the Desktop.

3   Press the spacebar to play the finished project in the Canvas.

   As you can see, the leaves grow, change color, and then fall off the tree, all in a mere 10 seconds.

Analyzing the Project on the Layers Tab

Rather than dive right into this complex particle system, let's take a moment to analyze the finished project on the Layers tab. It will be easier for you to re-create this particle system once you understand how it was built.

1   Press Cmd-4 to open the Layers tab.

   The project includes two layers: Leaves and Tree.

2   On the Layers tab, click the Leaves disclosure triangle to view the contents of the layer.

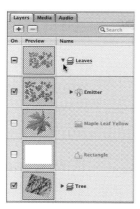

The Leaves layer includes an Emitter object, a Maple Leaf Yellow object that has been turned off (the original object), and a Rectangle object that has also been turned off. The rectangle shape was used to create the emitter shape so that the leaves spread out over the entire frame.

Let's look inside the Emitter object.

3   Click the Emitter disclosure triangle to view the contents of the emitter.

The Emitter object includes a Maple Leaf Yellow particle cell.

4   Click the Maple Leaf Yellow disclosure triangle to view the contents of the particle cell.

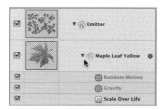

The Maple Leaf Yellow cell includes three behaviors: Random Motion, Gravity, and Scale Over Life.

Let's select each behavior to see when it begins and ends in the mini-Timeline.

5   On the Layers tab, select the Random Motion behavior.

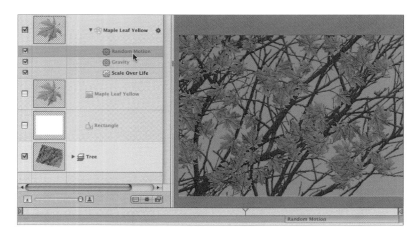

The Random Motion behavior starts toward the end of the project, so the leaves won't begin moving until the playhead reaches the start of the behavior in the mini-Timeline.

6   Select the Gravity behavior.

Notice that it also starts toward the end of the project in the mini-Timeline. The Gravity behavior causes the leaves to fall, and the Random Motion behavior makes each leaf particle move randomly as it falls out of the frame.

7   Select the Scale Over Life behavior to view it in the mini-Timeline.

This behavior starts at the beginning of the project in the mini-Timeline and ends before the other two behaviors start. Why? Because the Scale Over Life behavior makes the leaves grow, and we want the growth to stop before the leaves fall from the tree.

8   On the Layers tab, select the Emitter object.

The Emitter tab opens in the Inspector. Notice that the Image Source for the Emitter object is the rectangle.

9 Scroll down in the Inspector until you can see the Color Mode parameters.

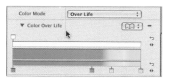

In the Color Mode pop-up menu, Over Life is selected, and the gradient in the Gradient Editor starts with green and then moves to yellow and then to orange. The particles will change colors to match the colors of the gradient from left to right throughout the duration of their life.

Now that you understand how the particle emitter was created and modified, it's your turn to try it.

10 On the Layers tab, select the Emitter object, if it is not already selected.

11 Press Delete to delete the emitter.

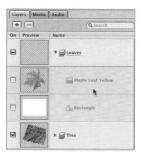

The entire particle system has been deleted from the project.

Creating a Complex Particle System

Let's rebuild the particle system that you just analyzed. First, you'll create the particles. Then you'll modify the particle emitter shape and color mode. The next step is to add behaviors to the particle cell, starting with the Scale Over Life behavior and ending with the Random Motion and Gravity behaviors.

1   On the Layers tab, select the Maple Leaf Yellow object.

It's okay if the object is turned off. An object does not need to be active for you to create a particle emitter from it.

2   Press E to create a particle emitter from the selected object.

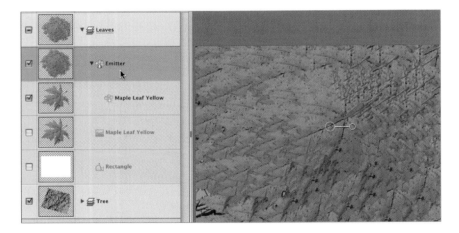

The frame fills with leaves, all looking exactly alike. Let's set the Birth Rate to 0 and the Initial Number to 100.

3   On the Emitter tab in the Inspector, drag the Birth Rate slider to the left until the value is 0.00.

All of the leaves disappear from the Canvas.

4   Type *100* in the Initial Number value field and press Return.

A ball of 100 leaves appears in the frame.

5   Drag the Life slider all the way to the right to set the Life value to the full duration of the project, 10.00 (10 seconds).

Next, you'll need to set the speed to 0 so the leaves won't move away from each other. Then you'll change the emitter shape to the rectangle image.

6   On the Emitter tab in the Inspector, drag the Speed slider to the left to set the value to 0.

7   At the top of the Emitter tab, open the Emitter Shape pop-up menu and choose Image.

8   Drag the Rectangle object from the Layers tab to the Emitter tab and drop it in the Image Source well for the Emitter Shape parameter.

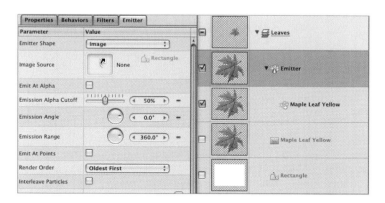

The leaf particles now spread out across the entire rectangular frame.

9   Press Cmd-S to save your progress.

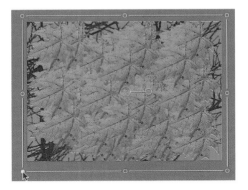

Scaling Particles over the Life of the Particles

You have set many of the initial parameters for your particles. Now let's change the scale over the life of the leaves.

First, you need to decide on the final size that you want the leaves to become; then you can apply and set the parameters of the Scale Over Life behavior. The Scale Over Life behavior can be applied only to a particle cell, so you'll also need to open the Layers tab and select the particle cell before applying the behavior.

The leaves are a little too large at 100 percent, so let's scale them down to 60 percent of their original size.

1   On the Layers tab, select Emitter. Then, in the Inspector, near the bottom of the Emitter tab, change the Scale value slider to 60%.

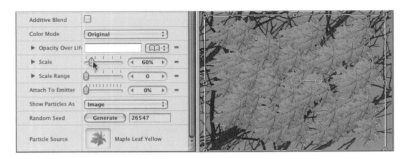

The leaves change to 60 percent of their original size.

2   Press Cmd-4 to open the Layers tab.

3   On the Layers tab, select the Maple Leaf Yellow particle cell.

4   On the toolbar, click the Add Behavior pop-up menu and choose Particles > Scale Over Life.

The Scale Over Life behavior appears below the Maple Leaf Yellow particle cell on the Layers tab, and on the Behaviors tab in the Inspector.

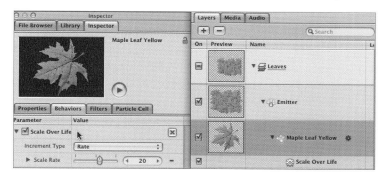

The Scale Over Life behavior has a default setting of a Scale Rate of 20, which means that the leaves grow by 20 percent over their life. Instead, let's change the Increment Type from a constant rate of growth to specific birth and death values.

5 On the Behaviors tab, click the Increment Type pop-up menu and choose Birth and Death Values.

The Scale Over Life parameters on the Behaviors tab change to include Scale At Birth and Scale At Death parameters.

The goal is to have the leaves grow from nothing to leaves that are the size you determine. To have them start at nothing, the Scale At Birth value should be 0%, which means 0 percent of the original scale. To have the particles grow up and reach the scale you set previously (60 percent of the original object size), the Scale At Death value needs to be 100%, which means 100 percent of the scale that you set for the particles in the cell controls.

6 Press the spacebar to pause playback, if it is not already paused.

7 Press Home to move the playhead to the first frame of the project.

> **TIP** ▶ It's a good idea to stop playback while setting birth and death values so that you can determine exactly what the scale should be on the first and last frame of the project or the behavior.

There are no leaves visible in the first frame of the project because their scale at birth is set to 0 percent.

Now let's set the death value of the leaves and the location where we want the leaves to stop growing.

8   On the Canvas, in the Current Playhead field, type *7.00* and press Return to move the playhead to 7;00 (7 seconds).

9   On the Layers tab, select the Scale Over Life behavior.

The purple Scale Over Life region appears in the mini-Timeline.

Let's change the Out point of the region to the playhead position so that the behavior ends at 7 seconds.

10   Press O to set the Out point of the Scale Over Life behavior.

11   Press Cmd-S to save your progress.

Finishing the Project

All we need to do now to finish the project is to add a little color and variety to the leaves and add the behaviors to make the leaves fall. Let's add the behaviors first; then we'll modify the color of the leaf particles.

1   On the Layers tab, select the Maple Leaf Yellow cell.

2   On the toolbar, click the Add Behavior pop-up menu and choose Simulations > Random Motion.

The Random Motion behavior appears on the Behaviors tab in the Inspector, below the particle cell on the Layers tab, and as a purple region in the mini-Timeline.

Notice that the purple Random Motion region in the mini-Timeline begins at the start of the project. Let's change the In point of the region so that the behavior starts at the playhead position (7 seconds).

3   Press I to change the In point of the region in the mini-Timeline to the playhead position.

Let's do the same thing with a Gravity behavior.

4   On the toolbar, click the Add Behavior pop-up menu and choose Simulations > Gravity.

5   Press I to change the Gravity behavior In point to the playhead position.

6   Press the spacebar to play the project in the Canvas.

It's working. However, the Gravity behavior isn't quite strong enough to pull the leaves all the way out of the frame. Let's increase the intensity of the Gravity behavior.

7   Press D to open the Gravity Dashboard.

8   In the Gravity Dashboard, drag the Acceleration slider all the way to the right to increase the gravity to the maximum value in the Dashboard (100).

Now the force of gravity pulls the leaves all the way out of the frame.

Changing the Color over the Life of the Particles

You've added the behaviors, and the leaves are growing and falling. It's time to change the leaves' color so that they start green and slowly turn yellow and then orange at the end of their short particle lives.

To make the color change over the life of the particles, all you need to do is change the Color Mode value in the Inspector to Over Life and then set the colors you want in the Gradient Editor. Let's try it.

1   On the Layers tab, select the Emitter object.

2   Click the Emitter tab in the Inspector to open it.

3   On the Emitter tab, open the Color Mode pop-up menu and choose Over Life.

4   Click the Color Over Life disclosure triangle to view the Gradient Editor.

The default colors in the Gradient Editor are red and blue.

5   In the Gradient Editor, click the first color tag (red) to apply the tag's color to the Color well.

6   Click the red Color well below the gradient to open the Colors window.

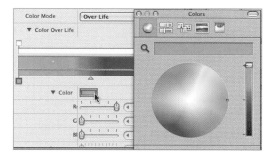

7   In the Colors window, select a nice green color from the color wheel.

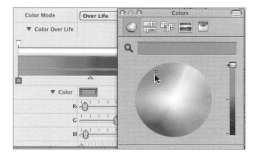

The gradient starts with the selected green color.

8   Click the blue color tag on the right side of the Gradient Editor to apply the tag's color to the Color well.

The color in the Color well and in the Colors window changes to blue to match the selected color tag.

9   In the Colors window, select a dark orange on the color wheel.

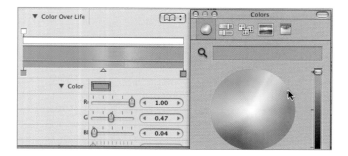

The right side of the gradient changes to orange.

Now let's add a transitional yellow color in the Gradient Editor between the green and the orange to make the transition look more natural.

To add another color tag, you simply click the lower part of the Gradient Editor.

10   Click the lower center of the Gradient Editor to add a new color tag.

11   Click the new color tag to select the color in the Colors window.

12   In the Colors window, select a yellow on the color wheel.

You will need to drag the Brightness slider in the Colors window upward to select a bright yellow color.

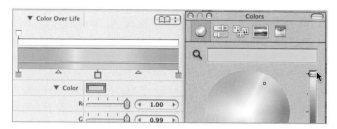

The color change works pretty well; however, the leaves need to stay green longer.

To change the proportions of a particular color in the Gradient Editor, you can drag the color tags and the gradient transition triangles located below the gradient.

13 Drag the yellow color tag toward the right until the yellow color starts at around the last quarter of the gradient.

Dragging a color tag moves the color to a new location. You can also change where the transition occurs between two colors by dragging the Location control, which looks like a small triangle.

14 Drag the Location control between the green and yellow colors toward the right until the yellow color starts at around the last third of the gradient.

About two-thirds into their life, the leaves change color.

15 Press Cmd-S to save your progress.

Adding Variety to the Particles

The last step to making this project look more natural is to add a little variety to the size and angle of the leaves. I don't know about you, but I've never seen a tree on which all of the leaves are the exact same size and pointing in the exact same direction. Let's change the Scale Range and Angle Range parameters to make the leaf particles appear more random and natural.

1   On the Emitter tab in the Inspector, change the Angle Range value to 90.0 so that the angle of the leaf particles is in the range of 90 degrees from the original value.

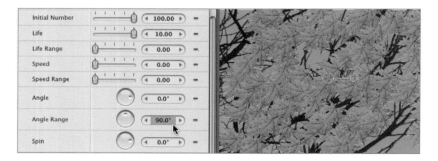

The leaf particles now point in a wide range of angles in the Canvas.

2   Near the bottom of the Emitter tab, change the Scale Range value to 25 so that the leaves vary in size 25 percent larger and smaller than the original.

3   On the Emitter tab, click the Random Seed Generate button to change the random seed until you find a random leaf pattern that you like.

4   Press Cmd-S to save the finished project.

Saving Particle Systems in the Library

The last project turned out so well, it would be a shame not to save it. In fact, that same particle system would look really good in the Master Project. If you want to save your favorite particle systems that you create or modify, all you have to do is drag the Emitter object from the Layers tab to the Favorites folder in the Library. Favorites are stored as part of your Motion preferences, so you can use them in any future Motion project. Let's try it.

1   Press Cmd-2 to open the Library tab in the Inspector.

The Favorites folder is located near the bottom of the upper pane in the Library.

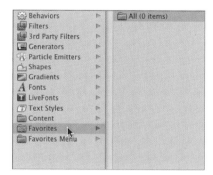

Before you add the emitter to the Favorites folder, let's name it Leaves Life Cycle.

2   On the Layers tab, double-click the Emitter object's name field and type *Leaves Life Cycle*; then press Return.

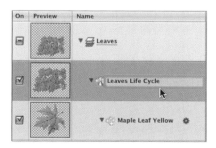

The name of the emitter changes to Leaves Life Cycle on the Layers tab.

3 Drag the Leaves Life Cycle particle emitter from the Layers tab to the Library and drop it on the Favorites folder.

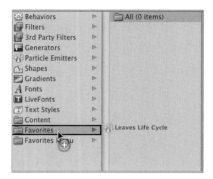

The Leaves Life Cycle emitter appears in the lower pane of the Library.

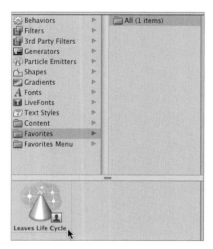

Emitters that you create or modify and save as Favorites include a little icon of a person's head next to the Emitter icon to show that it was customized by you, the Motion user.

Congratulations! You now have a working knowledge of particles and can start adding them to your own projects.

What You've Learned

- ▶ Motion comes with more than 100 particle emitters in the Library. These emitters are organized into categories, including Nature, Pyro, and Sparkles.

- ▶ Particle systems include three elements: an original object that is used as a mold, an emitter that mass-produces particles that are replicas of the original object, and a particle cell that represents the actual particles that are emitted.

- ▶ You can change the Project preferences so that new objects are created either at the playhead position or at the start of the project. If the playhead is moving, objects are automatically placed at the start of the project, which is also the default setting.

- ▶ You can create a particle emitter from virtually any selected object by pressing E or clicking the Make Particles button on the toolbar.

- ▶ When you create particles from an object, the original object becomes inactive on the Layers tab.

- ▶ Particle settings modify the particles as if they were living objects, with parameters like Birth Rate, Life, Scale At Birth, and Scale At Death.

- ▶ If you have only one particle cell in a system, the particle cell parameters are available on both the Emitter tab and the Particle Cell tab in the Inspector.

- ▶ You can modify the shape of a particle emitter so that it emits particles in a point, a line, a circle, a filled circle, a shape, or an image.

- ▶ You can apply behaviors to the particle emitter to modify the location where the particles appear in the frame, or you can apply behaviors to the particle cell to apply them to the individual particles.

- ▶ Particles assume the size and color of the original object. You can modify the scale and color with the cell controls in the Inspector. You can apply different color modes to the particles, including Solid, Pick From Range, and Over Life.

▶ You can replace the original object in a particle system with another object to change the particles without changing any of the other parameters in the system.

▶ Motion's particle generator combines random variables to create particles. Each set of random variables is assigned a number called the random seed. To change the random variables, you can generate a new random seed by clicking the Generate button on the Random Seed parameter in the Inspector.

▶ You can save your customized particle emitters in the Favorites folder on the Library tab.

Master Project Tasks

Your Master Project tasks for this lesson consist of adding two particles to your project. First, you'll add snow to the scene, with the snow beginning when the first two leaves fall from the tree. The second particles you will apply will be the Leaves Life Cycle particles that you created. If you're up for the challenge, you can also re-create the Leaves Life Cycle particles from scratch for practice.

To help you along, I've included a finished movie and a finished Master Project file for this lesson for you to use as a guide. Good luck, and have fun.

Let's start by opening your Master Project in the My Motion Projects folder. If you didn't complete the Master Project tasks in the previous lesson, you can open **06 Master Project start** in the Master_Project folder.

1   Open your Master Project or the **06 Master Project start** project.

2   In the File Browser, navigate to the Master_Project folder in your MOTION_INTRO Book Files folder. Then double-click the Master_Project folder to open it in the File Browser.

3   Select the **06 MP Finished.mov** file in the File Browser to preview the finished Master Project tasks.

The final movie includes snow particles and the leaves that you created earlier.

4   Move the play range Out point to 18;15.

5   In the Still Images & Objects area of the Project preferences window, select Create Objects At: Current frame.

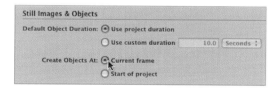

The goal is to have snow start to fall as soon as the first two leaves have cleared the frame at the beginning of the project.

6   Use the arrow keys to move the playhead to the point in the mini-Timeline where the first two leaves have cleared the frame (approximately 4;12).

7   Find the Snow Blizzard particle emitter in the Nature category of the Library.

8   Select the Weather layer on the Layers tab.

9   Apply the Snow Blizzard particle emitter to the Weather layer so that it starts at the playhead position.

10   Adjust the timing of the Snow Blizzard region in the mini-Timeline so that the snowflakes appear as the first two leaves disappear from the frame.

11 Change the Out point of the Snow Blizzard object to 7 seconds (7;00) so that the snowfall ends shortly after the clouds appear behind the tree image.

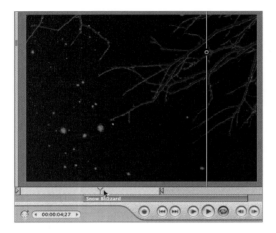

Now that you have added the snow, let's add a new tree image and the Leaves Life Cycle emitter. The second tree image will start at 8;15 in the Timeline.

12 On the Layers tab, select the Tree layer.

13 In the mini-Timeline, extend the region for the Tree layer to the play range Out point.

14 Move the playhead to 8;00 in the mini-Timeline.

15 In the File Browser, find the **IMG_2242.tif** file in the Master Project folder.

16 Drag the **IMG_2242.tif** file from the File Browser to the Tree layer on the Layers tab.

17 On the Inspector tab, change the Transform parameters of the IMG_2242 object as follows:

▶ Position: 284.84,148.86

▶ Rotation: –17.6

▶ Scale: 99

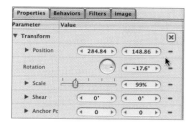

18 Change the Out point for the IMG_2242 object so that it ends at the play range Out point, 18;15.

19 Add a Fade In/Fade Out behavior to the IMG_2242 object. The default settings are fine.

20 Select the Leaves layer on the Layers tab.

21 Move the playhead to 8;15 and apply the Leaves Life Cycle particle emitter from the Favorites folder in the Library. The emitter should start at 8;15 and end at the play range Out point.

22 Press Cmd-S to save your Master Project.

7

Lesson Files

Time

This lesson takes approximately 1 hour to complete.

Goals

Create shapes with the Bezier and BSpline tools

Apply and modify generators from the Library

Add outline and drop-shadow styles to text

Customize and save a gradient preset

Preview and apply LiveFonts

Create particles from text

Working with Shapes, Text, and Generators

Manipulating objects and images with filters, behaviors, and particles can give your projects a professional, high-quality look. Now that you understand how to use those tools, it's time to focus on conveying information as well as attracting attention. A motion graphics composite without titles is like a movie without sound. It may be interesting to look at, but it's very difficult to convey the who, what, where, when, why, and how without words. Of course, we're not going to settle for plain old white text, either. Motion's Library includes generators to create background objects from scratch, gradients to add a splash of color, and LiveFonts to bring your text to life.

In the three projects in this lesson, you'll explore shapes, text, and generators in Motion. First, you'll work with the Bezier and BSpline tools to create free-form shapes. Then, in the second project, you'll generate a color background to enhance professional-looking titles for a news bumper. Finally, you'll create and animate text using filters, behaviors, gradients, and particles. Along the way, you'll explore Motion's generators in the Library, using them to create and customize gradients that you'll apply to the text and the project background.

Creating Free-form Shapes

You've already created geometrical shapes using the Motion Create tool set. In Lesson 1, you created a circle with the Create Circle tool, and in Lesson 5 you used the Circle Mask tool to create a circle-shaped mask. As you've discovered, creating circles and rectangles is pretty easy using the tools from the toolbar. Motion also includes two free-form tools that you can use to create any shape you want.

The free-form tools are the Bezier tool and the BSpline tool. So what do they do? Do you remember trying a connect-the-dots drawing as a child? By drawing a line from one numbered dot to the next, you ended up with the outline of a shape. Sometimes the shapes were simple—for instance, a beach ball—and sometimes the shapes were much more complicated—for instance, a dolphin doing a backflip in the moonlight. The more dots you connected, the easier it became to identify the object. Why am I reminiscing about connect-the-dots drawings? Because the free-form tools work in a very similar way.

Previewing the Finished Project

The best way to understand how the free-form tools work is to actually try them. Let's start by opening the completed **7-2 B-Shapes finished** project to see what you're aiming for in this exercise.

You'll find the **7-2 B-Shapes finished** project in the Lesson_07 folder.

1   In the File Browser, open the Lesson_07 folder.

2   Open the **7-2 B-Shapes finished** project in the Finder.

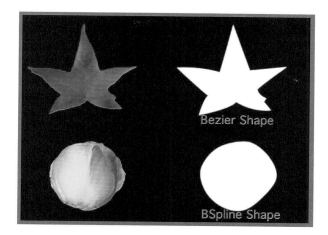

The B-Shapes finished project opens in the Canvas. On the left side of the frame are two objects from the Content folder in the Library. On the right side of the frame are shapes resembling those objects. The shapes were created using the free-form tools.

As you can see, the Bezier shape is a combination of straight and curved lines. The BSpline shape, on the other hand, is curved, with no straight lines.

Now let's take a look at the points (dots) that were used to create these shapes.

3   Ctrl-click the Bezier shape to open the contextual menu for that shape.

4   Select Edit Points from the contextual menu.

The Bezier points used to create this shape become visible. A red line connects each point to create the shape. Now let's view the points for the BSpline shape.

5   Ctrl-click the BSpline shape and choose Edit Points from the contextual menu.

Thin, straight lines connect the points in the BSpline shape. The points don't *create* the shape; instead, they *restrict* a curved shape within the lines. Huh? Imagine a blob of lava slowly creeping along, spreading in all directions. As the blob moves, its edges remain curved. To constrict the movement of the blob, you can place walls or other barriers. BSpline shapes are curved shapes that are contained and restricted by the barriers you create using points. This will make more sense when you actually try it.

6   Choose File > Close to close the finished project.

Opening and Saving the Project

Now that you've seen an example of finished free-form shapes, let's try creating them using the Bezier and BSpline tools. First, let's open the 7-1 B-Shapes start project using a contextual menu in the File Browser.

1   In the Lesson_07 folder, Ctrl-click the 7-1 B-Shapes start project and select Reveal in Finder from the contextual menu.

The Finder opens with the 7-1 B-Shapes start project already selected.

2   Double-click the 7-1 B-Shapes start project in the Finder to open the project in Motion.

The 7-1 B-Shapes start project opens.

3   Choose File > Save As and save the 7-1 B-Shapes start project in the My Motion Projects folder on the Desktop.

Mastering these tools can take some time, so to make things easier, let's use existing objects as a guide.

Working with the Bezier Tool

The first free-form tool that you'll work with is the Bezier tool. The Bezier tool allows you to create shapes with both straight and curved lines.

When you set the Bezier control points, remember the connect-the-dots drawings. The idea isn't to draw everything, just the outline of the shape. A good rule to remember is to set a new control point each time the outline of the shape changes direction. Just like in a connect-the-dots drawing, you need to place the control points in order either clockwise or counterclockwise around the object. When you make it all the way around the shape, click the first control point again to complete the shape. Once the outline of the shape is complete, it will automatically be filled with white color to create a solid shape. You can then change the fill color, just as you change the color of a circle or rectangle shape.

Since this is an exercise, don't worry about catching every detailed ripple in the leaf. You can always refine your shape later.

The first step in creating a free-form shape with the Bezier tool is to select the tool. There are two ways to select the Bezier tool:

► Press B (for Bezier tool).

► Select the Bezier tool from the Create tool set on the toolbar.

1   Press B to select the Bezier tool.

Bezier tool on the toolbar

Bezier tool

Two things happen when you press B: The Bezier tool icon becomes highlighted in the toolbar, and your pointer becomes a Bezier tool that looks like the head of a fountain pen.

Now that you have the tool, let's set some control points. Your goal is to create a shape that looks like the leaf in the upper left of the frame.

2   Starting at the top of the leaf and working your way around the shape clockwise, click the Bezier tool around the outer edge of the leaf at each place where the leaf shape changes direction.

3   After you have set control points all the way around the leaf, click the first point to close the shape.

The Bezier control points are connected by red lines to create a shape filled with the default color: white.

4   Press Cmd-S to save your progress.

Modifying the Bezier Vertices

Now that you've set the Bezier control points to create a rough shape, you can clean it up by adjusting the Bezier point vertices. What are vertices? The word is the plural form of *vertex*. A vertex is the point at which two sides of a plane figure or an angle intersect. Your elbow is a vertex at which your forearm and upper arm intersect. Your elbows are vertices of your body shape. You can keep a vertex linear (a straight angle) or make it smooth (curved) like the curve of your neck as it connects to your shoulders.

Motion provides three ways to modify the Bezier shape. You can move the control point to a new location, which will change the shape accordingly; you can add another control point (vertex) by Ctrl-clicking anywhere along the outside of the shape; and you can smooth the point by adding a Bezier handle. Let's try all three methods.

1   Drag one of the control points on the shape up, down, right, or left to reposition it along the leaf shape.

2   Ctrl-click along the outline of the shape (the red line) and select Add
Point from the contextual menu.

The new control point includes a handle that you can use to curve lines
extending from that point.

You can also delete control points by Ctrl-clicking them and selecting
Delete Point from the contextual menu.

3   Ctrl-click the new point and select Delete Point from the contextual menu.

Now let's try smoothing the point on the lower-center vertex of the shape.

4   Ctrl-click the point in the lower center and select Smooth from the contextual menu.

The lines on the left and right of the selected vertex are smooth (curved),
and two gray Bezier handles appear on the left and right sides of the
selected point. You can drag the Bezier handles to manipulate the shape
and curvature of the lines. Bending the handle bends the corresponding
line of the shape; extending the handle extends the curvature of the line.

Let's try it.

5   Drag the right Bezier handle downward to bend the right side of the vertex.

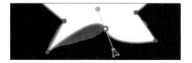

To bend the lines to the left and right of the vertex independently, you can hold down the Command key while you drag the handle.

6   Hold down Command and drag the left Bezier handle downward to curve the line to the left of the selected vertex.

7   Experiment with the different points to finish the leaf shape using the Bezier tool.

8   Press Cmd-S to save your progress.

Working with the BSpline Tool

Now that you've had a chance to use the Bezier tool, let's move on to the BSpline tool. The BSpline and Bezier tools are very similar in the initial stages of creating a shape. The first step is to select the tool and set the points in the shape that you want to create. The difference becomes apparent after you finish setting the last point. There are two ways to select the BSpline tool:

▶   Press B (this toggles between the Bezier and BSpline tools).

▶   Select the BSpline tool on the toolbar.

In this exercise, you'll use the BSpline tool to create a shape similar to the image in the lower left of the frame.

1   Press B to toggle from the Bezier tool to the BSpline tool.

The BSpline tool looks like the Bezier (pen) tool with the addition of an arcing curve.

2   Starting at the top of the yellow petal image, click the BSpline tool on the outer edge of the image. Move clockwise and continue setting control points until you arrive back at the first point. Then click the first control point to close the shape.

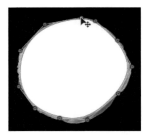

Modifying the BSpline Vertices

To modify the BSpline vertices, you simply drag the control points. The curved shape within the boundaries of the control points is attracted to the boundary lines, so wherever you drag the control points, the curvature of the shape will follow. To add a new point, you can Ctrl-click the lines between points and select Add Point from the contextual menu.

1   Experiment with the different BSpline control points to manipulate the shape.

2   Press Cmd-S to save your progress.

> **NOTE ▸** You can also modify the BSpline vertex by selecting the point, holding down the Command key, and dragging. This will flatten the arc.

Transforming a Free-form Shape

Once you've completed your shape, you can use the Select/Transform tool to move and resize the shape just as you would any other object in Motion.

Let's select each shape with the Select/Transform tool and move the shapes to different positions on the screen.

1   Press Tab or Shift-S to choose the Select/Transform tool.

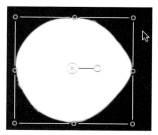

A bounding box appears around the selected shape.

2   Drag the BSpline petal shape to the right side of the frame.

3   Select the Bezier leaf shape and drag it to the right side of the frame.

4   Press Cmd-S to save the finished project.

5   Choose File > Close to close the project.

Now that you know how to use the free-form Create tools, you won't be limited to circles and rectangles as you add shapes to your projects.

Opening the Frances Project

In Lesson 5, you added filters and an image mask to the Hurricane Frances news bumper. In the next series of exercises, you'll learn to create the dynamic titles that were used to create that project. Let's open the **7-3 Frances start** project and then look at the finished movie.

1   Open the project **7-3 Frances start**.

2   Choose File > Save As and save the project in the My Motion Projects folder.

3   In the File Browser, select **Frances final.mov** to view it in the Preview area.

The text in this project includes two features that you haven't worked with yet: a solid-color object created by one of Motion's generators and an out-line around both text objects.

Previewing Generators in the Library

The Library includes a Generators folder that contains a selection of checker-boards, gradients, noise patterns, and other computer-generated elements for use in your projects. They are called generators because they don't exist as objects until you add them to a project, and therefore Motion generates that item specifically for your project. You can add generators to your projects as you would any other object. Let's preview some of the generators in the Library. The Generators icon looks like a screen with a color-bar test pattern.

1   Press Cmd-2 to open the Library tab.

2   Select Generators in the upper pane of the Library.

The lower pane of the Library lists 12 generators.

3   Select the first generator in the lower pane of the Library to view it in the Preview area.

4   Press the down arrow (if in List view) to view the next selection until you preview all 12 generators.

As you can see, the generators include static images like Gradient and Color Solid and moving images like Cellular and Swirly.

Applying a Solid Color to the Project

Now that you've previewed the various generators in the Library, let's apply a Color Solid generator to the project. Your goal in this exercise is to create the red bar that sits below the word *FRANCES* in the composite. First, you'll apply the Color Solid generator to the project; then you'll crop the generator and change the color.

First, let's look at the project in the Canvas and on the Layers tab.

1   Click the Canvas window to select the Canvas; then press the spacebar to begin playback.

The project includes two text objects with text behaviors applied.

2   Press Cmd-4 to open the Layers tab.

3   Drag the right edge of the Layers tab to resize the tab so that you can read the layer names.

The project includes four layers: Titles, Center Square, Stills, and Background. Let's add the Color Solid generator to the Titles layer.

4   On the Layers tab, select the Titles layer.

5   In the Library, select the Color Solid generator.

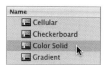

6   Click the Apply button in the Preview area of the Library to apply the Color Solid generator to the project.

Color Solid appears in the Titles layer as a generator object. The Color Solid object also covers the entire frame. Let's move the FRANCES text object above the Color Solid generator on the Layers tab.

7   On the Layers tab, drag the FRANCES text object above the Color Solid generator.

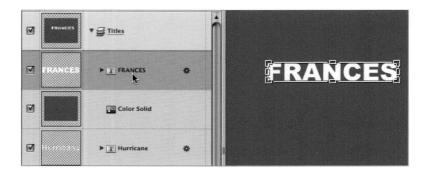

The FRANCES text object is the only thing showing above the Color Solid generator in the Canvas.

Modifying a Generator in the Inspector

You can modify generators in the Canvas the same way that you modify other objects in Motion. Generators also come with a convenient set of parameters that you can modify in the Inspector. Let's resize the Color Solid generator and change the color in the Inspector.

1   On the Layers tab, select the Color Solid generator; then press Cmd-4 to close the Layers tab.

2   Press Cmd-3 to open the Inspector to the Generator tab.

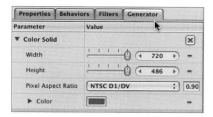

Your goal is to change the height of the Color Solid generator until it is just slightly higher than the FRANCES text object.

3   On the Generator tab in the Inspector, drag the Height slider toward the left to resize the height of the Color Solid generator.

4   Use the incremental arrows to the left or right of the Height field to change the value to exactly 100.

5   On the Canvas, drag the Color Solid generator upward until it fits directly below the FRANCES text object.

You've adjusted the height and position of the generator. Now let's change the color.

6   On the Generator tab in the Inspector, click the Color well.

The Colors window opens.

7 In the Colors window, choose a bright red color.

The Color Solid generator in the Canvas changes to bright red.

8 Close the Colors window.

The Color Solid generator looks pretty good in the Canvas, but it would look even better if you lowered the opacity so the background shows through the band of color.

9 Press D to open the Dashboard.

10 On the Dashboard, drag the Opacity slider toward the left to lower the opacity of the Color Solid generator to 50 percent.

11 Press Cmd-S to save your progress.

Now that you've completed modifying the Color Solid generator in your project, let's modify the FRANCES text object so that it stands out better against the red band of color.

Exploring the Text Tab in the Inspector

The Text tab in the Inspector has three text control panes: Format, Style, and Layout. Each pane has a corresponding button located on the Text tab. Let's look at the Text tab panes before we modify the look of the FRANCES text object.

1   Press Cmd-4 to open the Layers tab.

2   On the Layers tab, select the FRANCES text object.

   The contextual tab in the Inspector changes from a Generator tab to a Text tab to represent the selected object.

3   On the Text tab in the Inspector, click the Format button to open the Format pane, if it's not already open.

   The Format pane includes the font, size, tracking, scale, and other format-related parameters. Many of these parameters are also available in the Dashboard.

4   Click the Style button to view the Style pane.

   The Style pane offers four styles that you can apply to your text objects: Face, Outline, Glow, and Drop Shadow.

5   Click the Layout button to view the Layout pane.

   The Layout pane offers Alignment and Justification parameters.

6   Click the Style button again to return to the Style pane.

Applying an Outline Style to Text

To apply a different style to your text in the Style pane, you first need to make the style active by selecting the box next to the style. By default, all new text created in Motion is filled with the color white. The text fill color uses the Face style.

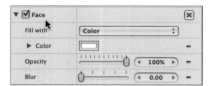

You can also modify the Face style parameters in the Dashboard.

The Outline, Glow, and Drop Shadow text styles cannot be added or modified in the Dashboard.

Let's apply a black outline to the FRANCES text object.

1   In the Style pane of the Text tab in the Inspector, click the Outline check box to activate the Outline style.

    The default outline color is red, so the outline will be difficult to see in the Canvas until you change the color.

2   Click the Color well for the Outline style to open the Colors window.

3   In the Colors window, drag the brightness slider to the lowest setting to change the selected color to black. Then close the Colors window.

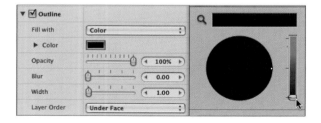

The Outline style parameters include Opacity, Blur, and Width. You can combine these parameters to create many different outline looks.

4   Experiment with the Opacity, Blur, and Width parameters.

Our goal is to make the word *FRANCES* stand out against the red bar, without losing the boldness of the letters. You've had a chance to experiment; now change the settings to the ones I used for the final project.

5   Change the Outline parameters as follows:

▶   Opacity: 100%

▶   Blur: 2.00

▶   Width: 3.00

6   Press Cmd-S to save your progress.

Applying a Second Outline

You've applied Outline parameters to the FRANCES text object; now you'll apply an Outline style to the Hurricane text. Unlike the FRANCES text, the Hurricane text is not placed over a bright red band to attract attention. Your goal is to add an outline that helps the Hurricane text stand out against the blowing trees in the background but does not overpower the FRANCES text. One technique is to create a really wide outline with a heavy blur. This combination of parameters places the text in a soft outline that separates it from the background, without drawing attention to the outline. Let's try it.

1   In the Canvas, click the Hurricane text object to select it.

2   In the Style pane of the Text tab in the Inspector, select the Outline check box to apply an outline to the Hurricane text.

A red outline appears around the Hurricane text object in the Canvas.

3 Click the Outline Color well to open the Colors window.

4 In the Colors window, change the color to black; then close the Colors window.

5 Set the Outline Width value to 15.00 and the Blur value to 30.00.

Notice that each of the letters in the word *Hurricane* is surrounded by a soft black blur, just enough to make it easy to read over a busy background.

6 Press Cmd-S to save the finished project.

7 Choose File > Close to close the project.

Now you can add Color Solid generators and Outline text styles to your bag of Motion tricks.

Planning the Right Text for the Job

Before you dive into the last project, this is a good time to mention another graphic design rule.

Rule #5: Text is the lead character and narrator of your motion graphics scene, so cast the right text for the part.

Text is usually the most important element in a graphics composite, so you need to select your text carefully. Think of the text as talent that you are casting for your project, and choose accordingly. If your project involves something exciting, you might choose a bold font and dress it up with bright colors and dramatic behaviors. If your project is about something like ballet, you might choose a more delicate font; soft, pastel colors; and smooth, graceful behaviors. Remember as you apply text to your projects that text is the actor, the color and styles are the costumes, and the behaviors are the choreography or action in the scene. Experiment with different combinations to cast the perfect text for your projects.

Opening the Animated Text Project

The last project that you'll work on in this Lesson is called **7-5 Animated Text start**. Over the next series of exercises, you'll incorporate many of Motion's features, including generators, text styles, LiveFonts, behaviors, filters, and particles, to create an animated text sequence. First, let's open the project and preview the finished movie.

1   Open 7-5 **Animated Text start**, located in the Lesson_07 folder.

> **NOTE ▶** If a window opens asking for a missing font, click Cancel to open the project without the missing font.

2   Choose File > Save As and save the project in the My Motion Projects folder.

3   In the File Browser, double-click the **Animated Text.mov** file to open it in the Viewer.

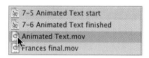

4   Play the finished movie in the Viewer to see what you're aiming for in this project.

5   Close the Viewer window.

As you can see, there are three text objects, each animated in a unique fashion that works with the actual word. WATER ripples, FIRE burns, RAIN drops in and out of the screen. All of the content in this project came from the Library or was created in Motion.

Let's take a look at the unfinished version of the project to see what elements you have to work with.

6   Press the spacebar to play the project in the Canvas.

Since you're starting with the WATER text object, let's pause playback and move the playhead so that this object is clearly visible in the Canvas.

7   Press the spacebar to pause playback; then move the playhead to 00;15 on the mini-Timeline.

Working with Gradient Presets

Before you start working with the text, let's apply a Gradient generator to the background of the project. Gradients are a classy alternative to a solid-colored background and come in 14 premade varieties in the Library. You can also customize gradients in the Gradient Editor and save them as Favorites.

In this exercise, you'll apply a Gradient generator to the Background layer of the project; then you'll modify the color using one of Motion's gradients in the Library. First, let's take a look at the project on the Layers tab.

1   Press Cmd-4 to open the Layers tab. The project includes four layers: Rain, Fire, Water, and Background.

2   Click the disclosure triangle for each layer to view the contents.

The Rain layer includes a Rain particle system and a RAIN text object. The Fire layer includes a Fire Crawl movie file and a FIRE text object. The Water layer includes a WATER text object and a Water Bubbles-Large movie file.

All of the text objects have text behaviors applied to them.

The Background layer is currently empty. Let's apply a Gradient generator to the background.

3   On the Layers tab, select the Background layer.

4   In the Library, select the Generators icon; then choose Gradient from the lower pane of the Library.

5   Drag the Gradient generator from the Library to the Background layer on the Layers tab.

The Gradient generator appears on the Background layer of the Layers tab, and a red and blue gradient appears in the background of the project in the Canvas.

Applying a Gradient Preset from the Library

The default gradient is red to blue, which may be great for a Fourth of July banner but doesn't quite fit with the animated text theme of this project. In this exercise, you'll preview the various preset gradients in the Library and apply one to the Gradient generator in the project.

1   Select the Gradients icon in the upper pane of the Library.

The lower pane of the Library lists 14 gradient presets, with interesting names like Atlantic Blue, Chrome, and Radioactive.

2 Select the Atlantic Blue gradient preset in the Library to see it in the Preview area.

3 Press the down arrow to view each of the gradient presets.

Since the final project includes water and rain, a blue, waterlike gradient might look nice.

4 Select the Blue Sky gradient preset in the Library; then click the Apply button in the Preview area to apply it to the selected object on the Layers tab.

The Gradient generator in the project changes to the Blue Sky gradient color pattern.

That was easy. You can also apply gradient presets to text and objects.

Applying a Gradient Preset to Text

To apply a gradient preset to a text object, you simply select the text object and then apply the gradient preset. Then you can modify the gradient parameters in the Inspector. Let's apply a gradient to the WATER text object.

1 On the Layers tab, select the WATER text object in the Water layer.

2 In the Library, select the Grayscale gradient preset; then click the Apply button to apply it to the selected text object.

The Grayscale gradient preset appears in the WATER text object in the Canvas.

3   Press Cmd-S to save your progress.

Modifying Gradients in the Inspector

Once you've applied a gradient preset to an object, you can modify it in the Inspector. If the gradient preset is applied to a text object, you can modify it in the Face controls of the Styles pane on the Text tab.

1   Press Cmd-3 to open the WATER text object in the Inspector.

2   In the Inspector, click the Text tab; then click the Style button to view the Style pane.

At the top of the Style pane, the Grayscale gradient preset appears in the Face controls.

To edit the gradient, you can click the Gradient disclosure triangle to open the Gradient Editor. Let's open the Gradient Editor and change the black value to a blue that matches the Gradient generator.

3   Click the Gradient disclosure triangle to open the Gradient Editor.

4   In the Gradient Editor, click the black color tag to select the black color of the gradient.

5 Click the Color well to open the Colors window; then drag the color picker (the magnifying glass) over the Canvas and select the dark blue from the image in the Canvas.

The Gradient Editor and the gradient in the WATER text object change to reflect the modified gradient.

6 Close the Colors window. Then press Cmd-S to save your progress.

Saving a Customized Gradient Preset

Now that you've created your own customized gradient preset, let's save it so that you can use it another time. To save a gradient preset, you first need to open the Gradient pop-up menu in the Style pane of the Inspector.

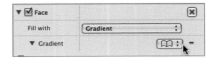

The Gradient pop-up menu displays the Library icon (an open book), because this menu provides quick access to all of the gradient presets in the Library.

1 In the Style pane of the Text tab, click the Gradient pop-up menu.

Notice all of the gradient presets from the Library in the pop-up menu.

2   Select Save Gradient at the top of the Gradient pop-up menu.

A Save Preset to Library window appears so that you can name your preset before you save it.

3   Type *Water white to blue* in the name field; then click the Save button to save the preset.

Congratulations! You're the proud creator of a new gradient preset. Your new preset now appears with the other gradient presets in the Library and in the Gradient pop-up menu. Let's take a look.

4   Click the Gradient pop-up menu to see the Water white to blue gradient preset at the bottom of the alphabetized list.

5   Press Cmd-2 to open the Library.

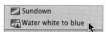

Your customized Water white to blue gradient preset appears at the bottom of the gradient presets list in the Library. Notice the icon of a person on the new preset, indicating that this is a preset that you customized.

Adding a Drop Shadow to Text

The WATER text object is really starting to look great; however, it would be even better if it had a light drop shadow to separate it from the background. Drop Shadow is one of the Style controls that you can add to your text in the Inspector. Let's return to the Text tab in the Inspector and apply a drop shadow to the WATER text object.

1   Press Cmd-3 to open the Inspector.

2   In the Style pane of the Text tab, scroll down to the bottom of the pane to view the Drop Shadow controls.

3   Select the Drop Shadow check box to turn on the Drop Shadow style for the selected text object.

The default drop shadow appears on the WATER text object in the Canvas.

I like the subtle look of the default drop shadow; however, feel free to adjust the other Drop Shadow parameters in the Inspector to modify the shadow.

4   Press Cmd-S to save your progress.

Adding a Filter to Text

With the behaviors, drop shadow, and gradient, the WATER text object has really come to life. If only we could make it ripple like it's actually made of water. Why not? You can also apply filters to your text, including distortion filters like Ripple. Let's try it. First, let's change the play range Out point so that we can isolate the WATER text object in the mini-Timeline.

1   Press Shift-O to move the playhead to the end of the WATER region in the mini-Timeline.

2   Press Option-Cmd-O to set the play range Out point to the playhead position.

3   Press the spacebar to preview the new play range in the Canvas.

Now let's add the Ripple filter from the Distortion category of filters.

4   On the toolbar at the top of the Canvas, click the Add Filter pop-up menu and choose Distortion > Ripple.

5   Press Cmd-S to save your project.

Now *that's* water text.

Exploring Fonts, LiveFonts, and Text Styles in the Library

The Motion Library also includes fonts, LiveFonts, and text styles that you can apply to your text objects. Let's explore the various text features in the Library.

1   Press Cmd-2 to open the Library tab in the Inspector.

2   On the Library tab, click the Fonts icon to view the font categories and choices.

    The fonts are organized into categories ranging from Classic to Web. To view all of the available fonts, click the All Fonts folder in the upper pane of the Library.

    You can view a font in the Preview area of the Library by selecting it in the lower pane of the Library.

3   In the lower pane of the Library, click one of the fonts to see it in the Preview area.

4   Press the down arrow to move down the list of fonts and preview additional selections.

    You can also access all of the fonts in the Dashboard and the Inspector.

Working with LiveFonts

Live Fonts are pre-animated fonts that you can use to add excitement and life to the text in your projects. The LiveFonts are located in the Library below the Fonts icon and can also be applied directly in the Inspector. In this exercise, you'll preview the LiveFonts in the Library and then apply one to the FIRE text object in your project.

> **NOTE ▶** LiveFonts are not included with the trial version of the software. If you're using the trial version, you can apply a colorful gradient to the FIRE text object instead of a LiveFont.

Setting a New Play Range

First, let's change the project play range to isolate the FIRE text object.

1   Press Cmd-4 to open the Layers tab; then select the FIRE text object on the Fire layer.

The FIRE text object region appears in the mini-Timeline.

2   Select the FIRE region in the mini-Timeline.

3   Press Shift-I to move the playhead to the beginning of the selected region.

4   Press Option-Cmd-I to set the play range In point to the playhead position.

5   Press Shift-O to move the playhead to the end of the selected region; then press Option-Cmd-O to set the play range Out point to the playhead position.

6   Press the spacebar to see the new play range in the Canvas.

Previewing and Applying LiveFonts

Now let's preview some of the LiveFonts that you can use for your text.

1   In the Library, click the LiveFonts icon.

Motion offers 37 LiveFonts for you to choose from.

2   Select the first LiveFont in the lower pane of the Library to see it in the Preview area.

The Bar LiveFont makes the letters look like they are made of 3D glistening gold bars. Let's preview the remaining LiveFonts and find one that would be appropriate for the FIRE text object.

3   Press the down arrow to see the remaining LiveFonts in the Preview area.

The Burn Barrel LiveFont makes the text look like it's on fire. That seems like a winner for this project.

4   Select the Burn Barrel LiveFont in the Library; then click the Apply button in the Preview area to apply it to the selected text object.

You can view and change the LiveFonts applied to a text object in the Inspector.

5   Press Cmd-3 to open the Inspector; then click the Text tab.

6   Click the Format button to display the Format pane, if it is not already displayed.

At the top of the Format pane is the Font Type pop-up menu. This pop-up menu allows you to select between System Fonts and LiveFonts.

The Collection pop-up menu, below the Font Type parameter, lets you choose from fonts that are grouped together in descriptive categories such as Fun, Classic, and Modern, and the Family pop-up menu lets you choose the system font or LiveFont that you want applied to the selected text.

7   Press Cmd-S to save your progress.

Creating Text Particles

You can also create particles from any text object by selecting the object and clicking the Make Particles button in the toolbar. In this exercise, you'll create rain particles using the RAIN text object. First, let's change the play range in the mini-Timeline to isolate the Rain layer.

1   On the Layers tab, select the RAIN text object on the Rain layer.

2   Press Shift-I to move the playhead to the beginning of the selected object in the mini-Timeline; then press Option-Cmd-I to set the play range In point.

3   Press Shift-O to move the playhead to the end of the selected object; then press Option-Cmd-O to set the play range Out point.

4   Press the spacebar to play the Rain section of the project.

The goal in this exercise is to create rain from the word *RAIN*. There are two ways to accomplish this. You could select the RAIN text object and create particles from it. The downside of that technique is that you would have to set all of the particle parameters to achieve a rainlike effect. The alternative approach is to duplicate the Rain emitter—which currently showers the frame with raindrops—and replace the raindrop object in the duplicate emitter with the RAIN text object. That sounds much easier. Let's try it. First, let's clean up the Layers tab to make it easier to focus on the Rain layer.

5   On the Layers tab, click the disclosure triangle to close all of the open layers except for the Rain layer.

6   On the Rain layer of the Layers tab, Ctrl-click the Rain emitter and choose Duplicate from the contextual menu.

A copy of the Rain emitter appears on the Layers tab. It's also good idea to duplicate the RAIN text object and remove any behaviors from it before you replace the emitter object.

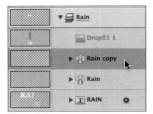

7   Ctrl-click the RAIN text object and select Duplicate from the contextual menu.

8   Click the disclosure triangle for the RAIN copy text object to view the behaviors applied to the object.

You can delete the behaviors by selecting them on the Layers tab and pressing the Delete key.

9   Select and delete the behaviors from the RAIN copy text object.

Now you're ready to replace the object for the Rain copy emitter with the RAIN copy text object.

10   Click the disclosure triangle for the Rain copy emitter to view the contents of the emitter.

You'll drag the RAIN copy text object to the Drop01 copy 1 particle cell to change the object from a drop to the word *RAIN*.

11   Drag the RAIN copy text object upward and release it on the Drop01 copy 1 particle cell.

The particle cell changes to RAIN, and the Canvas updates to a shower of rain.

Notice that you can see two RAIN text objects in the Canvas. Since you replaced the particle cell instead of the original object, you'll need to turn off the original RAIN copy text object on the Layers tab.

12 Select the Activation check box for the RAIN copy text object on the Layers tab to turn it off.

You can use this method to turn virtually any object into rain, including text and AquaBalls—even cats and dogs.

Modifying the RAIN Text Particles in the Dashboard

Now that you've created a RAIN text particle cell, let's modify the parameters in the Dashboard to a light drizzle rather than a downpour of words on the screen.

1   Press D to open the Dashboard for the modified particle cell.

2   On the Dashboard, drag the Birth Rate slider toward the left to reduce the number of particles born per second from 1200 to around 200.

3   Press Cmd-S to save your progress.

Applying Text Styles

The last step to complete the Rain section of this project is to apply a text style from the Library to the RAIN text object. Text styles are very similar to gradient presets; however, they are designed specifically to fit on a piece of text, rather than to function as full background gradients. To preview the text styles, all you need to do is select the Text Styles icon in the Library and select the styles in the lower pane of the Library.

1   Press Cmd-2 to open the Library tab; then select the Text Styles icon in the upper pane of the Library.

2   Preview the various text styles and choose one that you think will work well for the RAIN text object.

I like the Chrome Text style for this project.

3   Select the RAIN text object on the Layers tab; then click the Apply button to apply the selected text style to the selected text object.

4   In the Inspector, click the Style button on the Text tab to view the Style controls.

5   In the Face controls, open the "Fill with" pop-up menu and choose Gradient, if it's not already selected.

There you have it. You can now apply gradients, text styles, LiveFonts, drop shadows, outlines, and a whole lot of creativity to your projects.

What You've Learned

▶   The Bezier and BSpline tools can be used to create free-form shapes by setting points and modifying the vertices around the shape. The Bezier tool can create both straight and curved lines; the BSpline tool creates only curved lines.

▶   Generators are objects in the Library that you add to your project, often as a background. They are called generators because they don't exist as objects until you add them to a project, and therefore Motion generates that item specifically for your project. Motion comes with 12 generators: Cellular, Checkerboard, Color Solid, Gradient, Noise, Op Art 1, Op Art 2, Op Art 3, Soft Gradient, Star, Stripes, and Swirly.

▶   Generators can be applied to a project and modified just like any other object.

▶   Motion also includes 14 gradient presets that you can apply to objects, generators, and text within your project.

▶   Gradient presets can be applied from the Library or the Inspector and can be customized using the Gradient Editor.

▶   You can save your customized gradients in the Library by choosing Save Gradient Preset from the Gradient pop-up menu in the Inspector.

▶   The Text tab in the Inspector has Format, Style, and Layout panes with controls for modifying text.

▶   The Format pane includes controls for changing the font, size, text, and other parameters also available on the Dashboard.

▶   The Style pane contains style controls including Face, Outline, Glow, and Drop Shadow.

Master Project Tasks

Your Master Project tasks for this lesson consist of adding two text objects at the end of the project. First, you'll set a play range in the mini-Timeline to isolate the end of the project. Then you'll apply what you've learned in this lesson to add exciting and dynamic text to your Master Project. In the previous Master Project tasks, I gave you a lot of specifics. For this exercise, I encourage you to use your imagination and Motion skills to create text for this project. The rules are that there are no rules. You don't even have to use the same text as I did for the project. I intentionally created a generic Master Project so that you could make it about anything you desire.

Let's start by opening your Master Project in the My Motion Projects folder. If you didn't complete the Master Project tasks in the previous lesson, you can open **07 Master Project start** in the Master_Project folder.

1   Open your Master Project or the **07 Master Project start** project in the File Browser.

2   Select the **07 MP finished.mov** file in the File Browser to preview the finished Master Project task.

The final movie includes both LiveFont and System Font text objects, as well as behaviors. The goal is to place your text so that it begins right after the Leaf particles fall from the frame.

3   Set a play range in the mini-Timeline with a play range In point of 16;15 and a play range Out point of 22;15.

4   Use the Text tool to create text; then modify the text using the skills that you learned in this lesson.

5   Save your finished project.

8

Lesson Files

Time

This lesson takes approximately 1 hour to complete.

Goals

Add objects to the Timeline

Modify regions in the Timeline

Work with markers

Edit objects and layers in the Timeline

Insert, overwrite, and exchange objects

Move, delete, and collapse layers

Work with templates

Working in the Timeline

If you've been following along with the lessons in this book, you've already built more than a dozen projects using the Canvas and the Layers tab in the Project pane. In this lesson, you'll expand your Motion horizons as you learn to create and modify a project on the Timeline tab, located in the Timing pane.

Those of you who are video editors are already accustomed to working in a timeline environment. The Timeline in Motion includes many of the features of professional editing software such as Final Cut Pro. You're already familiar with the mini-Timeline, which is actually a condensed version of the Timeline. The difference is that the mini-Timeline shows only one region at a time, whereas the Timeline in the Timing pane shows tracks for all the elements in the project.

In this lesson, you'll work with three projects to hone your Timeline skills. You'll practice moving, importing, replacing, marking, and compositing clips within the various Timeline tracks.

First, you'll compare the Layers and Timeline tabs as you add files to a project. Then you'll organize and modify a more complicated project in the Timeline. Finally, you'll open a Motion template and modify it in the Timeline with your own media. You'll also use markers in the Timeline to help choreograph the elements of your composite scene. We'll start with a quick tour of the Timeline tab.

Opening the Timeline Project

The first project you'll be working with as you get to know the Timeline tab is the **8-1 Timeline start** project, located in the Lesson_08 folder.

1   In the File Browser, open the Lesson_08 folder; then open the project **8-1 Timeline start**.

2   Choose File > Save As and save the project to your My Motion Projects folder on the Desktop.

3   Click the Icon view button to change the File Browser to Icon view, if it's not already in Icon view.

Comparing the Timeline and Layers Tabs

Over the last six lessons, you've gained a lot of experience working on the Layers tab. Now it's time to learn how to work with the Timeline tab, which is located in the Timing pane. Since you are so familiar with the Layers tab, let's compare it to the Timeline tab to see their similarities and differences.

We'll start with an empty Layer; then we'll add several video clips and create a transition (fade) from one video clip to the next. First, let's open the Timeline tab in the Timing pane.

If you recall, Cmd-1, Cmd-2, and Cmd-3 open the tabs in the Utility window; Cmd-4, Cmd-5, and Cmd-6 open the corresponding tabs in the Project pane. The Motion designers were very consistent in developing an easy-to-learn interface, so Cmd-7, Cmd-8, and Cmd-9 open the corresponding tabs in the Timing pane. Let's try it.

1   Press Cmd-7 to open the Timeline tab in the Timing pane.

The Timeline tab opens in the Timing pane below the Canvas window.

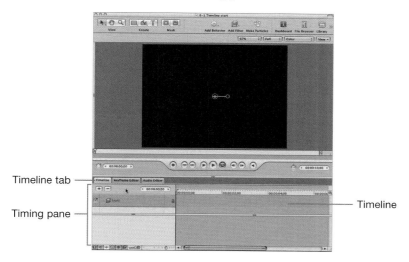

Timeline tab

Timing pane

Timeline

Now let's open the Layers tab for comparison.

2   Press Cmd-4 to open the Layers tab in the Project pane.

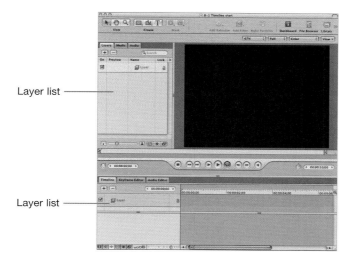

Layer list

Layer list

Both project views include a Layer list that shows one empty layer.

The Layer list on the Timeline tab works exactly the same as the Layer list on the Layers tab. Let's add an object to the empty layer on the Timeline tab.

3 In the File Browser, locate the **surf_1_SD_jpg.mov** file.

4 Drag the surf_1_SD_jpg.mov file from the File Browser to the Timeline tab and drop it on the empty layer in the Layer list.

You added the surf_1_SD_jpg object to the project, and it appeared simultaneously on the Layers tab, on the Timeline tab, and in the Canvas.

Of course, this isn't anything new. In fact, you've been adding objects to the Timeline tab in this way since Lesson 1; you just weren't focusing on that part of the interface.

5   Press Cmd-Z, or choose Edit > Undo Media Import, to undo the last step.

Normally, it's counterproductive to undo each step as you build a project; however, in this case, it's easier to start the next exercise with an empty project.

Importing Multiple Objects to the Project at the Same Time

Now that you've seen that dragging an object to the Layer list on the Timeline tab is virtually the same as dragging an object to the Layer list on the Layers tab, let's try bringing in two objects. That's right. We've never tried importing two objects at the same time. To select more than one file in the File Browser, you simply hold down the Command key as you select the multiple files. To drag more than one selected file to the Layer list, all you need to do is drag one of the selected files, and both will move in tandem to the Layer list.

1   In the lower pane of the File Browser, select the surf_1_SD_jpg.mov file (if it's not already selected); then Cmd-click the surf_2_SD_jpg.mov file to select the second file.

2   Drag the surf_1_SD_jpg.mov file from the File Browser to the Timeline tab and drop it on the empty layer.

Both of the surf movie files appear on the layer on the Timeline tab and the Layers tab.

The Timeline itself is the area to the right of the Layer list on the Timeline tab. Previously, you've worked with the mini-Timeline, which is a condensed version of the real Timeline. The mini-Timeline shows regions for only the selected object or layer in a project. The actual Timeline shows horizontal regions for every element of the project, graphically representing each element's length and position as they occur over the duration of the project.

Notice in the Timeline that the movie files are stacked on top of one another, just as they appear on the Layer list. The surf_2_SD_jpg movie is visible in the Canvas, because it is above the surf_1_SD_jpg movie. You can't see both movies in the Canvas at the same time unless you resize them or use a blend mode to combine them.

When one file is above another file in the Timeline, it is referred to as *superimposed*. When one file is superimposed on another, you'll generally want to see them both at the same time, so you'll want to resize, crop, key, or apply a blend mode. Titles are usually superimposed on (placed above) other objects or layers.

Analyzing Tracks in the Timeline

Before you move on to the next Timeline experiment, let's analyze the different *tracks*. What's a track? Tracks are the horizontal gray areas within the Timeline that represent the adjacent elements in the Layer list. Motion creates a track for every element in the project, and if you delete an element, you delete the track as well. Tracks match the organization of your Layer list, with one large track for each layer, and smaller tracks for each object on the layer. If you click the disclosure triangle for a layer and hide (collapse) the contents, you'll also hide the associated tracks in the Timeline. Let's try it.

1   In the Layer list on the Timeline tab, click the Layer disclosure triangle to collapse the layer and hide its contents.

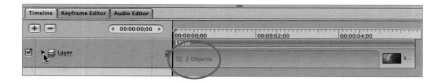

The Layer list shows only one layer, with a corresponding Layer track in the Timeline. The contents of the collapsed layer are identified as 2 Objects.

Notice that the Layer list on the Layers tab has not been modified and still shows a layer with two objects inside. That's because both Layer lists contain the same information, but they can be modified independently.

2   Press Cmd-Z to undo the file import and return the project to one empty layer.

Dragging Files to the Timeline

Now let's try a multifile importing maneuver that is possible only if you drag files to the Timeline. Remember: The Timeline is the long, horizontal area to the right of the Layer list on the Timeline tab.

First, let's get a better understanding of the different places that you can import a file in the Timeline. If you drag an individual file to the Layer track, you'll simply add the file to that layer. If you drag more than one file to the Layer track, a drop menu appears with two choices: Composite and Sequential.

If you choose Composite, Motion will import the objects one on top of the other; if you choose Sequential, Motion will import them one after the other. By default, if you drag multiple files to the Layer list, Motion imports them as a composite (one atop the other).

Let's drag the same two files to the Layer track in the Timeline and choose Sequential from the drop menu. To use the drop menu, you simply drag your files to the Timeline and hold down the mouse button for a moment until you see the drop menu; then release the mouse over the menu selection that you want.

1   Select both of the surf video files in the File Browser, if they aren't already selected.

    You need to drag only one of the two selected files to import both files at the same time.

2   Drag the surf_1_SD_jpg.mov file from the File Browser to the beginning (00;00) of the Layer track in the Timeline and choose Sequential from the drop menu.

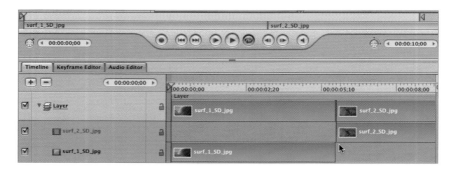

The two surf movie files appear one after the other in both the Timeline and the mini-Timeline.

Now that you've compared the Layers tab and the Timeline tab, let's close the Layers tab. You can always open it again later.

3   Press Cmd-4 to close the Layers tab.

4   Press Cmd-S to save your progress.

Overlapping Video Clips in the Timeline

Before you move any objects in the Timeline, it's a good idea to know what you are trying to accomplish. Your overall goal in this exercise is to dissolve (fade) from the first surf clip to the second. At the moment, the two video clips are aligned one after the other in the Timeline. That means that you'll see the first clip and then the second. To dissolve or fade from one clip to the next, they'll need to overlap. First, let's play the current project.

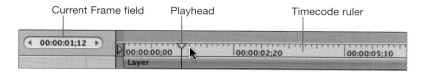

The Timeline includes a full-size playhead that extends vertically to play all tracks simultaneously. Previously, you've worked with the playhead in the mini-Timeline. The playhead in the Timeline works exactly the same way; it's just a larger version.

The Timeline also includes a Current Frame field that displays the current playhead position and can be used for playhead navigation. A handy timecode ruler displays the project timecode from the first frame to the last frame.

Let's play the project in the Timeline; then we'll overlap the second video clip.

1   Press the spacebar to play the project in the Timeline and see it in the Canvas.

Notice that the playhead in the Timeline scrubs along the tracks as it plays.

2   Press the spacebar to stop playback.

Objects in the Timeline are also referred to as clips, as in video clips. When you move a clip in the Timeline, all selected items move with it. When a clip is selected, it becomes a darker color. For example, both surf movie clips are currently selected in the Timeline, and both are a darker shade of blue. To deselect a clip, click the empty space below it in the Timeline.

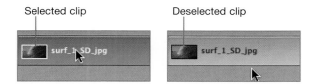

Selected clip   Deselected clip

3 Click the empty space below the clips in the Timeline or press Shift-Cmd-A to deselect all elements in the project.

In the Timeline, let's check the timecode where the first clip ends and the second begins. To drag (scrub) the playhead, you need to drag the colored triangle on the timecode ruler. The point in the Timeline where one element ends and another begins is called the *edit point*.

4 Drag the playhead to the beginning of the surf_2_SD_jpg movie clip (05;26).

If you have trouble moving the playhead to the beginning of the clip, you can always snap it into position. Snap? If you hold down the Shift key while you drag the playhead, the playhead will snap to the beginning or end of the elements in the Timeline. Let's try again.

5 Click anywhere on the timecode ruler to jump the playhead to that position in the Timeline.

6 Press and hold down Shift; then drag the playhead to the beginning of the surf_2_SD_jpg clip.

Snap.

A 1-second (30 frame) dissolve would look very nice as a transition from one video clip to the next. To create a 30-frame dissolve, you first need to make sure that the two clips overlap by at least 30 frames. Let's move the playhead 30 frames earlier in the Timeline and then drag the second surf clip to the new playhead position. Remember: To move the playhead 10 frames at a time, you hold down the Shift key and then press the right or left arrow key.

7   Press Shift-left arrow three times to move the playhead left (reverse) a total of 30 frames, or 1 second. The new timecode position will be 4;26.

You can not only snap the playhead to elements in the Timeline, but also snap elements such as clips to the playhead. The playhead darkens when you snap something to it, to show that you've reached the playhead position. All you need to do is hold down the Shift key while you drag.

Before you drag the second surf clip, it's important to know exactly what you are supposed to drag. You want to drag the surf_2_SD_jpg clip that is in the surf_2_SD_jpg track. How do you know if you're on the right track (so to speak)? Just look at the name on the Layer list to the left of each track.

8   Select the surf_2_SD_jpg clip in the Timeline; then Shift-drag it to the left until the clip snaps to the playhead.

The playhead darkens to show that you've snapped to the right position, and a tooltip window appears to show you that the new In point is 4;26, the new Out point is 9;25, and the amount of change is −1;00 (1 second earlier).

Applying Behaviors in the Timeline

The last step in creating a transition from the first clip to the second is to apply the Fade In/Fade Out behavior to the upper clip in the Timeline. Why the upper clip? The same reason that you always apply opacity or blend modes to the upper clip. The upper clip is physically above the lower clip. By applying an effect to the upper clip, you'll be able to see through it to the clip below. You apply behaviors to elements in the Timeline the same way that you apply them in the Canvas or on the Layers tab. Since you already have the surf_2_SD_jpg clip selected, let's use the Apply Filter button on the toolbar.

1   With the surf_2_SD_jpg clip selected in the Timeline, click the Add Behavior button on the toolbar and choose Basic Motion > Fade In/Fade Out from the pop-up menu.

A purple Fade In/Fade Out behavior region appears in the Timeline below the surf_2_SD_jpg clip. The behavior also appears below the object in the Layer list, just as it would on the Layers tab.

Let's adjust the length of the Fade In/Fade Out behavior in the Dashboard.

2   Press D to open the Dashboard.

3   Drag the left side (fade in) of the Fade In/Fade Out parameter display in the Dashboard to change the value to 30 frames.

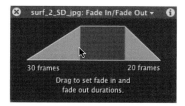

4   Press Cmd-S to save your finished project; then press the spacebar to pre-view it in the Canvas.

5   Press Cmd-7 to close the Timing pane to view the project in the full-size Canvas.

6   Choose File > Close to close the finished project.

Great work! Now, on to a more complicated version of the project.

Opening the Oakley Project

The second project you'll be working with should look familiar, since you've created it from scratch in previous lessons. During the next series of exercises, you'll import additional media into the project, create and organize layers, duplicate tracks, and learn how to use markers. Let's open the **8-3 Oakley start** project, located in the Lesson_08 folder.

1   Open the project **8-3 Oakley start**.

2   Choose File > Save As and save the project to your My Motion Projects folder on the Desktop.

3   Play the project in the Canvas to remind yourself of the various elements that you have applied to the project so far; then pause playback.

Analyzing the Project in the Timeline

Let's take a look at the Oakley project in the Timeline to see all of the elements and the current organization.

1   Press Cmd-7 to open the Timeline tab.

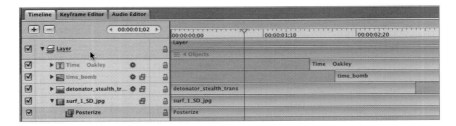

The Layer list includes one layer with four objects. How can you tell? You can count the blue object regions (clips) in the Timeline, or just look at the lower-left area of the Layer region in the Timeline; Motion always shows you how many objects are within a layer. In this case, Motion displays 4 Objects. If you look below the Layer object in the Layer list, you'll see a text object, two still-image objects, and one video object.

Just like the Layer list on the Layers tab, the Layer list on the Timeline tab includes buttons to enable behaviors and filters, and activation boxes to turn elements on and off.

Let's move the playhead to the beginning of the project and look at the elements in the Layer list a little more closely.

2   Press the Home key to move the playhead to the first frame of the project.

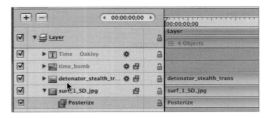

On the Timeline, the playhead is over two objects (blue regions): detonator_stealth_trans and surf_1_SD_jpg.

Notice that these objects have colored icons on the Layer list. Whenever the playhead is over an element in the Timeline, the icons for those elements appear in color in the Layer list. This is also true for the Layer list on the Layers tab.

Let's test this by moving the playhead farther into the project.

3   Type *2.20* in the Current Frame field and press Return to move the playhead forward to 2;20 in the Timeline.

The playhead is over all four objects in the Timeline, and all of their icons appear in color in the Layer list.

Disabling Filters in the Timeline

The filters really add a nice touch to the final look of the project. However, they also require more video RAM to process each time you play the project. Let's temporarily disable the filters while we edit the project in the Timeline. We'll turn them back on when we need them.

To disable all of the filters for an object, you simply click the Filter enable/disable button in the Layer list.

1   In the Layer list on the Timeline tab, click the Filter enable/disable button for the time_bomb, detonator_stealth_trans, and surf_1_SD_jpg objects to disable all of the filters for each object.

A diagonal red line appears over each Filter enable/disable button to show that the filters have been disabled.

2   Play the project to see it without the filters enabled; then pause playback.

Working with the Timeline Tab Buttons

The Timeline tab includes a set of Show/Hide buttons to help you show and hide various elements in the Timeline.

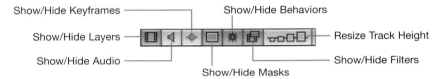

By default, the Show/Hide buttons for layers, masks, behaviors, and filters are set to Show. Let's hide the filters and behaviors by clicking the corresponding buttons on the Timeline tab.

1   On the Timeline tab, click the Show/Hide Behaviors button to hide the behaviors in the Timeline.

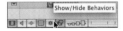

The buttons appear a lighter gray color when they are in the Hide position.

2   Click the Show/Hide Filters button to hide the filters in the Timeline.

Any filters that were showing in the Timeline are now hidden. Also, notice that the disclosure triangles for the objects in the project are now hidden. Why? Because if you hide all of the behaviors and filters, there isn't anything for the disclosure triangles to disclose. Don't worry; the disclosure triangles will return later in this lesson when you show the behaviors and filters again.

Keep in mind that all you've done is hide the behaviors and filters. The behaviors are all still active in the project; you just don't see them in the Layer list or the Timeline.

NOTE ▶ The Layers tab in the Project pane also includes Show/Hide buttons for behaviors, filters, and masks.

Changing Track Height

You'll be working primarily in the Timeline for the remainder of this lesson. To make your work easier, you'll control how you view the elements in the Timeline.

You can control the height of the tracks by clicking the various Resize Track Height buttons. The Resize Track Height buttons look like a series of blocks ranging from small to large; the four blocks represent the four preset track heights. To change the height of the tracks, you simply click the height button that represents the track height you want to use. Let's try it.

1   Click the largest Resize Track Height button to view the tracks in the Timeline at the largest size.

The rows in the Layer list and the corresponding tracks in the Timeline change to the largest size.

2 Click the other three Resize Track Height buttons to see the different track height options.

3 Select whichever track height you want to work with; you can always change it as needed.

Zooming in the Timeline

Now you know how to adjust the height of the tracks. You can also zoom into and out of the Timeline to change your view of the Timeline. Motion provides three different tools that you can use to modify the Timeline zoom level: the Zoom slider, the Zoom/Scroll control, and the Zoom to Fit button.

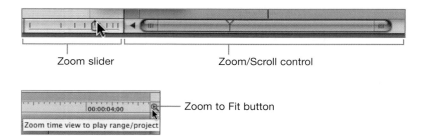

Zoom slider   Zoom/Scroll control

Zoom to Fit button

Zoom time view to play range/project

Let's try the different zoom controls to see how they work.

1 Drag the Zoom slider toward the left and then toward the right to zoom into and out of the tracks in the Timeline.

Notice that as you zoom in or out, the playhead always remains in the same position.

Now let's try the Zoom/Scroll control. If you drag the edges of the Zoom/Scroll control left or right, you change the zoom level of the Timeline. If you drag the center of the Zoom/Scroll control left or right, you scroll the Timeline view.

2   Drag the left edge of the Zoom/Scroll control to the right to zoom into the Timeline.

The more you zoom in (drag to the right), the shorter the Zoom/Scroll control becomes. It becomes shorter because the size of the Zoom/Scroll control is relative to the length of the regions in the Timeline. In other words, the Zoom/Scroll control looks shorter because the tracks are so much longer when you zoom all the way in. Think of the Zoom/Scroll control as a person standing in front of a highway. The farther the person is from the highway, the larger the person appears compared with the highway in the distance. The closer the person is to the highway, the smaller the person appears relative to the highway.

You've zoomed; now try scrolling with the Zoom/Scroll control.

3   Drag the center of the Zoom/Scroll control toward the right to scroll through the Timeline until you see the play range Out point.

The last control to try is the Zoom to Fit button. It's the little magnifying glass at the upper right of the Timeline.

4   Click the Zoom to Fit button to compress the entire Timeline to show everything within the play range.

NOTE ▶ You'll find the same Zoom slider and Zoom/Scroll Timeline controls in Final Cut Pro and Final Cut Express.

Creating and Organizing Layers

You know how to change your Timeline view; now let's focus on organizing the project. Your goal in this exercise is to organize the project to make it easier to add more media files. First, you'll add two new layers; then you'll rename them. You add and rename layers on the Timeline tab the same as you do on the Layers tab. It's also a good idea to resize the Timing pane while you're organizing the layers.

To resize the Timing pane, you simply drag the top edge of the pane.

1   Move the pointer over the top edge of the Timing pane until the cursor changes from an arrow to the Resize tool.

2   Drag the top edge of the Timing pane upward to create a larger Timeline workspace.

Notice that the Canvas window gets smaller to accommodate the larger Timing pane.

3   Click the Add new layer button (+) at the upper left of the Timeline tab to add a new layer to the Layer list.

4   Repeat step 3 to add another new layer.

5   Double-click the name field for each layer and rename all three layers, from top to bottom, as *Text*, *Stills*, and *Video*.

Now that the layers have been created and named, let's move the various elements to the appropriate layers to organize the project. You can move objects in the Layer list on the Timeline tab the same way you did on the Layers tab in the Project pane.

6   Move the Time Oakley text object from the Video layer up to the Text layer.

7   Click the time_bomb object to select it; then Cmd-click the detonator_stealth_trans object to select it along with the first object.

8   Drag the selected objects from the Video layer up to the Stills layer.

9   Click the disclosure triangles for each layer to collapse them and hide the contents.

10   Resize the Timing pane so it's just slightly taller than the three tracks.

11   Press Cmd-S to save your progress.

Your project is now organized and ready for you to add more media.

NOTE ▸ It is not necessary to organize a project before you add media or move elements in the Timeline. Organization just makes the process a little easier in the long run.

Working with Markers in the Timeline

You don't have to guess, estimate, or drag clips aimlessly through the Timeline searching for the right place to move them. Sure, it's okay to experiment and move things without knowing exactly what you want. On the other hand, if you already know where you want things to go, you can place markers in the Timeline as guides. Markers are like Post-it notes that you place on the Timeline as reminders or comments or to mark specific frames. Let's place some markers in the Timeline that we can use as guides as we add and move media within the Timeline.

Planning the Project Updates

The current project has a duration of 5;26, which is also the duration of the surf_1_SD_jpg clip. Your overall goal is to extend the project to make room for a third Oakley watch—but 5 seconds and 26 frames is not much time to show two watches effectively, let alone three watches, so you'll first add another video clip to the video layer. The first two watches are on the screen for approximately 3 seconds each, so you'll want to add at least 3 more seconds of video. Also, you need room to overlap the video clips, to add a fade transition between them. You also need to decide where the third watch element will begin in the Timeline.

In the next exercise, you'll plan where each of these elements should occur in the Timeline and set a marker to use as a guide for each maneuver.

Applying Markers

To apply a marker in the Timeline, all you need to do is move the playhead to the position where you want to place the marker and then press the M key to set the marker.

The first playhead position we need to mark is the place we want the second video clip to start. Let's move the playhead into position and then set a marker. First, we'll extend the project duration to 9 seconds (9;00).

1   In the Project Duration field, type *9.00* and press Return to change the project duration.

Now let's reset the play range to fit the entire duration of the project.

2   Press Option-X to reset the play range; then click the Zoom to Fit button on the Timeline tab to fit the full play range into the Timeline.

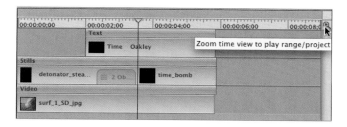

The last 2 seconds of the surf_1_SD_jpg video clip include a wall of water washing over the camera. I like the way the water covers the frame at the beginning, but a little water goes a long way, so let's set a marker at the point when the water first covers the entire frame; that's where we'll start the second video clip.

3   Scrub the playhead over the last few seconds of the video clip in the Timeline until you see the water completely fill the video portion of the frame (4;15).

NOTE ▶ You could choose a frame or two before 4;15, but when you keep project elements timed to whole or half seconds (15 frames), you can calculate the timing of the overall project more easily.

4   Press Shift-Cmd-A to deselect everything; then press M to set a marker at the playhead position on the Timeline ruler.

A green marker appears above the playhead.

Editing Markers

Now that you've set your first marker, you can label it and even change the color. To edit a marker, you simply double-click it, or Ctrl-click the marker and select Edit Marker from the contextual menu.

1   Double-click the marker to open the Edit Marker window.

2   In the Name field, type *Surf 2*; then press Return to save the changes and close the window.

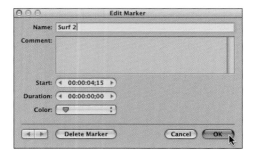

The marker's name (Surf 2) appears next to the marker above the Timeline ruler.

Let's set another marker. This time, let's set a marker at the beginning of the time_bomb still object. Just for fun, let's also change the color of the marker to blue.

3 Click the Stills disclosure triangle to show the contents of the layer.

4 Shift-drag the playhead to the beginning of the time_bomb clip so that it snaps to the clip In point (2;11).

5 Press M to set a marker; then double-click the marker to open the Edit Marker window.

6 In the Name field, type *Time Bomb*.

7 Click the Color pop-up menu in the Edit Marker window and select the blue marker.

8 Click OK or press Return to close the window.

The marker turns blue, and the name Time Bomb appears in the Timeline.

Now let's set the remaining two markers. The first marker will be for the third watch, and the last marker will show where to end the text. Why? Because once you extend the length of the project with extra media, the Time Oakley title will seem to end prematurely. If you extend it so that it ends 1½ seconds from the end of the project, it will look and feel like you planned it that way all along. I'll give you the timecode to place the markers; feel free to make the markers any color you like.

9   Move the playhead to 5;00 in the Timeline; then press M to set a marker.

10   Double-click the new marker to open it in the Edit Marker window;
then name the marker *GMT*. Press Return when you finish editing
the marker.

11   Move the playhead to 7;15 in the Timeline; then press Shift-M to set
a marker.

12   Double-click the new marker to open it in the Edit Marker window; then
name the marker *End Text*. Press Return when you finish editing the
marker.

13   Press Cmd-S to save your progress.

> **TIP** ▶ If you'll be using a lot of markers in your projects, you may want
> to come up with a color code for your markers. You may, for instance,
> want to choose one color for text markers, another for video clips, another
> for stills, and another for behaviors and filters. You can use a fifth color for
> notes to yourself, like "replace this shot" or "remember to crop and resize
> this object" or "feed the dog."

Navigating to Markers

Now that you've set four markers in the Timeline, what do you do with them?
You can navigate quickly forward to the next marker by pressing Option-Cmd-
right arrow. You can also press Option-Cmd-left arrow to navigate back to the
previous marker. Once the playhead is over a marker, you can then extend or
edit elements in the Timeline to the playhead position. We'll try this method
to move the playhead to the End Text marker; then we'll change the Out point

of the text object to the playhead position. First, let's try moving the playhead to the various markers in the Timeline.

1   Press Option-Cmd-left arrow to move the playhead back to the previous markers.

2   Press Option-Cmd-right arrow to move the playhead to the End Text marker.

When a layer is closed, you can still select the contents within the layer in the Timeline. A closed layer includes two regions. The narrow top region represents the layer, and the lower, thicker region represents the elements within the layer.

3   Select the Time Oakley object in the Timeline.

4   Press O to extend the Out point of the Time Oakley text layer to the play-head position (End Text marker).

5   Click the Text disclosure triangle in the Layer list to view the contents of the newly extended layer.

The layer and its contents both have been extended to the playhead position.

Dragging Media into the Timeline

The next step in extending the project is to add the second surf video clip to the Timeline. Dragging a single media file to the Timeline will also open a drop menu. If you drag a file to a layer track in the Timeline, the drop menu will give you three choices: Composite, Insert, and Overwrite.

NOTE ▶ The Insert and Overwrite functions in the Motion Timeline work the same as the Insert and Overwrite functions in the Final Cut Pro and Final Cut Express Timelines.

Composite places the new object on the layer above the other objects. Insert places the new object in the Timeline at the playhead position and pushes all of the other objects in the Timeline toward the right so that they resume after the inserted object. Overwrite places the new object at the playhead position in place of the other media in the same position on that track; in other words, Overwrite writes over any media in its path.

Layer track drop menu

Dragging a file to an object track opens a drop menu with four choices: Composite, Insert, Overwrite, and Exchange.

Object track drop menu

The Exchange selection replaces the media on the track with the new media file, just as you can replace media on the Layers tab.

For this exercise, you'll use the Composite selection from the drop menu to place the second surf clip above the first so that the clips overlap. Before adding media to the Timeline, it's a good idea to change the project preferences so that new media is created at the playhead position.

1   Choose Motion > Preferences to open the Preferences window.

2   In the Project pane in the Preferences window, select Create Objects At:
    Current frame and then close the Preferences window.

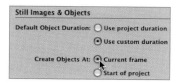

Now let's drag the second surf clip to the Surf 2 marker position on the
Video layer track in the Timeline.

3   Drag surf_2_SD_jpg from the File Browser to the Surf 2 marker on
    the Video layer track in the Timeline; then choose Composite from the
    drop menu.

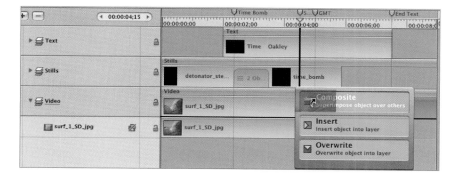

The surf_2_SD_jpg clip appears at the Surf 2 marker on the Video layer
on a new track above the surf_1_SD_jpg object.

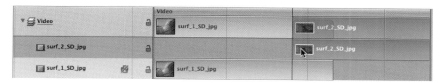

4 Press Cmd-S to save your progress.

5 Play the project in the Timeline to see your progress; then pause playback.

The second video clip starts right on cue, but it doesn't fade in—and worse, it covers the right half of the frame. Looks like we'll need to crop before we move on.

Cropping the Video Clip in the Canvas

Let's take a moment to hide the Timing pane and crop the surf_2_SD_jpg image in the Canvas. Of course, you don't have to close the Timing pane to crop, but your work may be easier if you have a larger Canvas window.

1 Move the playhead to the Surf 2 marker in the Timeline.

2 Press Cmd-7 to close the Timing pane; then press Cmd-3 to open the Inspector.

3 Press Cmd-– (hyphen) to zoom out of the Canvas.

4 Ctrl-click the surf_2_SD_jpg object in the Canvas and choose Crop from the contextual menu.

The goal is to move the surfer image toward the left to keep the surfer on the left side of the frame and then to crop the excess image from the right side of the frame. First, let's move the image in the Canvas.

5 Drag the middle of the surf_2_SD_jpg object toward the left until the Position indicator in the Inspector shows the coordinates –120,0.

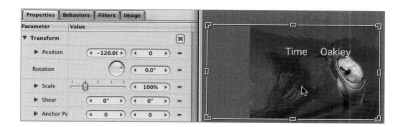

6 Drag the right edge (crop handle) of the image toward the left to crop the image to the center of the frame (Right 324).

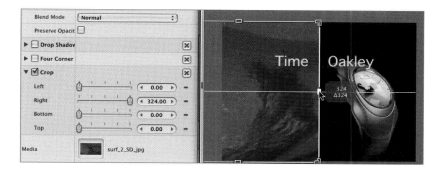

7 Press Tab to toggle from the Crop tool to the Select/Transform tool.

Great! The video image has been cropped. Now let's reopen the Timing pane so we can continue our work.

8 Press Cmd-7 to open the Timeline tab in the Timing pane.

Adding a Behavior to the Upper Clip

While the surf_2_SD_jpg clip is selected in the Timeline, let's add a Fade In/Fade Out behavior to the clip.

1 On the toolbar, click the Add Behavior button and choose Basic Motion > Fade In/Fade Out.

2 Press D to open the Dashboard; extend the Fade In parameter to 30 frames.

3 Press Cmd-S to save your progress.

Modifying Filters in the Timeline

Now that the new video clip has been added to the project, let's enable the filters and see how the two video clips look when played in the Canvas. While we're at it, we'll enable all of the filters in the project.

To enable the filters, you'll need to click the Filter enable/disable buttons in the Layer list. It's also a good idea to set the Show/Hide Behaviors and Show/Hide Filters buttons to Show so you can see all of the different elements in the Timeline.

1 Click the Stills layer disclosure triangle to view the contents of the Stills layer.

2 Click all three of the Filter enable/disable buttons in the Layer list to enable the filters for all of the objects in the Timeline.

Filter enable/disable button

3 Click the Show/Hide Behaviors and Show/Hide Filters buttons at the bottom of the Timeline tab to show behaviors and filters.

The Show/Hide buttons appear darker gray when they are in the Show position.

4 On the Timeline Layer list, click the surf_1_SD_jpg disclosure triangle to see all of the Posterize filter. Then play the project once in the Canvas.

The Posterize filter still looks great on the first video clip, but it would be even better if it were used on both video clips. You could copy and paste the filter to the second video clip, or just move the filter to the Video layer so it applies to all of the contents in the Video layer. Let's try it.

5 On the Layer list, drag the Posterize filter upward from the surf_1_SD_jpg object and drop it on the Video layer.

The Posterize filter appears at the top of the Video layer, and a purple Posterize region appears on a track below the Video track in the Timeline.

The Posterize filter needs to be extended to cover the full duration of the project.

6 Press the End key to move the playhead to the end of the project; then press O to extend the Out point of the Posterize filter to the playhead.

7 Press the spacebar to play the project.

The Posterize filter is definitely over both video clips. However, the Posterize filter is so strong on the second clip that you can't tell what you're looking at. Let's modify the Posterize filter in the Dashboard to take it down a notch or two so you get the effect and can also recognize what you're looking at in the video clip.

8   Press D to open the Posterize Dashboard, if it's not already open; then drag the Levels slider toward the right to 11.

Feel free to modify the Posterize level to whatever you think looks best.

9   Click the Video layer disclosure triangle to collapse the layer and hide the contents.

10   Press Cmd-S to save your progress.

Duplicating and Moving Objects in the Timeline

It's time to add another watch still to the project. Rather than start from scratch, let's just duplicate one of the existing watch objects and replace the media with the new watch. Your goal in this exercise is to add the GMT watch to the project and then modify the behaviors and filters as needed.

1   Click the Stills disclosure triangle to view the contents of the layer in the Timeline, if they're not already visible.

2   Ctrl-click the detonator_stealth_trans clip in the Timeline and choose Duplicate from the contextual menu.

A new track appears above the detonator_stealth_trans track with a clip called detonator_stealth_trans copy. Let's change the name of the new track to GMT.

3   In the Layer list on the Timeline tab, double-click the track name detonator_stealth_trans copy and change it to *GMT*.

The name of the clip in the GMT region changes to GMT. Now let's move the GMT clip in the Timeline to the GMT marker.

Moving a Clip to the Playhead

You can drag a clip along a track in the Timeline to move it, or you can Shift-drag a clip to align it with another element in the Timeline. You can also jump a selected element to the playhead by pressing Shift and the left or right bracket key. How do you know which bracket to use? The [(left bracket) represents the In point of a clip, and the] (right bracket) represents the Out point. If you want to move the beginning (In point) of the selected clip to the playhead, you press Shift-[(left bracket). Let's try it.

1   Select the GMT clip in the Timeline, if it's not already selected.

2   Press Option-Cmd-right arrow to move the playhead to the GMT marker.

3   Press Shift-[(left bracket) to move the In point of the selected GMT clip to the playhead (GMT marker).

4   Press Cmd-S to save your progress.

Exchanging Media in the Timeline

You duplicated the Detonator watch and all of its behaviors and filters and then changed the name of the duplicate clip in the Timeline. Now it's time to replace the media with the GMT still by using the Exchange option on the drop menu. To get to the Exchange option on the drop menu, you need to drag the new media file to the object on the object's track in the Timeline.

1   Press Cmd-1 to open the File Browser tab in the Utility window.

2   Drag the GMT.00_trans.psd file from the File Browser to the beginning of the GMT object on the GMT track in the Timeline, and hold down the mouse until the drop menu appears. Then choose Exchange from the drop menu.

The GMT watch is now the media on the GMT track in the Timeline.

3   Play the project to see it in the Canvas.

Changing the Track Position in the Timeline

The GMT watch appears below the Time Bomb watch instead of above it. Let's reposition the GMT and Time Bomb tracks so the GMT track is above the time_bomb track in the Timeline.

You can reposition a track by dragging the objects on the Layer list, just as you reposition objects on the Layers tab in the Project pane.

1 In the Timeline Layer list, drag the GMT object upward until the position indicator appears above the time_bomb object. Release the mouse.

The GMT clip now appears above the time_bomb clip in the Timeline.

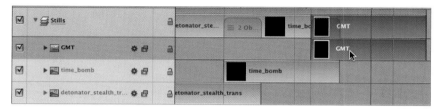

The project is nearly perfect. The GMT watch appears and moves as if you had planned it that way all along. The only thing distracting to me is the color of the GMT watch; it has the exact same color tint as the Detonator watch. Let's select the Colorize filter for the GMT clip in the Timeline and modify the color in the Dashboard.

2 Click the GMT disclosure triangle to view all of the filters and behaviors applied to the object.

3 Select the purple Colorize filter region in the Timeline below the GMT track.

4   Press D to open the Dashboard, if it's not already open, and select a new
color for the third watch.

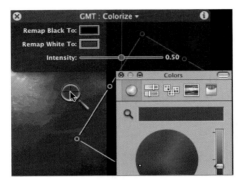

I used the color picker to select an aqua green color from the
surf_2_SD_jpg clip in the Canvas. Choose any color you wish to
accent the GMT watch.

5   Press Cmd-7 to close the Timing pane; then watch the finished project in
the Canvas.

6   Press Cmd-S to save the finished project.

7   Choose File > Close to close the finished project.

Now you have all of the skills you need to import, edit, and modify a project in
the Timeline.

Working with Motion Templates

For the last exercise in this lesson, you'll create a new project from one of
Motion's exciting templates and customize it for your own purposes. Motion
templates are premade projects that are set up for easy customization. Best of
all, the premade templates are royalty free, so you can use them at will for your
professional projects. Each template contains backgrounds, text objects, and
premade graphics that you can use as is or replace with your own media.

Motion's built-in templates are organized in the Template Browser, which you can open from the File menu. Let's open the Template Browser and preview some of the exciting prebuilt templates.

1   Choose File > Open Template to open the Template Browser.

The Template Browser window opens.

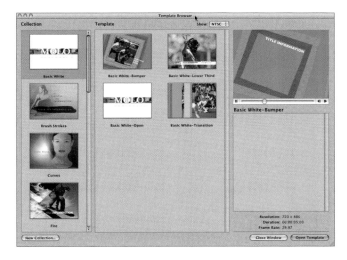

Template Browser

The templates are organized in the Collection list on the left side of the window. Each collection includes several different templates that have the same theme. When you select a collection, the templates appear in the Template area in the center of the window. You can also preview templates in the Preview area on the right side of the window.

The Collection list on the left side of the window shows all of the templates that are available.

2   Click a template collection to display its contents in the center of the window.

3 Click a template from the collection you selected to see it in the Preview area, along with the template's resolution, duration, and frame rate.

4 Click through the various categories and preview the templates in the Template Browser.

NOTE ▶ The Motion content in the Library is conveniently organized into categories that match the various template collections.

Analyzing a Template in the Timeline

Now that you have opened the Template Browser and previewed some of the templates, let's use one as the foundation for a short presentation introduction.

If you're using the trial version of the software, you can install the Weave template by dragging the Weave folder from the Additional Motion Content folder to the Users > Shared > Motion > Templates folder on your hard drive.

1 Select the Weave collection; then click the Weave-Bumper template to see it in the Preview area.

This is a simple template with only one still photograph for media, but it's a good place to start learning how to use templates.

2 Click the Open Template button in the lower right of the window to open the template as a new, untitled project.

The untitled project opens in the Canvas.

3   Press the spacebar to play the template in the Canvas.

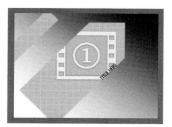

The template includes large, moving arrows that are used as masks to reveal an image. The grid pattern with a numbered clip icon is a place-holder to show you where you can place your own media file. The titles in the template are generic—TITLE HERE and DAY 1—to make them easy to replace.

Let's take a look at the template on the Timeline tab.

4   Press Cmd-7 to open the Timeline tab in the Timing pane.

The project includes two collapsed layers: Weave-Bumper and Background.

There is also a series of dots (keyframes) below the Weave-Bumper layer in the Timeline. You'll learn more about keyframes in the next lesson. For now, let's hide the keyframes.

5   Click the Show/Hide Keyframes button at the bottom of the Timeline tab to hide the keyframes in the Timeline.

Now let's take a look inside the Weave-Bumper layer. The contents may seem a bit intimidating at first. Look a little more carefully and you'll see that the entire template was built using skills that you've already learned in this book. Really.

6   Click the Weave-Bumper disclosure triangle to reveal the contents of the layer.

7   Click the Zoom to Fit button in the upper-right corner of the Timeline so that you can see the tracks for the entire length of the project.

8   Press the spacebar to start playback, if the project is not already playing.

Watch the playhead scrub across the various tracks and elements in the Timeline as you preview the project in the Canvas. See; it's not such a big deal—just a lot of thick arrow objects that were created using the Bezier tool, some masks, a few titles, and a familiar gradient in the background layer. Piece of cake. Okay, a big cake with a lot of layers—but still cake.

Replacing Text and Media in a Template

Now that you've seen what the empty template looks like, let's change the titles and add a photograph to finish the project. First, let's find the elements that we're going to modify.

1   Look at the names of the tracks in the Timeline Layer list.

Let's change the contents of three of the layers, starting with the Text objects.

2   Select the TITLE HERE object at the top of the Timeline Layer list.

Where do you change the title? Well, you could double-click it in the Canvas and change it with the Text tool, or you could change the text in the Inspector. Since you've never used the Inspector text-changing method, let's give it a try.

3   Press Cmd-3 to open the selected TITLE HERE object in the Inspector.

4   Click the Text tab to open the Text parameters.

The Text field at the bottom of the Format pane allows you to edit the text.

5   Type *PHOTOGRAPHY* in the Text field to change the title.

The text in the Preview area and the Canvas both update to the new text. That was easy. Let's change the DAY 1 text object as well.

6   Select the DAY 1 text object on the Timeline Layer list toward the bottom of the list.

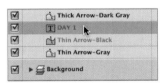

The DAY 1 text object appears in the Inspector.

7   In the Text tab's Format pane, change the text in the Text field to *Jeffrey A. Graves*.

The text in the Canvas and the Preview area automatically updates to the new text.

TIP You can copy text from another application and paste it into the Text field in the Inspector. You can paste words, sentences, or entire paragraphs into the field to create your text objects.

The last step in finishing this project is to replace the media. How do you know which objects to replace? Look for the objects conveniently named Replace.

8   In the Timeline Layer list, select the Replace object.

9   Press Cmd-1 to open the File Browser tab in the Utility window.

Let's replace the media in the Replace object with the Big Ben London.jpg file in the lower pane of the Browser.

10 Drag the **Big Ben London.jpg** file from the File Browser to the Replace object in the Timeline Layer list.

11 Choose File > Save As and save the project as *Big Ben* in the My Motion Projects folder.

12 Press Cmd-7 to close the Timing pane.

13 Press the spacebar to preview the project in the Canvas.

As you can see, Motion templates look really great and are easy to use.

Attending to the Details

You've come so far throughout this book; it wouldn't be right to leave this project without fixing a few details. Sure, it's only an exercise, but it's the thought that counts. Your work is your calling card, and your reputation. Now that you know how to fix the little things, you have no excuse for letting them go. So what needs fixing? Well, for one, the picture of Big Ben isn't framed very well at the end of the project. Also, the word *PHOTOGRAPHY* doesn't show up very well over the image in the first half of the project. Let's take an extra moment and touch up these two details.

1   Pause playback; then move the playhead to 4;00 in the Timeline so you can see the position of the Big Ben London.jpg image in the Canvas.

2   Click the Big Ben London.jpg image in the upper-right corner of the Canvas to select the object.

3   In the Canvas, drag the selected object upward until you clearly see the Big Ben clock tower.

Much better. What's the point of having a great photograph masked off for display in the frame if you can't see the interesting part of the image?

Now let's fix the PHOTOGRAPHY text object.

4   Move the playhead to 2;15 to see the PHOTOGRAPHY text object over the image.

It's very difficult to see the blue text over the blue background. Let's change the color of the text to something that stands out better over blue. Perhaps yellow? Let's use the color picker to grab a gold color from the image.

5   Press Shift-Cmd-A to deselect everything in the Canvas.

6   Click the PHOTOGRAPHY object in the Canvas to select it; then press D to open the Dashboard. Press D again until you see the Text: TITLE HERE Dashboard.

7   Click the Color well on the Dashboard to open the Colors window; then use the color picker (magnifying glass) to pick a gold color from the Big Ben London.jpg image in the Canvas.

All the text needs now is a drop shadow.

8   In the Dashboard header bar, click the Inspector button (i) to open the Inspector.

9   In the Inspector, click the Text tab and then the Style button; then select the Drop Shadow check box to apply a drop shadow to the text.

Now *that's* a great-looking title. Nice work.

10 Close the Dashboard and the Colors window; then press Cmd-S to save your finished project.

11 Press F8 to view the finished project in full-screen mode; then press the spacebar. Press F8 again when you're finished to return to the interface.

That's it for this lesson. Now you can maneuver like a pro in the Timeline and modify the Motion prebuilt templates to make them your own.

What You've Learned

▶ You can open the Timeline tab in the Timing pane by pressing Cmd-7.

▶ The Timeline tab includes a Timeline Layer list that works the same as the Layer list on the Layers tab. It also includes a Timeline, a timecode ruler, and a Current Frame field.

▶ You can enable and disable filters and behaviors in the Timeline Layer list, and also show and hide filters, behaviors, and other elements.

▶ Motion provides three tools for zooming into and out of the Timeline: the Zoom slider, the Zoom/Scroll control, and the Zoom to Fit button (which fits the entire play range into the Timeline window).

▶ The Timeline consists of tracks for each layer, object, behavior, and filter. You can collapse a layer by clicking its disclosure triangle. The number of objects that a layer contains is listed on a collapsed layer in the Timeline.

▶ If you drag multiple files to the Timeline, you can import them as a composite (one over the other) or sequentially (one after the other).

▶ Motion provides three options for importing media into the Timeline. You choose the import option from the drop menu that appears when you drag a file to the Timeline. The drop menu options are Composite, Insert, and Overwrite.

▶ You can use markers to align clips in the Timeline. You can set markers in the Timeline at the playhead position by pressing Shift-M. You can name and colorize markers in the Edit Marker window.

▶ You can move a clip to the playhead by pressing the bracket keys. Pressing Shift-[(left bracket) moves the In point of the selected clip to the play-head position. Pressing Shift-] (right bracket) moves the Out point of the selected clip to the playhead position.

▶ Motion includes premade templates that are organized in the Template Browser. The premade templates are royalty free, and you can modify them with your own media.

▶ Templates include generic titles and objects that you can replace with your own text and media.

Master Project Tasks

Your Master Project task for this lesson requires you to work in the Timeline to extend the project. Your goal is to extend the project to a duration of 25 seconds. How? Good question. In the real world, if a client asks you to make a project longer, you don't ask how—you just come up with a creative way to make it happen. In this case, I left a few bread crumbs in the form of markers in the Timeline for you to follow in the **08 Master Project finished** project.

Now that you're familiar with the Timeline, your goal is to compare the **08 Master Project finished** project with your Master Project file and make the appropriate changes. Or, if you're up for the challenge, you can simply watch the **08 MP finished.mov** file and try to emulate it without seeing the Timeline. You can also devise your own project enhancements to lengthen the project. Whatever you come up with, the overall goal is to make the project a total of 25 seconds long, without cheating. Cheating? That would be simply extending the titles to elongate the project.

Let's start by opening your Master Project in the My Motion Projects folder. If you didn't complete the Master Project tasks in the previous lesson, you can open **08 Master Project start** in the Master_Project folder.

1   Open your Master Project or the **08 Master Project start** project.

   NOTE ▸ If a window opens asking for a missing font, click Cancel to open the project without the missing font.

2   In the File Browser, navigate to the Master_Project folder in your MOTION_INTRO Book Files folder. Double-click the Master_Project folder to open it in the File Browser.

3   Select the **08 MP finished.mov** file in the File Browser to preview the finished Master Project tasks.

   Now it's your turn to extend the Master Project. Don't forget: If you need a little help, open the **08 Master Project finished** project and analyze the changes in the Timeline.

9

Lesson Files

Time

This lesson takes approximately 1 hour to complete.

Goals

Import audio files into a Motion project

Adjust audio levels in the Project pane

Work with keyframes in the Audio Editor

Animate objects with keyframes

Group particles with an object in the Timeline

Add keyframes to Transform parameters in the Inspector

Show keyframes in the Timeline

Record keyframes in the Canvas

Working with Audio and Keyframe Basics

In previous lessons, you applied behaviors to animate objects, layers, and text. While behaviors are easy to apply and manipulate, sometimes you need a little more precision as you manipulate parameters in a project. What if you need to set a precise parameter value at a specific frame? If your project requires exact timing, you'll probably need to add keyframes to get the job done. Ah yes, the dreaded keyframe. Many hours, days, and years have been dedicated to keyframing projects— not out of joy, but necessity. Fortunately, the Motion interface offers several user-friendly methods for applying keyframes.

So why combine audio and basic keyframing in the same lesson? Because one of the most common uses of basic keyframing is to adjust audio levels. So we'll start our Keyframing 101 course with Audio parameters; then we'll graduate to keyframing Transform parameters in the Canvas.

This lesson includes two projects. The first focuses on working with audio, the second on manipulating images with keyframes. Both projects are based on real-world keyframing exercises.

Opening the Frances Project

First, let's open the **9-1 Frances start** project, located in the Lesson_09 folder.

1   Close any open Motion projects; then change the File Browser to List view.

2   In the File Browser, open the Lesson_09 folder; then open the project **9-1 Frances start**.

   This is an updated version of the Frances project that you finished in Lesson 7.

3   Choose File > Save As and save your project in the My Motion Projects folder on the Desktop.

   I've made a few modifications to the project since your last visit. Let's take a look at the Layers tab to see what I've changed.

4   Press Cmd-4 to open the Layers tab in the Project pane. Then click the disclosure triangle for the Movie layer to view the layer contents, if they're not already visible.

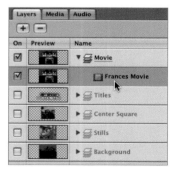

What do you think of the new Movie layer with the Frances Movie object inside? As you can see, I've done a little baking since you last worked with this project. What did I bake? A fresh, new QuickTime file of the finished project. Notice that all of the other layers in the project have been turned off. Why? Because now that you've finished the visual portion of this project, there's no sense making the computer calculate all of those layers, objects, and effects parameters if it doesn't need to.

The process of exporting a finished portion of a project as a movie file and then bringing it back into a project is often referred to as *baking*—just like baking in a kitchen. Once you have all of the ingredients mixed together properly, you bake the dish. You then combine all of the baked dishes to create the final meal. You'll learn more about exporting files in Lesson 11. For now, just be aware that you're watching the finished QuickTime movie file in the Canvas rather than all of the individual layers, objects, and effects.

Importing Audio into a Project

The Frances project is nearly complete. All it needs is some dramatic news-bumper music. You already imported music into a project in Lesson 2, but since that was seven lessons ago, let's try it again as a refresher.

The first step in importing music is to locate the music file that you want to import. The music file you'll use for this project is named **Frances Music** and is conveniently located in the Lesson_09 folder that you have open in the File Browser. Once you've selected a music file, you can import it by clicking the Import button, or you can drag it to the project and drop it on the Canvas, the Layers tab, or the Timeline tab.

Exploring the Audio Tab

Before you add music, let's take a look at the Audio tab in the Project pane. The Audio tab is the third tab in the Project pane and can be opened by clicking the tab or pressing Cmd-6.

1   Press Cmd-6 to open the Audio tab.

     The Audio tab lists all of the objects in your project that contain audio. Let's add an audio file to the project and see how it appears on the Audio tab.

2   Press the spacebar to start playback in the Canvas, if the project is not already playing.

3   In the File Browser, locate the **Frances Music.aif** file and drag it to
the Canvas.

A green Frances Music region appears in the mini-Timeline, and the file
also appears on the Audio tab.

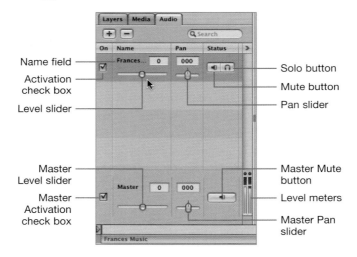

The Audio tab contains two types of audio controls: object audio controls
and master audio controls. Each object that contains audio includes a set
of object audio controls for adjusting its volume and panning levels. You
use the master audio controls to modify the volume and panning levels for
the overall project.

The levels represent the perceived volume of the track in the form of deci-
bels (dB). Any audio that you import into the project is assigned a level of
0 dB. The 0 dB level is relative to the level of the individual track you
imported. The lowest level you can apply to an audio track is –96 dB
(silence), and the highest is 6 dB.

Let's test the Frances Music track controls.

4   Drag the Level slider on the Frances Music track all the way to the left (–96).

The Frances Music track is now silent.

5   Type *0* in the field above the Level slider and press Return to reset the level to 0 dB.

The Pan slider controls the position of the audio track in the left and right stereo fields. A pan value of 000 creates a centered track, with equal sound coming out of the left and right speakers. Dragging the Pan slider all the way left (–100) moves the sound to the left speaker; dragging the slider all the way right (100) moves the sound to the right speaker.

6   Drag the Pan slider all the way to the right (100) to hear the sound out of only the right speaker.

7   Type *0* in the field above the Pan slider and press Return to reset the pan position to centered (000).

You can also adjust the audio levels in the Audio Editor.

8   Press Cmd-S to save your progress.

Exploring Audio on the Timeline Tab

You've imported an audio file into the project; let's see what it looks like in the Timing pane. The Timing pane includes two places where you can modify your audio files: the Timeline tab and the Audio Editor tab.

1   Press Cmd-7 to open the Timeline tab in the Timing pane.

The Timeline tab opens, but where is the audio track? It's hidden by default, but you can reveal it at any time by clicking the Show/Hide Audio button at the bottom of the Timeline tab. It's the button that looks like a speaker.

2   Click the Show/Hide Audio button to display the audio track in the Timeline.

The green audio clip appears in the Timeline. Audio tracks always appear below the horizontal gray separator bar that separates video and audio tracks. You can see the audio waveform (graphical display of audio) within the green audio clip in the Timeline when the track height is set to any of the larger track sizes.

3   Click one of the middle track height buttons to increase the track height and see the waveform within the audio clip, if you're not already viewing a larger track height.

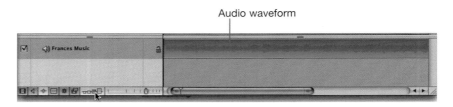

You can drag the separator bar up or down to expand or contract the track section. Since this project has only one audio track, let's lower the separator bar to limit the audio track section to just the size necessary for the Frances Music track.

4   Drag the separator bar downward until the Frances Music track is at the bottom of the Timing pane.

You move and resize an audio clip in the Timeline the same way that you modify other project elements.

Exploring the Audio Editor

The Audio Editor tab in the Timing pane shows the audio waveform (the graphical display of audio waves) for a selected object or for the master track. You can also modify the audio levels, scrub audio, and trim the audio region in the Audio Editor. Let's take a look at the Frances Music clip on the Audio Editor tab.

1   Click the Audio Editor tab or press Cmd-9 to open the Audio Editor tab in the Timing pane.

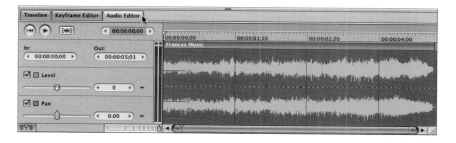

The Frances Music object appears in the Audio Editor because you selected it on the Audio tab of the Project pane. The name of the selected audio track appears in the green bar at the top of the Audio Editor. Let's change the audio selection in the Audio Editor to the master audio by selecting it on the Audio tab.

2   On the Audio tab of the Project pane, click anywhere on the master audio
controls at the bottom of the window to select the master audio track.

The name in the Audio Editor changes to Master to show that the master
audio track has been selected.

Let's import another audio file and then use the Audio Editor to modify
the levels.

Importing a Second Audio File

So you've added some dramatic music to the Frances news bumper and seen
where the audio appears in the Project and Timing panes. Now you'll modify
an audio file. It so happens that the producers of the Frances news bumper
want you to add siren sound effects to the project to make it more dramatic.
Sirens? Okay. If it's sirens they want, it's sirens they get. Don't laugh; this
actually happened to me on a real project.

Let's add some sirens.

1   Press the spacebar to begin playback, if the project is not already
playing.

2   In the File Browser, select the **Bumper Sirens.aif** file and drag it to
the Canvas.

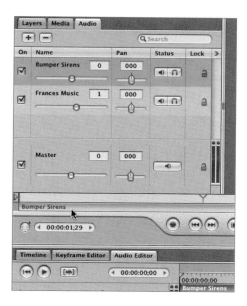

Voilà! Not only do you *hear* sirens, but you also can *see* the Bumper Sirens object at the top of the Audio tab in the Project pane and in the Audio Editor in the Timing pane.

3   Press Cmd-S to save your progress.

> **NOTE** ▶ I created the original score for this piece using Apple's Soundtrack software. Fortunately, Soundtrack includes a siren sound effect among the 4000 royalty-free music loops that come with the application.

Scrubbing in the Audio Editor

Previously you dragged the playhead in the mini-Timeline to scrub the playhead and preview the project in the Canvas. You can also scrub the playhead in the Audio Editor so that you can hear the audio and see the waveform at the same time. The difference between playing and scrubbing is that you control scrubbing manually, by dragging the playhead back and forth to hear a piece of audio or view a piece of video. When you play a project, it proceeds automatically, at one speed and in one direction: forward. Let's scrub the playhead over the Bumper Sirens clip in the Audio Editor to hear the sirens forward, reversed, fast, and in slow motion.

1   In the Audio Editor, drag the playhead right and left over the Bumper Sirens clip to scrub the audio.

You can hear the audio no matter what speed or direction you scrub the playhead. This is great if you're trying to isolate a sound, and annoying if you're just trying to edit something using the visual waveform as a guide. You can turn off audio scrubbing by clicking the Audio scrubbing button in the lower-left corner of the Audio Editor tab. When audio scrubbing is turned off, you won't hear any sound when you scrub the playhead.

2   Scrub the playhead again with audio scrubbing off.

Silence.

3   Click the Audio Scrubbing button once again to turn audio scrubbing back on.

Working with Audio Curves

You can modify the Level and Pan values for your audio tracks numerically and graphically on the Audio Editor tab. You can use the audio controls on the left side of the Audio Editor tab to raise or lower the Level and Pan values, just as you did on the Audio tab in the Project pane.

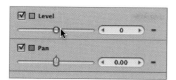

The Level and Pan values for a track are displayed graphically in the Audio Editor with colored lines called curves. Why is a straight line called a curve? Because you can bend it to change the value dynamically over time. We'll get to that in a few moments. First, let's identify the curves in the Audio Editor.

The Level control has a purple box next to the word *Level* to indicate that the color of the Level curve is purple. The Pan control has a blue box next to the word *Pan* to indicate that the color of the Pan curve is blue.

When learning to work with curves, it's a good idea to isolate the curve that you want to focus on. Let's start with the purple Level curve. To isolate the Level curve, you need to turn off the Pan curve by clicking the Pan check box.

1 Click the Pan check box to turn off the Pan curve in the editor.

Notice the purple dotted line in the Audio Editor. That line is the Level curve.

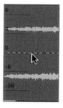

The numbers on the left side of the Audio Editor represent the audio levels, from highest (6) to lowest (–96). The purple Level curve is currently at the 0 position, which is the default, just as it is on the Audio tab.

2   In the Audio Editor, drag the Level control all the way to the left to change the audio level to –96.

The Level curve (purple line) moves to the bottom of the Audio Editor graph, to the value –96.

3   Press the spacebar to stop playback, if the project is playing—to save your ears from the next step.

4   Drag the Level control all the way to the right to change the value to 6.

The Level curve moves to the top of the Audio Editor, to the value 6.

5   Type *0* in the Level value slider and press Return to reset the Level value to 0.

The Level curve moves back to the center (0).

Keyframing in the Audio Editor

You are now familiar with the Audio Editor controls and the Level curve. Your goal in this exercise is to fade in the Bumper Sirens audio at the beginning of the project, and fade it out at the end. You can accomplish this goal by keyframing the Level curve in the Audio Editor. What's keyframing? Great question. Keyframing is the process of assigning a specific parameter value to a specific frame. Why? So that the values can change over time. If the values on the Level curve change, the curve bends to show the different values over time. For example, to fade in an audio track, you can assign the audio level a value of –96 dB (the lowest audio level) at the first frame of the track, and a value of 0 dB 1 second later in the track. The result when you play the track is that it will start silent and gradually fade up to a normal volume level of 0 dB 1 second later. Let's try it.

First, though, you need to learn how to set a keyframe. There are many ways to set keyframes in Motion. For this exercise, you'll set keyframes in the Audio Editor controls and on the curve itself. Let's start with the Audio Editor controls.

1   In the Audio Editor, move the playhead to the beginning of the project.

The Audio Editor includes a Current Frame field to make it easy to maneuver the playhead within the Audio Editor. The current frame should be 00:00:00;00.

NOTE ► The playhead needs to be paused to use this keyframing method.

2   Drag the Level slider all the way to the left (–96).

Now you need to set a keyframe to assign the value of –96 dB to the first frame of audio. To set a keyframe, you click and hold down the keyframe pop-up menu. Where is the pop-up menu? Hidden to the right of the Level value field. The pop-up menu button looks like a dash until you roll over it.

Keyframe pop-up menu hidden   Keyframe pop-up menu showing

3   Click the Level keyframe pop-up menu and choose Add Keyframe.

A black diamond (a keyframe indicator) appears in place of the dash to show that a keyframe has been added to the frame. The actual keyframe (purple dot) appears at the playhead position on the Level curve.

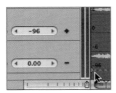

Now let's set another keyframe 1 second later.

4   In the Audio Editor Current Frame field, type *1.00* and press Return to move the playhead forward 1 second.

5   Click the Level keyframe pop-up menu and choose Add Keyframe.

A new keyframe appears on the Level curve at the playhead position (1;00).

Now that you've set the keyframe, you can change its value.

6   Change the Level control to a value of 0.

The Level curve bends so that the level changes from −96 dB to 0 dB over a 1-second period of time.

7 Scrub the playhead over the first second of audio in the Audio Editor to hear the value change.

You can also play the audio in the Audio Editor by clicking the Play button located in the upper left of the Audio Editor tab.

8 Press Cmd-S to save your progress.

That wasn't so difficult. You can also use the keyframe pop-up menu to delete keyframes by choosing Delete Keyframe from the menu.

Trimming Audio in the Audio Editor

Before you fade out the Bumper Sirens clip using keyframes, you should trim any blank space from the end of the clip. If you look carefully at the end of the Bumper Sirens waveform in the Audio Editor, you'll see a straight, horizontal line. A flat line in an audio waveform means the same thing as a flat line on a heart monitor: dead silence. So let's trim off the right edge of the clip. There are two methods for trimming clips in the Audio Editor: You can drag the edges of the green bar at the top of the editor, or you can use the handy In and Out value sliders.

For this exercise, let's just drag the right edge of the clip (the green bar) to trim the clip. We'll set a marker first, to use as a guide for the trimming operation.

1   In the Audio Editor, move the playhead to 4;00. Press M to set a marker at the playhead position.

A red marker appears *on* the clip. If a clip is selected when you press M, the marker appears on the clip, rather than on the timecode ruler.

2   Move the pointer to the right edge of the clip (the green bar) in the Audio Editor until the pointer becomes a Trim tool.

3   Drag the right edge of the clip toward the left, to the red marker on the clip.

The marker disappears because it has also been trimmed. That's okay—the marker served its purpose.

Now you can keyframe the last second of the clip and know that you'll be keyframing the portion of the clip that has audio, instead of silence.

Keyframing on the Level Curve

Let's try a different keyframing method to fade out the level at the end of the clip. Instead of using the keyframe pop-up menu to set keyframes, let's set them directly on the Level curve. How? Easy; just double-click the curve where you want to set a keyframe. You can also drag a keyframe to a new value.

1   In the Audio Editor, move the playhead to 3;00.

2   Double-click the Level curve at the playhead position to set a new keyframe.

You don't have to move the playhead to set a keyframe. This time, you'll set one without using the playhead as a guide.

3   Double-click the Level curve near the end of the clip to set the last keyframe.

> **TIP** ▶ Try not to set a keyframe too close to the edge of a clip, or it will be difficult to grab and move. You can always drag a keyframe to the edge of a clip once you've created the keyframe.

4   Drag the new keyframe at the end of the clip downward to a level of −96 dB.

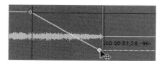

5   Press Cmd-S to save your progress.

6   Press Cmd-9 to close the Audio Editor.

7   Press the spacebar to see and hear the finished project in the Canvas, sirens and all.

The Level values for the Bumper Sirens clip on the Audio tab change to reflect the new keyframed values of the Level curve.

8   Choose File > Close to close the project.

Congratulations! You just created an audio fade-in and fade-out by keyframing the Level parameters in the Audio Editor.

Creating Keyframed Animation in the Canvas

You are now familiar with the concept of keyframing audio to modify levels over time. You can also apply keyframes to other object parameters to create more complex animation. Motion's behaviors provide an easy way to apply animation parameters to objects. However, sometimes you may want to create a combination of parameter changes over time, and it's easier to apply keyframes than to combine and modify a lot of different behaviors.

In the next series of exercises, you'll learn to record keyframes to animate two static images—doesn't sound too exciting until you see the project. You're about to re-create my first professional Motion project. Here's the backstory in a nutshell. The week that the Motion application shipped, I had just finished editing a new promotion piece for my client, Universal Studios Florida Production Group (USFPG). At the same time, USFPG announced its brand-new 22A division for producing and servicing national and international film and television productions. The executive decision was made to combine the USFPG logo with the new 22A logo at the beginning of the promo. "No problem," I said, because that's what you always say when a client asks you to do something. Then, of course, you have to live up to your words. Fortunately, I had just installed Motion on my computer and was able to use it to combine the logos in record time.

Opening the 22A Project

Let's take a look at the two logos in the **9-3 22A start** project so you know what you'll be working with for the remainder of this lesson.

1   In the File Browser, open the Lesson_09 folder, if it's not already open; then open the project **9-3 22A start**.

    The start version of the project includes both logos without any modification.

2   Choose File > Save As and save your project in the My Motion Projects folder on the Desktop.

3 Press the spacebar to play the project.

Animated logo   Static image

As you can see, the Universal Studios Florida Production Group logo is fully animated and exciting, while the 22A logo is just a static image. All you have to do now is come up with a creative way to combine them. As I said, no problem.

Searching for Similarities in the Objects

Combining two objects that seem so dramatically different takes a little practice and creativity. It doesn't hurt to implement one of my rules, either.

Rule #6: You can make objects seem like they belong together if you emphasize their similarities rather than their differences.

Similarities can be anything from a common color to a shape or even a letter of text. If you can find even one similarity, then you have something that you can use as a transition point between the two objects in the project.

As you watch the project in the Timeline, look for any similarities in the two logos. Usually, the best options are the things you notice first.

At first glance, I see a large, predominantly blue globe as the focal point of the animated USFPG logo. The 22A logo has a retro-futuristic look that includes a large blue circle behind the letter *A*. Bingo! We have a winner. All we have to do now is fade the globe from the first logo into the blue circled *A* on the second logo, and we're on the way to a really cool logo combo. Sound difficult? Not if you use keyframes to animate the parameters on the 22A logo.

First, let's take a look at the finished animated logo so you can see what you're aiming for with this project.

1   In the File Browser, double-click the **Logos finished.mov** file to open the finished logo movie in the Viewer.

2   Play the finished movie in the Viewer.

The two logos were combined in the same project by creating a transition between the blue circles in each logo.

3   Close the Viewer.

Planning the Project

Now that you've seen the finished project, it's time to dive in and re-create it yourself. First, it's a good idea to have a plan. This project will also help you review some of your other Motion skills as you use various features to accomplish your goal. Here are the steps you'll follow to finish the project:

1.   Modify the timing of the elements in the Timeline.

2.   Apply a Fade Out behavior to the object with the globe so that it fades out, revealing the A object below.

3.   Transform the A object over the globe image in the Canvas to match their sizes and positions.

4. Add a particle emitter to the A object to match the glowing animation of the globe.

5. Animate the A object with keyframes to move it from the starting position to its final size and position.

6. Animate the 22 object and move it to its final position.

7. Tweak to taste.

That's the plan.

Resizing Clips in the Timeline

Let's start with the first step. We'll resize the different objects in the Timeline. To save time, I have already set markers that you can use as guides for choreographing the elements in the scene.

1 Press Cmd-7 to open the Timeline tab in the Timing pane; then click the Zoom to Fit button to see the entire play range in the Timeline.

The Timeline contains three markers: start A, end USFPG logo, and end 22A animation. Let's resize each of the elements to the various markers, starting with the USFPG logo.

2 Move the playhead to the end USFPG logo marker in the Timeline.

3 Select the USFPG logo clip in the Timeline.

4 Press O to extend the Out point (end) of the USFPG logo clip to the playhead position.

5 Drag the A clip in the Timeline toward the right until it begins at the start
A marker.

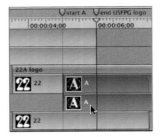

6 Drag the 22 clip to the end USFPG logo marker.

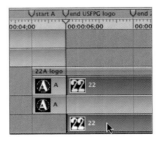

7 Press Shift-O to move the playhead to the play range Out point (8;29).

8   Select the objects on the 22A layer; then press O to change the Out points of the layer and its objects to the playhead position.

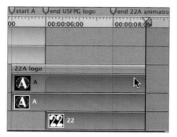

9   Press Cmd-S to save your progress.

Applying a Fade to the Upper Object

You've finished moving and resizing all of project elements in the Timeline. Now let's apply a Fade In/Fade Out behavior to the USFPG logo object to create a 1-second (30 frame) fade-out at the end of the clip. The USFPG logo overlaps the 22A logo by 1 second, so you'll be able to use the fade to see both objects at the same time.

1   In the Timeline, select the USFPG logo clip; then click the Add Behavior icon in the toolbar and select Basic Motion > Fade In/Fade Out from the pop-up menu.

A purple Fade In/Fade Out region appears below the USFPG logo clip in the Timeline.

2   Press D to open the Fade In/Fade Out Dashboard; then drag the parameters in the Dashboard so the Fade In value is 0 frames and the Fade Out value is 30 frames.

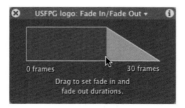

3   Move the playhead to 5;15 in the Timeline to see both objects simultaneously.

The 5;15 position is halfway through the 1-second fade, so the upper clip is at 50 percent opacity, allowing you to see both logos at the same time.

4   Press Cmd-S to save your progress.

Transforming the Lower Object

Now that you can see both objects, let's change the position and scale properties of the A object to match the image of the globe.

You will be able to manipulate the A object in the Canvas more easily if you close the Timing pane.

1   Select the A object in the Timeline, if it's not already selected.

2   Press Cmd-7 to close the Timeline tab and the Timing pane.

3   Press Option-Z to resize the frame in the Canvas to 100 percent.

The Option-Z method allows you to see the empty space around the edge of the frame, while the Shift-Z method fits the frame to the Canvas window, without showing any empty space.

4   In the Canvas, drag the A object to the center of the globe image.

The globe is not centered in the frame exactly, so the Dynamic Guides will not show you the exact center of the globe. Use your best spatial judgment to align the *A* over the center of the globe.

NOTE ▶ If you're having trouble moving the object exactly where you want to because of the Dynamic Guides, you can turn them off in the View pop-up menu located at the upper right of the Canvas.

Now it's time to change the scale of the A object to match the globe image.

5   Option-Shift-drag any corner of the A object to transform the scale from the center of the object. Your goal is to make the A object the same size as the globe image.

You may need to move the object a little to change the center if you were off a bit originally. Tweak until the images are perfectly aligned in the Canvas.

6   Press Cmd-S to save your progress.

7   Press the spacebar to play the project and see the transition between the first two logos.

Not bad. In fact, the transition between the globe and the A looks pretty good. All it needs are some particles to liven it up a bit.

Working with Particles in the Timeline

Nothing brings a static object to life faster than a little particle enhancement. Let's browse the Library to find a particle emitter that will give the A object a healthy, flaming glow to match the animated globe.

1   Press Cmd-2 to open the Library tab in the Utility window; then select the Particle Emitters icon in the Library.

2   Select the Pyro category of particle emitters; then select the Corona emitter from the list in the lower pane of the Library.

It's a little extreme, but with some minor particle modification this will look great behind the static A object.

Changing the Project Preferences

Before you add the particle emitter to the project, do you know where it will appear in the Timeline? Because this project requires precision timing, it's a good idea to set the Project preferences to create new objects at the playhead position.

1   Choose Motion > Preferences to open the Preferences window.

2   In the Project pane of the Preferences window, change the Still Images & Objects setting to Create Objects At: Current frame, if that's not already the current setting.

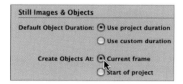

3   Press Cmd-7 to open the Timeline tab.

4   Move the playhead to the beginning of the 22A layer (5;00).

Applying and Modifying the Particle Emitter

With the playhead in position, it's time to apply the Corona particle emitter. The easiest way to do that is simply to click the Apply button in the Preview area of the Library.

1   Select the A object if it's not already selected; then in the Preview area of the Library tab, click the Apply button.

The Corona emitter appears on the 22A logo layer in the Timeline.

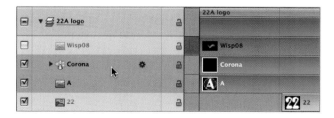

2   Scrub the playhead forward in the Timeline to 6;00 to view the Corona emitter over the A object.

Okay, it's a little small, but that's easy to fix. Let's modify the scale of the emitter to make it almost the same size as the circle in the A object. You'll be placing the emitter behind the A object shortly, so you should keep it slightly smaller than the object that will be above it.

3   In the Timeline Layer list, click the Corona emitter to select it in the Canvas.

4   In the Canvas, Option-Shift-drag any corner of the Corona bounding box to resize it to approximately 175 percent.

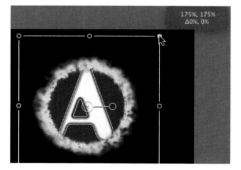

Now let's change the position of the emitter and the A object on the layer so that the A is above the Corona emitter.

5   In the Timeline Layer list, drag the A object upward until the position indicator appears above the Wisp08 object (the original object for the Corona emitter).

The Corona emitter now appears behind the A object in the Canvas.

The flaming particles on the animated globe were mostly white. Let's change the particle colors of the Corona emitter so that they are also mostly white, to match.

6   In the Timeline Layer list, click the Corona emitter to select it; then press Cmd-3 to view the Corona emitter in the Inspector.

7   On the Emitter tab of the Inspector, scroll downward to the Color controls.

8   Change the color tags in the Gradient Editor to light orange and white; then close the Colors window.

While you're in the Inspector, let's lower the particle birthrate to 30 to limit the flames to match the globe image.

9   Change the Birth Rate value to 30.

The project is looking good. Let's add a blur filter to the Corona emitter to blur the particles.

10 Click the Add Filter icon in the toolbar and choose Blur > Gaussian Blur from the pop-up menu.

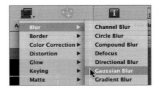

11 Play the project in the Canvas to see how it looks so far.

The transition between the globe image and the A object looks great. Now all you need to do is animate the 22A objects to finish the project.

12 Press Cmd-S to save your progress.

Adding Keyframes to the Transform Parameters

Earlier in this lesson, you used keyframes to change the values of the audio Level curve in the Audio Editor. You can use that same technique to modify virtually any parameter in Motion. For this exercise, you'll set keyframes for the Scale and Position Transform parameters. You can manually set each parameter by moving the playhead and clicking the keyframe pop-up menu next to the parameter, or you can turn on the Record button in the transport controls to record all parameter changes at the playhead position. The best part about recording keyframes with the Record feature is that you can make your changes with the Transform tool in the Canvas, and you never have to visit the Inspector to set keyframes.

Your goal is to keyframe the Scale and Position parameters for the 22 and A objects so that the objects move into their final positions in the frame. Let's start with the A object, since you're most familiar with it.

Grouping Elements Before Animating Them

One point to consider before you go haphazardly keyframing the A object is that whatever you apply to the A object, you also need to apply to the Corona emitter to keep the two in sync. The easiest way to keep these objects in sync is to group them. Then you can apply keyframes to the grouped sublayer rather than to each individual object.

1   In the Timeline Layer list, Cmd-click the A object to select it along with the Corona emitter (which should already be selected).

2   Choose Object > Group to group the two elements together on a sublayer.

    A sublayer named Layer containing the A object and the Corona emitter appears on the 22A logo layer.

3   Rename the sublayer *Flaming A* so you'll be able to identify it later.

Keyframing in the Inspector

Recording keyframes is the easiest way to keyframe your project's parameters. Still, it's a good idea to know how to add a keyframe in the Inspector, in case you ever need to do so. Think of this exercise as long division or algebra. You may not use it every day, but it's still a good idea to understand how it works.

Let's set two keyframes on the Flaming A layer to hold its initial size and position for 1 second. Why? Because any time you add keyframes, the animation begins with the parameter settings for the first frame of the object and moves forward to the new keyframes. In this case, you want the A object to maintain its original scale and position between the first frame and the 30th frame. Adding a keyframe on the 30th frame with the exact same parameter settings as the first frame maintains those settings for the first 30 frames. Let's set keyframes for the size and position parameters on the 30th frame. Remember that the goal is to maintain the same settings as the first frame, so you won't need to change the value of the parameters. All you will do is set the keyframes to lock in the parameter values on that frame.

1   On the Properties tab of the Inspector, locate the Transform parameters.

2   In the Timeline, move the playhead to the end USFPG logo marker.

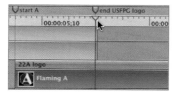

If you set Position and Scale keyframes for the sublayer in this frame, you are locking both parameters from the first frame to the keyframe (for 30 frames) at the current values. That's exactly what you want to do.

How do you set keyframes in the Inspector? The same way that you did in the Audio Editor. You simply click the keyframe pop-up menu and choose Add Keyframe.

3   On the Properties tab of the Inspector, click the Position keyframe pop-up menu and choose Add Keyframe.

A black diamond appears in place of the Position pop-up menu to show that a keyframe has been applied to that parameter at that specific time-code position.

4   Click the keyframe pop-up menu for the Scale parameter and select Add Keyframe from the menu.

5   Press Cmd-S to save your progress.

Viewing Keyframes in the Timing Pane

You can view the keyframes in the Timeline by clicking the Show/Hide Keyframes button at the bottom of the Timeline tab. Let's show the keyframes in the Timeline.

1 Click the Show/Hide Keyframes button at the bottom of the Timeline tab to show keyframes in the Timeline.

The keyframes appear at the playhead position, below the keyframed elements in the Timeline.

You can also view and modify the keyframes in the Keyframe Editor, which is the middle tab on the Timing pane.

2 Press Cmd-8 to open the Keyframe Editor, or simply click the Keyframe Editor tab.

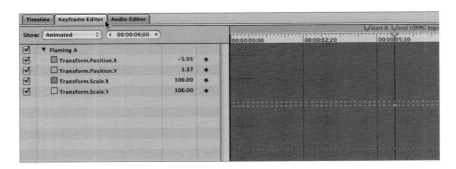

The keyframed parameters appear in the list on the left side of the Keyframe Editor tab. The Keyframe Editor should seem familiar, because it works exactly like the Audio Editor—except that the Audio Editor shows only the Audio parameter keyframes, whereas the Keyframe Editor shows all parameters that can be keyframed.

You can add, move, and delete parameter keyframes in the Keyframe Editor.

Because manipulating keyframes is more of an advanced Motion feature, let's focus on applying keyframes to finish the project.

3   Click the Timeline tab to go back to the Timeline tab in the Timing pane.

Recording Keyframes in the Canvas

Finally—the moment you've been waiting for: recording keyframes using the Record button in the transport controls. How does it work? You can record keyframes with the playhead stationary or moving. The easiest and most controlled way to record keyframes is to keep the playhead stationary, so that's what you'll do in this exercise.

Remember that your goal is to have the Flaming A sublayer become smaller as it moves toward the right of the frame, until it forms the final 22A logo. The playhead is already in the first position, so all you need to do to get started is start recording.

1   Make sure that the Flaming A sublayer is selected and the playhead is at 6;00 in the Timeline.

2   In the transport controls, click the Record button.

Keyframes have now been recorded for all parameters at their current values at the playhead position (6;00). Do not turn off the Record button.

3   Press Option-Cmd-right arrow to move the playhead to the end 22A animation marker in the Timeline (8;00).

Any changes you make to the project in the Canvas will set new keyframe values for those parameters at the new playhead position.

4   Press Cmd-7 to close the Timing pane.

5   Option-Shift-drag the corner of the Flaming A bounding box and resize it to 75 percent to match the scale of the 22 object.

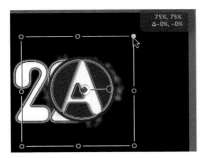

6   Drag the center of the Flaming A sublayer in the Canvas toward the right and position the sublayer so that it rests next to the 22 object in the frame.

Use your best judgment for positioning the sublayer.

7   Click the Record button to turn off keyframe recording.

That was very easy. Let's look at the Flaming A move in the Canvas. Then we'll animate the 22 object.

8   Press Shift-Cmd-A to deselect all objects.

9   Press Cmd-S to save your progress; then press the spacebar to preview your work in the Canvas.

The Flaming A animation is complete; now all you need to do is animate the 22 object, and the project will be finished.

Animating a Second Object in the Canvas

Let's apply all of your new keyframe skills to the 22 object. The first step will be to select the object that you want to animate. Then you'll move the playhead to the desired position. Finally, you'll click the Record button and change the parameters. Your goal in this exercise is to change the starting position of the 22 object to hide it behind the A object, and then cause it to appear from behind the A object and move toward the left to its final position. Since it's already in its final position, you may as well set a keyframe for the Position parameter first.

1   Press Cmd-7 to open the Timeline tab; then move the playhead to the end 22A animation marker (8;00) in the Timeline.

2   Select the 22 clip in the Timeline.

3   On the Properties tab of the Inspector, add a Position keyframe to set the final position of the 22 object.

4   Press Option-Cmd-left arrow to move the playhead to the previous marker (end USFPG logo).

5   Press Cmd-7 to close the Timing pane.

6   Click the Record button to begin keyframe recording at the starting position of the 22 object.

7   In the Canvas, drag the center of the selected 22 object toward the right until the object is centered behind the Flaming A sublayer.

8   Click the Record button again to stop recording.

9   Press Cmd-S to save your progress.

10 Press Shift-Cmd-A to deselect all objects.

11 Press the Home key to move the playhead to the beginning of the project; then press the spacebar to preview the project.

Amazing, isn't it? In a few minutes, you created a complex animated logo sequence. That would have taken hours or even days in the good ol' days before Motion. All the project needs is a little music.

Adding Music to the Project

Just for fun, and to remind you how to apply music, I included the actual **Logos Music.aif** file that I created to go along with this animated logo sequence.

1   Press the spacebar to begin playback, if the project is not already playing.

2   Press Cmd-1 to open the File Browser.

3   Drag the **Logos Music.aif** file from the File Browser to the Canvas and release the mouse to import the music into the project.

4   Play the project in the Canvas to hear the music and watch the animated logos.

5   Press Cmd-S to save the project with the music.

> **TIP** It's a good idea to end an animated company logo like this without a transition. That makes the finished animated logo more flexible so it can be applied in other projects, such as the beginning of a promotional piece. Then, when the finished project is imported into an editing system like Final Cut Pro, the editor can add the animated logo to the project with any transition. If you fade out the end of the sequence in Motion, you are limiting the editor's options.

What You've Learned

▶   Audio controls, including Level and Pan, are located on the Audio tab of the Project pane and on the Audio Editor tab of the Timing pane.

▶   The Level control adjusts the perceived volume of an audio file and always imports at a relative level of 0 dB. The lowest audio level is –96 dB (silence), and the highest (loudest) audio level is 6 dB.

▶   The Pan control adjusts the left and right placement of the sound in the stereo field. The default value is 0, which is centered, or equal sound from both the left and right speakers. A Pan value of –100 pans all the way to the left speaker, and a value of 100 pans all the way to the right speaker.

▶   The Master audio controls on the Audio tab can be used to change the Level and Pan values for the overall project.

▶ Audio parameters are displayed in the Audio Editor as Level and Pan curves. These curves are dotted lines on a graph and represent the parameter values over time.

▶ A keyframe is a specific value on the curve at a specific frame in the timecode. You can set keyframes along the parameter curves in the Audio Editor by choosing Add Keyframe from the keyframe pop-up menu or double-clicking the curve in the Audio Editor.

▶ The Audio Editor in the Timing pane shows only the audio parameters, while the Keyframe Editor shows curves for all parameters.

▶ You can show keyframes in the Timeline by clicking the Show/Hide Keyframes button.

▶ You can add keyframes to virtually any parameter in the Inspector by adding keyframes with the individual parameter keyframe pop-up menus. You can also record keyframes with the Record button in the transport controls.

▶ When the Record keyframes feature is on, Motion records keyframes for any parameter change at the current playhead position.

Master Project Tasks

Your Master Project tasks for this lesson consist of adding a piece of music to your project, and then fading the levels in at the beginning of the project and out at the end of the project. I've included a piece of music called Master Trees Music.aif in the Master_Project folder that you can use—or, feel free to choose another selection from your own music collection.

Let's start by opening your Master Project in the My Motion Projects folder. If you didn't complete the Master Project tasks in the previous lessons, you can open **09 Master Project start** in the Master_Project folder.

1   Open your Master Project or the **09 Master Project start** project.

2   In the File Browser, navigate to the Master_Project folder in your MOTION_INTRO Book Files folder. Then double-click the Master_Project folder to open it in the File Browser.

3   Select the **Master Trees Music.aif** file from the File Browser and apply it to the project.

4   Open the Audio Editor in the Timing pane and add keyframes to fade in the level for the first second of the project; then add keyframes to fade out the music for the last second of the project.

5   Save the finished Master Project in the My Motion Projects folder.

10

Lesson Files   Lesson_10 > 10-1 Reconnecting

Time   This lesson takes approximately 25 minutes to complete.

Goals   Reconnect missing media files to a project

Learn how to organize media files for a project

Create a RAM preview in the Canvas

Lesson 10
Managing Media

You've likely arrived at this lesson on managing media for one of two reasons. Either you've been following along in the book and have simply reached this lesson, or you've been working on your own and are looking for answers to common problems. Well, however you ended up here, you'll be glad that you did. The title of this lesson may sound a bit boring, but the lesson is actually packed full of useful information. You'll learn how to reconnect media files to a project, organize your media and project files, and create a RAM preview—to perform the preventive maintenance for your projects that allows you to focus on the fun stuff.

Reconnecting Media to a Project

Whenever you add a file to your project, a corresponding object appears in the Canvas, in the Timeline, and on the Layers tab. Adding a file to a Motion project does not create duplicate files for it. Instead, it creates connections to the original file on your hard drive. Each object in the project is always connected to the corresponding media file on your computer.

A media file that is connected to a project is referred to as being *online*. You can think of all the objects in a project as a family. Some projects consist of a small family of objects that all live together in the same folder on the computer, and some projects consist of large, extended families of objects living on multiple drives and in multiple locations on the computer. In either case, as long as the objects (family members) don't move after they've been added to a project, they will remain connected to the project.

What happens if a file is moved to a different location on the computer after it has been added to the project? The object becomes disconnected from the project, or *offline*. When you open a project that includes offline media, a window appears to alert you that some of the project files are missing. What do you do if a member of your family is missing? You dial 911 and send out a search party. Motion also lets you search for missing media files and reconnect them to the project.

For this exercise, you'll open the **10-1 Reconnecting** project. To make sure that the files appear offline, I moved the entire folder of media files out of the Lesson_10 folder while the project was closed.

1   Close any open Motion projects.

2   In the File Browser, open the Lesson_10 folder; then open the project **10-1 Reconnecting**.

A window with a detailed list of all the missing files for this project appears.

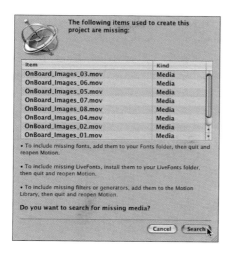

3   Click the Search button at the lower right of the window to begin your search.

A Finder window opens, showing the original path of the project and files.

Like a diligent detective, Motion searches at the location of the last search. This may be different than the project location if the last search was run for another project. So it's up to you to remember where you put the files.

The files are in a folder called Lesson_10 Media, which is located in the MOTION_INTRO Book Files folder just below the Lesson_10 folder.

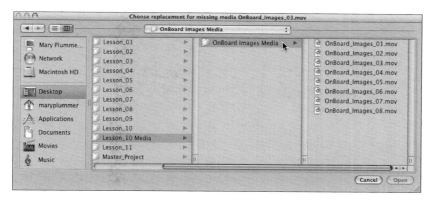

4   Click the Lesson_10 Media folder; then select the OnBoard Images Media folder to view the contents of that folder.

The OnBoard Images Media folder contains eight files. How do you know which one to reconnect? Just look at the filename at the top of the Finder window to see which specific file Motion is looking for. In this case, the window header reads "Choose replacement for missing media OnBoard_Images_03.mov." Motion looks for missing media in the order that the items appear on the Media tab, not alphabetically or numerically.

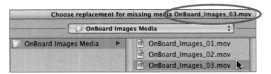

5   Select OnBoard_Images_03.mov; then click the Open button in the lower-right corner of the window to reconnect the file to the project.

If all missing files are in the same location, as they are here, Motion should reconnect all of the missing files at the same time. If the missing files are in different locations, you will need to find and connect additional files.

NOTE ▸ If all of the files do not reconnect, repeat step 5, but select the requested missing OnBoard Images file until you have reconnected all of the project's media.

Mission accomplished. You've located the missing files and reconnected them to the project. Now that you've reunited the project with its objects, you can play the finished project in the Canvas.

6   Play the project in the Canvas.

If the project plays too slowly on your computer, you can open the **Air Show Opening.mov** QuickTime file, located in the Lesson_10 folder in the File Browser, to see the finished movie in the Viewer.

The project for this exercise is based on a video created by Mark Magin of OnBoard Images for the International Council of Air Shows and was edited in Final Cut Pro. This project was exported from Final Cut Pro to

Motion. You'll learn more about exporting a project from Final Cut Pro to Motion in the next lesson. For now, let's save the project and learn a little more about project management.

7   Choose File > Save As and save your project in the My Motion Projects folder on the Desktop.

> **TIP▶** If you're having trouble locating a file and you know you haven't changed its filename, use the Search field in the Finder to search all local disks on your computer to find the missing file. Once you've found the location, you can follow that same path to reconnect the files in Motion.

Identifying Missing Media in a Project

What happens if you can't locate a missing file? You can still open a project even if you don't find and reconnect all of its missing files. All you need to do is skip the files that you can't find. When the project opens, a question mark will appear instead of a thumbnail on the Media and Layers tabs.

Missing file on the Layers tab

Missing file on the Media tab

If you can't find the original file at all, you can always replace it with a different file.

Tips for Keeping Media Connected

Here are some tips to help you keep your projects and their media connected:

▶ Place all of your media for a project in one folder before you build the project; then save your projects in the same folder as the media. The media can be organized into subfolders within the main folder, as long as everything is together. If the project and its media are all located in one folder, they'll be easier to manage and to move, if necessary, to another location, drive, or computer.

▶ Motion projects maintain a connection with all media listed on the Media tab. Remember that every object that you add to a project is listed on the Media tab even if you delete it from the project. If you delete media from a project, be sure to delete it from the list on the Media tab as well. To remove files from the media list, open the Media tab in the Project pane and select and delete any files that aren't being used in the final project. If you inadvertently select a file that is in use and try to delete it from the project, a dialog box will open to warn you that you're about to delete an active file.

▶ Don't rename media files on your hard drive after they have been added to a project. If you must rename a file, drag the renamed version of the file from the File Browser to the Layers tab and replace the file that has the old filename.

▶ Organizing your computer and cleaning up unnecessary files are good practices. However, to reduce the likelihood of lost, missing, or offline files, you should organize your media files before you begin your project and then reorganize your media files after you finish your Motion project.

Creating a RAM Preview

The real-time playback capabilities of your Motion projects are proportional to your computer's hardware. The system RAM determines the number of frames of animation that you can preview in real time; the CPU speed determines the number of simulations and complex behaviors that can be applied to composite objects in real time; and the VRAM (video RAM on the graphics card) determines the number of objects, filters, and effects in a composite that can be rendered in real time before a RAM preview is required. What is a RAM preview?

Motion performs many complex calculations to represent each frame when you play your project. The process of performing these calculations is referred to as *rendering*. A project plays back in the Canvas as quickly as possible, up to the specified frame rate for the project. With highly complex projects, the frame rate can drop significantly, making it difficult to see the project at its full frame rate. To get around this problem, instead of having Motion calculate the frames as you go, you can render parts of your project and store the frames in RAM. Then when you play your project, you see the rendered parts at their full frame rate. This view is called a *RAM preview*. The length of the RAM preview that Motion can perform is directly proportional to the amount of available RAM on your computer.

> **MORE INFO ▶** For more information about the hardware requirements for Motion, see the "Getting Started" section of this book and the documentation in the Help menu that came with the application.

Motion provides three RAM preview options: Play Range, Selection, or All (the entire project). The Play Range option renders only the frames within the play range as a RAM preview. Selection, on the other hand, renders the duration of the selected objects or layers. The current project is more than 20 seconds long. That's more than 600 frames, including multiple layers of video, which would require a lot of RAM to render from start to finish. So instead of rendering the entire project, let's render a play range, choosing the 6 seconds of the project starting at 11;00 and ending at 17;00.

1   Quit any open applications (other than Motion) to free up the system RAM on your computer.

2   Move the playhead to 11;00 and then press Option-Cmd-I to set the play range In point.

3   Move the playhead to 17;00 and then press Option-Cmd-O to set the play range Out point.

The RAM Preview controls are located at the bottom of the Mark menu.

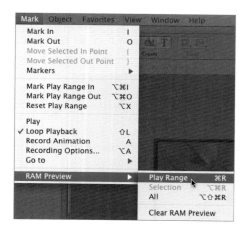

4   Choose Mark > RAM Preview > Play Range.

A RAM Preview window appears to keep you updated on the progress of your RAM preview.

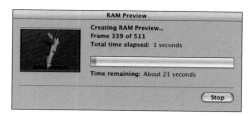

While you watch the estimated remaining time tick down on the progress bar, your computer is performing complex calculations that once required the use of a supercomputer. If you get tired of watching the RAM preview progress, you can watch the grass grow above the mini-Timeline. Okay, it's not grass, but it is a green bar that represents the frames in the RAM preview that have been rendered.

5   When the RAM preview is finished, press the spacebar to see the rendered play range in the Canvas.

You should see and hear the play range in real time. If the green bar didn't fill your entire play range, you didn't have enough system RAM to render a preview of the entire duration.

This is my favorite part of the opening and makes me appreciate all of those twisted, corkscrew, loop-the-loop roller coasters I've ridden over the years.

Unfortunately, the end of the play range is not very easy on the ears because it cuts off the music in the middle of a phrase. Let's extend the play range a bit to see what happens.

6   Drag the play range Out point toward the right for 1 second (to 18;00).

Notice that the play range is now longer than the rendered (green) portion of the project.

7   Press the spacebar to preview the extended play range.

You'll likely see a little bit of a hiccup or stutter in the images when you get to the unrendered portion—unless you have a super-fast, fully loaded, top-of-the-line, souped-up Mac, in which case you can gloat quietly to yourself.

To extend a RAM preview, you simply press Cmd-R or choose Mark > RAM Preview again.

8   Press Cmd-R to render the remaining portion of the play range.

If you have enough RAM left on your system, the green bar should extend to fill the rest of the play range.

9   Play the newly extended RAM preview in the Timeline.

Clearing the RAM Preview

If you make any changes in your project, you'll need to create a new RAM preview. Fortunately, each time you create a new RAM preview for the same frames, it overwrites the old render files for those frames. If you want to create a RAM preview for a different part of the project and want to maximize the amount of RAM available, you can clear the current RAM preview memory. To clear the RAM preview, you simply choose Clear RAM Preview from the RAM Preview submenu. Let's clear the RAM preview memory and then create a new play range to preview.

1   Choose Mark > RAM Preview > Clear RAM Preview.

The green bar within the play range in the Canvas disappears.

2   Set a new play range with a play range In point of 0;00 and a play range Out point of 8;00.

3   Press Cmd-R to render the play range in a RAM preview.

4   Watch the newly rendered play range in the Canvas.

5   Press Cmd-S to save your progress.

Tips for Maximizing Your RAM Preview

Here are some tips to help you maximize your computer's RAM preview capabilities:

▶   Close any other applications that are running on your computer to free up more RAM for Motion.

▶   Turn off any unneeded objects, layers, filters, or behaviors before you create your RAM preview. For example, if you want to create a RAM preview to see the timing of the behaviors, you probably don't need to see any filters or the background at the same time. By turning off those elements of the project, you free up RAM, which can be allocated to additional frames in your RAM preview.

▶   Clear your RAM preview when you no longer need it, to free up the RAM for other purposes.

▶   Enjoy your RAM preview while the project is open, because once you close the project, you flush the RAM.

▶   Add system RAM to your computer. On a G5 computer, Motion can utilize up to 4 GB of system RAM.

Working with Preferences

Before you move on to the next lesson, I recommend that you open Bonus 10, which is located in the MOTION_INTRO Book Files folder in PDF format. Bonus 10 discusses useful preferences settings that you can apply to your projects.

What You've Learned

▶ Media files can be located anywhere on the computer or on an additional internal or external drive.

▶ A media file that is added to a project is referred to as being *online*. When you add a media file to a project, a connection is made between the media file and the project. If you change the location of the media file on the disk or change the file's name, you may lose the connection between the file and the project. When the connection is lost, the media file is referred to as being *offline*.

▶ If you open a project with offline files, you will see a window with a list of all the missing files and have the opportunity to search for them. If all the missing files are in the same location on the disk, you need to reconnect only the first file; the others will be reconnected automatically.

▶ If you must rename a file after it has been added to a project, be sure to replace the older version of the file in the project with the new version so that the file doesn't go offline.

▶ The real-time playback capabilities of your Motion projects are proportional to your computer's hardware. One way to see a part of a complex project in real time is to create a RAM preview. The RAM preview options are located at the bottom of the Mark menu.

▶ A RAM preview is a frame-by-frame render file stored in your system RAM that allows you to play back the rendered frames in real time. You can create a RAM preview of a selection, a play range, or an entire project. The length of the RAM preview you can create is determined by the amount of system RAM available.

▶ The RAM preview (rendered frames) is indicated by a green bar within the play range and is available only while the project is open.

11

Lesson Files   Lesson_11 > 11-1 Air Show Open

Master_Project > 11 Master Project start

Time   This lesson takes approximately 20 minutes to complete.

Goals   Export a project as a QuickTime movie

Export a still frame

Explore the export presets

Exporting and Sharing Motion Projects

According to one common definition, *export* means to cause the spread of goods, ideas, values, or a way of life from one society, culture, or nation to another. But although Motion has had a great impact on the world of motion graphics, that's not the definition I am looking for. *Export* also means to convert data from one computer program into a form suitable for use by a different program. Now that definition fits our purposes better.

Up to this point, you've created many different projects that can be seen and heard only within the Motion application on *your* computer. That's great while you're building your projects, but sooner or later you'll want to convert those projects into a form that can be shared with the rest of the world, or at least your part of it. How? By rendering your project into a movie or a series of still frames through a process also known as exporting.

In this lesson, you'll explore the types of files to which you can export your Motion projects: QuickTime movies, image sequences, and still images. First, you'll export the 11-1 Air Show Open project as a finished QuickTime movie. Then you'll export a still image from the same project. Finally, you'll look at the Export presets options in the Preferences window.

Opening the Project

First, let's open the **11-1 Air Show Open** project located in the Lesson_11 folder. This is the same project that you worked with in the previous lesson, except I added a Lens Flare filter at the end.

1   Close any open Motion projects.

2   In the File Browser, open the Lesson_11 folder; then open the project **11-1 Air Show Open**.

3   Choose File > Save As and save your project in the My Motion Projects folder on the Desktop.

Now you can render the play range and see the lens flare effect at the end.

4   Press Cmd-R to create a RAM preview of the play range; then watch the rendered play range.

NOTE ▶ This flare effect was created by applying a Lens Flare filter and then keyframing the various filter parameters to make the flare follow the jet, grow larger, and then disappear.

Exploring Motion's Export Options

When you export a project, whether it's a draft or the final composite, all of the project's media, edits, behaviors, filters, particles, and animation are rendered to an export file (or series of files). Unlike the RAM preview, in which frames are rendered into temporary memory, an exported file is a self-contained media file that can be opened in other applications and on other computers.

Motion includes a variety of export presets for broadcast-quality and highly compressed QuickTime movies and for image sequences and still images.

Exporting a QuickTime Movie

When you export a Motion project as a QuickTime movie, you can include the entire duration of the project or just the play range. You also can choose whether to include video or audio or both in the QuickTime movie file.

To export a project, you start by choosing File > Export to open the Export window.

Let's export the entire **11-1 Air Show Open** project as a QuickTime movie.

1   Choose File > Export or press Cmd-E to open the Export window.

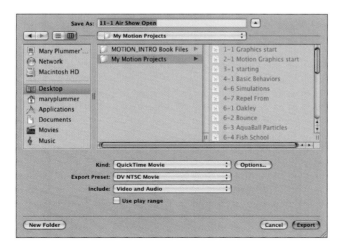

The Export window drops down from the title bar; the project name appears in the Save As field.

2   Select the Desktop as your destination; then change the name to *Air Show Open*.

In the lower portion of the Export window, you can specify the type of export file you want to create, using the Kind, Export Preset, and Include pop-up menus.

The default setting is a QuickTime movie using the project's preset (DV NTSC Movie) and including video and audio. The Use play range check box at the bottom of the window allows you to export the play range rather than the entire project. In this case, we want to export the entire project as a QuickTime movie, so we'll use the default settings.

3   Click the Export button to export the project as a QuickTime movie.

Once you click the Export button, Motion begins to render each frame to create a QuickTime movie. An export progress window appears to show you the status of your export.

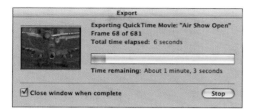

That's it. Let's hide Motion and find the new Air Show Open movie on your Desktop.

4   Press Cmd-H to hide Motion.

5   Locate the Air Show Open.mov QuickTime file on your Desktop, and double-click the file to open it in QuickTime.

6   Press the spacebar to play the movie with the QuickTime Player.

7   Press Cmd-Q to quit QuickTime.

8   Press and hold down the Command key, then tap Tab to see the open applications. Press the Tab key until you select the Motion application. Release the Command key to unhide Motion.

You can use Cmd-Tab to toggle between any open application in Mac OS X.

Now that you've seen how easy it is to export a QuickTime movie, let's try exporting a still image.

Exporting a Still Image

To export a still image from a Motion project, you first need to move the play-head to the frame that you want to export. Then you choose Export from the File menu or press Cmd-E to open the Export window. Finally, you choose Still Image from the Kind pop-up menu on the Export window. You can also click the Options button to choose the type of still image you want to export. When you export a still image or an image sequence, you can include only video. For this exercise, I placed a marker in the Timeline to indicate the frame that you'll export.

1 Shift-drag the playhead to the marker in the mini-Timeline (9;00).

2 Press Cmd-E to open the Export window.

3 Change the name in the Save As field to *Air Show Still*.

4   From the Kind pop-up menu, choose Still Image.

The default export preset for a still image is a JPEG file. Let's change the preset to a TIFF file.

5   From the Export Preset pop-up menu, choose TIFF.

Motion will now export the still image as a TIFF file. You can change the default export presets in the Preset pane of the Preferences window.

6   Click the Export button.

7   Press Cmd-H to hide Motion; then double-click the Air Show Still.tif file on your Desktop to preview it.

8   Press Cmd-Tab to unhide Motion; then close the current Motion project.

As you can see, it's quite easy to export a still image from Motion.

Exploring Motion's Export Presets

The Presets pane of the Preferences window includes project and export presets. Let's open the Preferences window one last time so you'll know where to find the presets for future projects.

1 Press Cmd-Tab to unhide Motion.

2 Choose Motion > Preferences.

3 Click the Presets button at the top of the Preferences window to open the Presets pane.

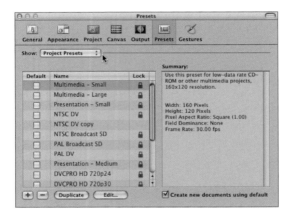

4 Open the Show pop-up menu and choose Export Presets.

The Presets pane lists the various export options. You can change the preset here or in the Export window when you choose Export from the File menu. Your preset may vary from the one shown here depending on your current presets settings.

5 Close the Preferences window.

Sharing Projects with Final Cut Pro

If you use Final Cut Pro, you can share your Motion projects with that application in several ways. The easiest method is to drag the Motion project directly into the Final Cut Pro Timeline. Final Cut Pro will read the Motion project as a clip. The Motion project will need to be rendered because it will be imported in the Animation codec (uncompressed).

You can also import a Final Cut Pro project directly into Motion. The Air Show promo project began as a Final Cut Pro project. After I imported it into Motion, I added the black frame and the Lens Flare filter at the end. Everything else, including the keyframed opacity, originated in Final Cut Pro.

> **MORE INFO** ▸ You can find more information on the integration between Motion and Final Cut Pro in the Motion documentation in the Help menu. I included the original Final Cut Pro project in the Soundtrack and FCPHD folder in the MOTION_INTRO Book Files folder so that you can see the original project and how it was integrated with Motion.

Continuing On with Motion

Well, this is the end of *Getting Started with Motion Graphics*. If you followed along with all of the lessons, you should feel comfortable with the basic Motion interface and such Motion features as behaviors, filters, and particles. You're now ready to go out and create projects from scratch. If you really enjoyed working with Motion and want to learn more about its advanced features, I strongly recommend another book in the Apple Pro Training Series, *Motion: Revolutionary Motion Graphics*, by Damian Allen, also published by Peachpit Press (2004).

Before you go, don't forget to finish the Master Project tasks for this lesson and to export your finished Master Project. You should also go through Bonus 11, located in the MOTION_INTRO Book Files folder in PDF format. Bonus 11 is a continuation of this lesson that discusses additional import and export formats that you can use with your Motion projects.

Good luck, have fun, and may your behaviors be plentiful and your particles have long and colorful lives.

What You've Learned

▶   You can export three kinds of files from Motion: QuickTime movies, still images, and image sequences.

▶   When you export a Motion project, all of the project's media, edits, behaviors, filters, particles, and animation is rendered as part of the export file or files. Unlike a RAM preview, in which frames are rendered into temporary memory, an exported file is a self-contained media file that can be opened in other applications and on other computers.

▶   Exporting as a QuickTime movie is the only method of exporting that includes audio. Motion includes a variety of QuickTime presets, from broadcast quality to highly compressed Web-friendly formats.

▶   Holding down the Command key and pressing Tab in Mac OS X allows you to toggle between opened applications, even if they are hidden.

▶   To export a still frame, you first move the playhead to the frame that you want to export and then open the Export window (Cmd-E) and select Still Image from the Kind pop-up menu. You can export a variety of still-image formats, including Photoshop, TIFF, and JPEG.

Master Project Tasks

This is it. You're about to export your Master Project so that you can share it with the world. If you ever feel like a little challenge, you can always go back to Lesson 3 and start the Master Project again. Your goal in this exercise is to export the finished Master Project as a QuickTime movie.

Let's start by opening your Master Project in the My Motion Projects folder. If you didn't complete the Master Project tasks in the previous lesson, you can open **11 Master Project start** in the Master_Project folder.

1   Open your Master Project or the **11 Master Project start** project in the File Browser.

2   Reset the play range if needed.

3   Choose File > Export.

4   Change the settings in the Export window to export a QuickTime movie with audio and video.

5   Export the finished project to the Desktop.

imation

action

reation

Index

Become a Certified Apple Pro!

Through the Apple Pro Training Series

The Apple Pro Training Series is the official training curriculum for Apple Pro applications.

Upon completing the course material in this book, you can become a certified Apple Pro by taking the certification exam at an Apple Authorized Training Center. Certification is offered in Final Cut Pro, DVD Studio Pro, Shake, and Logic. Successful certification as an Apple Pro gives you official recognition of your knowledge of Apple's professional applications while allowing you to market yourself to employers and clients as a skilled, pro-level user of Apple products.

To find an Authorized Training Center near you, visit:
www.apple.com/software/pro/training

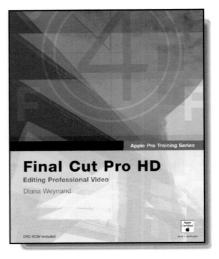

Final Cut Pro HD
Diana Weynand
0-321-25613-1 • $44.99

Advanced Editing and Finishing Techniques in Final Cut Pro HD
DigitalFilm Tree and Michael Wohl
0-321-25608-5 • $54.99

Final Cut Pro for Avid Editors
Diana Weynand
0-321-24577-6 • $44.99

Final Cut Express 2
Diana Weynand
0-321-25615-8 • $44.99

Optimizing Your Final Cut Pro System
Sean Cullen, Matthew Geller, Charles Roberts, and Adam Wilt
0-321-26871-7 • $49.99

Logic 7 and Logic Express 7
Martin Sitter
0-321-25614-X • $44.99

Shake 3
Marco Paolini
0-321-19725-9 • $44.99

DVD Studio Pro 3
Adrian Ramseier and Martin Sitter
0-321-25610-7 • $44.99

Color Management in Mac OS X
Joshua Weisberg
0-321-24576-8 • $44.99

Soundtrack
Mary Plummer
0-321-24690-X • $39.99

Motion
Damian Allen
0-321-27826-7 • $44.99

To order books or find out more about the Apple Pro Training Series, visit:
www.peachpit.com/applepro